Foundation Stage

Module A

Accounting Framework

Revision Series

Feb 97

British Library Cataloguing-in-Publication Data

A catalogue record for this book is available from the British Library.

Published by AT Foulks Lynch Ltd
Number 4
The Griffin Centre
Staines Road
Feltham
Middlesex
TW14 0HS

ISBN 0 7483 3540 4

© AT Foulks Lynch Ltd, 1997

Acknowledgements

The past ACCA examination questions are the copyright of the Association of Chartered Certified Accountants. The answers to the questions from June 1994 onwards are the answers produced by the examiners themselves and are the copyright of the Association of Chartered Certified Accountants. The answers to the questions prior to June 1994 have been produced by AT Foulks Lynch Ltd.

We are grateful to the Chartered Institute of Management Accountants and the Institute of Chartered Accountants in England and Wales for permission to reproduce past examination questions. The answers have been prepared by AT Foulks Lynch Ltd.

EXAMINER PLUS - THE EXAMINER'S OFFICIAL ANSWERS

At the end of this book we include all the new syllabus exams from June 94 to December 96 with the examiner's official answers, and at the end of each topic in the contents page below we indicate which of the questions from these exams are relevant to that topic.

For example, under the heading Bookkeeping and Accounting Techniques below, you will see that as well as the questions listed, question number 63, from the June 94 exam, and question number 80, from the December 96 exam, are also relevant.

CONTENTS

v

Note that the ACCA changes examiners from time to time and that there will be a new examiner for Paper 1 from June 1997. However, we ensure that the answers included here are those written by the original examiner who set the questions.

PREFACE

The new edition of the ACCA Revision Series published for the June and December 1997 examinations is an exciting product which incorporates 'Examiner Plus' - **all the new syllabus examinations from June 1994 up to and including December 1996 plus the Examiner's official answers.**

We have cross referenced all these questions to their topic headings in the contents pages so you can see at a glance what questions have been set on each syllabus area to date, topic by topic.

The inclusion of these questions and answers really does give students an unparalleled view of the way the new syllabus examinations are set and, even more importantly, a tremendous insight into the mind of the Examiner. The Examiner's answers are in some cases fairly lengthy and whilst the Examiner would not necessarily expect you to include all the points that his answers include, they do nevertheless give you an excellent insight into the sorts of things that the Examiner is looking for and will help you produce answers in line with the Examiner's thinking.

The Revision Series contains the following features;

- The Pilot Paper issued by the new examiner

- **Practice Questions and Answers -** a total bank of around 80 questions and answers

- An analysis of the past new syllabus exams - including all examinations since June 1994-providing a complete analysis of all examinations set under the New Syllabus

- Update notes which bring you up-to-date for new examinable documents and any changes to the Official Teaching Guide as at 1 December 1996

- Details of the format of the examination

- The Syllabus

- Formulae and tables where appropriate

- General Revision Guidance

- Key Revision Topics

- Examination Technique - an essential guide to ensure you approach the examinations correctly

---

CHANGES TO PAPER 1

Please note that there are three changes which affect Paper 1.

1   The examiner is changing with effect from the June 1997 examination.
2   The format of the exam is changing with effect from June 1997.
3   The syllabus is being modified with effect from December 1997.

In response to 1 and 2, ACCA have produced a new pilot paper which is reproduced on page xii.

As regards the change in syllabus, the changes are highlighted in the syllabus on page ix, and further details in the 'update section' on page lx.

---

1 SYLLABUS, EXAMINATION FORMAT AND PILOT PAPER

FORMAT OF THE EXAMINATION

The examination will have the following format:

	Number of marks
Section A: 2 compulsory questions	40
Section B: 3 (out of 4) questions of 20 marks each	60
	————
	100

Time allowed: 3 hours

The overall balance in the paper will be in the region of 60% technical and 40% conceptual. Supplementary information, for example an extract from an Accounting Standard, may be provided within the text of a question.

The examination format has changed with effect from June 1997. The main difference from the previous format is that multiple choice questions have been dropped.

Introduction

Please note the syllabus changes indicated for December 1997

Paper 1 provides a broad introduction and overview of the financial accounting process. The syllabus covers all the essential aspects, without reaching the depth of complexity or variety of applications of later studies.

(1) **THE ROLE AND PRINCIPLES OF FINANCIAL ACCOUNTING AND REPORTING**

    (a) Nature, principles and scope of accounting: role of financial accounting, management accounting, financial management and auditing.

    (b) Nature, principles and scope of financial accounting

        (i) the reasons for its current state of development
        (ii) the influences on possible future developments.

    (c) Nature, scope and purposes of financial and related records, accounts and statements.

    (d) The users of financial accounts and statements, and their information requirements

        (i) the adequacy of financial accounts and statements in meeting those needs
        (ii) introduction to alternative methods to meet those needs.

    (e) The structure of the regulatory system and its relationship to financial accounts and statements.

(f)   The nature of the accounting profession and the role of the accountant.

(g)   The nature and role of bodies which set accounting standards and guidelines.

(h)   Ethics and independence of the accounting and auditing professions.
(*Note:* this topic will be deleted from the syllabus with effect from December 1997.)

(i)   The nature, role and significance of

    (i)   accounting theories and principles
    (ii)   accounting conventions (to include SSAP2)
    (iii) accounting standards and guidelines (eg SSAPs, FRSs, IASs, SORPs)
    (iv)   Generally Accepted Accounting Practice (GAAP)
    (v)   legislative and quasi-legislative requirements.

(j)   Applications of information technology in processing financial and related information.

(2)   APPLICATIONS OF ACCOUNTING CONVENTIONS

(a)   The understanding, application and implications of accounting conventions.

(b)   Principles of the conceptual framework debate.

(c)   Standardisation versus accounting choice.

(3)   RECORDING, HANDLING AND SUMMARISING ACCOUNTING DATA

(a)   Double entry book-keeping and accounting systems

    (i)   form and content of accounting records (manual and computerised)
    (ii)   books of original entry, including journals
    (iii) sales and purchase ledgers
    (iv)   cash book
    (v)   general ledger
    (vi)   trial balance
    (vii) accruals, prepayments and adjustments.

(b)   Methods of classifying expenditure between capital and revenue.

(c)   Accounting treatment of

    (i)   fixed assets - tangible and intangible
       -    depreciation - reasons for, and methods of providing for it (to include SSAP12)
       -    research and development (to include SSAP13)
       -    goodwill
    (ii)   current assets
       -    stock (to include SSAP9 (except for long term contracts))
       -    debtors, including bad debts
       -    cash
    (iii) liabilities
    (iv)   provisions and reserves

        (v)   post balance sheet events (to include SSAP17)

        (vi)   contingencies (to include SSAP18).

  (d)   Confirming and correcting mechanisms

        (i)   control accounts

        (ii)   bank reconciliations

        (iii)   suspense accounts and the correction of errors.

(4) PREPARING FINANCIAL STATEMENTS FOR

  (a)   Sole traders: from simple incomplete records situations.

  (b)   Clubs or societies

        (i)   receipts and payments accounts

        (ii)   income and expenditure accounts.

  (c)   Partnerships: changes in the constitution of a partnership; admission, change in profit sharing ratio and retirement including elementary treatment of goodwill.
Note: from December 1997, dissolution of partnerships will be introduced into the syllabus. See the updates section of this book for more detail.

  (d)   Individual companies: profit and loss accounts and balance sheets for internal and external purposes in accordance with the Companies Act formats.

(5) INTERPRETING/USING FINANCIAL STATEMENTS

  (a)   Preparing cashflow statements in accordance with FRS1 and contrasting cash flow and funds flow concepts.

  (b)   Preparing significant ratios for financial statements.

  (c)   Appraising and communicating the position and prospects of a business based on given and prepared statements and ratios.

  (d)   Appraising the validity of available information for user purposes.

Accounting Framework

UK Pilot Paper

Question Paper:

Time allowed   3 hours

This paper is divided into two sections

Section A   BOTH questions are compulsory and
                                   MUST be answered

Section B   THREE questions ONLY to be answered

Do not open this paper until instructed by the supervisor

**This question paper must not be removed from the
examination hall**

Section A - BOTH questions are compulsory and MUST be attempted

1   The trial balance of Harmonica Limited at 31 December 1995 is given below.

Trial Balance 31 December 1995

	Dr £'000	Cr £'000
Purchases and sales	18,000	28,600
Stock at 1 January 1995	4,500	
Warehouse wages	850	
Salespersons' salaries and commission	1,850	
Administrative salaries	3,070	
General administrative expenses	580	
General distribution expenses	490	
Directors remuneration	870	
Debenture interest paid	100	
Dividends - interim dividend paid	40	
Fixed assets - cost	18,000	
- aggregate depreciation, 1 January 1995		3,900
Trade debtors and creditors	6900	3,800
Provision for doubtful debts at 1 January 1995		200
Balance at bank		2,080
10% Debentures (repayable 2010)		1,000
Called up share capital (£1 ordinary shares)		4,000
Share premium account		1,300
Profit and loss account, 1 January 1995		8,720
Suspense account (see Note 3 below)		1,650
	55,250	55,250

The following further information should be allowed for:

(1)   Closing stock amounted to £5m.

(2)   A review of the trade debtors total of £6.9m showed that it was necessary to write off debts totalling £0.4m, and that the provision for doubtful debts should be adjusted to 2% of the remaining trade debtors.

(3)   Two transactions have been entered in the company's cash record and transferred to the suspense account shown in the trial balance.

They are:

(a)   The receipt of £1.5m from the issue of 500,000 £1 ordinary shares at a premium of £2 per share.

(b)   The sale of some surplus plant. The plant had cost £1m and had a written down value of £100,000. The sale proceeds of £150,000 have been credited to the suspense account but no other entries have been made.

(4)   Depreciation should be charged at 10% per annum on cost at the end of the year and allocated 70% to distribution costs and 30% to administration.

(5)   The directors propose a final dividend of 4 pence per share on the shares in issue at the end of the year.

(6)   Accruals and prepayments still to be accounted for are:

	Prepayments £'000	*Accruals* £'000
General administrative expenses	70	140
General distribution expenses	40	90
	110	230

(7)   Directors' remuneration is to be analysed between distribution costs and administrative expenses as follows:

	£'000
- distribution	300
- administration	570
	870

(8)   Ignore taxation

Required:

(a)   Prepare the company's trading and profit and loss account for the year ended 31 December 1995 and balance sheet as at 31 December 1995 in a form suitable for publication. Notes to the accounts are not required.

(16 marks)

(b)   Explain the differences between the following pairs of terms or items which may be found in company accounting:

    (i)   Authorised share capital and called up share capital

    (ii)   A capital reserve and a revenue reserve.
           (Give one example of each type of reserve).

    (iii)   A rights issue and a bonus issue.

(6 marks)
(Total: 22 marks)

2   The draft final accounts of Upright for the year ended 31 October 1995 show a net profit of £48,200.

The trial balance still has a difference for which a suspense account has been opened. The suspense account appears in Upright's balance sheet as a debit balance of £1,175.

In the course of subsequent checking, the following errors and omissions were found:

(a)   At 1 November 1994 insurance of £1,305 has been prepaid, but the figure had not been brought down on the insurance account as an opening balance.

(b)   A vehicle held as a fixed asset, which had originally cost £22,000, was sold for £6,000. At 1

November 1994, depreciation of £17,600 had been provided on the vehicle. The £6,000 proceeds of sale had been credited to sales account, and no other entries had been made.

(c)   Depreciation on vehicles had been calculated at 20% (straight line basis, on the balance on the vehicles cost account. The charge for the year now needs to be adjusted for the effect of item (b) above.

(d)   At 31 October 1995, insurance of £1,500 paid in advance had not been allowed for in the insurance account.

(e)   The credit side of the rent receivable account had been undercast by £400.

(f)   A credit purchase of £360 had been correctly entered into the purchases day book but had been entered as £630 on the credit side of the supplier's account in the purchases ledger. Upright does not maintain a purchases ledger control account in the nominal ledger.

When these errors had been corrected, the suspense account balanced.

Required:

(a)   Prepare a statement showing the effect on Upright's profit of the correction of these errors.

(12 marks)

(b)   Show the suspense account as it would appear in Upright's records.

(6 marks)
(Total: 18 marks)

Section B - THREE questions ONLY to be attempted

3   The balance sheets of Grand Limited, a wholesaler, at 31 December 1995 and 1996 were as follows:

	31 December			
	1995		*1996*	
	£'000	£'000	£'000	£'000
Tangible fixed assets				
Cost or valuation	126,300		162,400	
Aggregate depreciation	(50,000)		(64,000)	
		76,300		98,400
Current assets				
Stock	12,000		15,000	
Debtors	10,500		14,000	
Cash	1,400		2,000	
	23,900		31,000	
Current liabilities				
Trade creditors	6,800		9,400	
Corporation tax	3,400		5,000	
Proposed dividend	4,000		6,000	
	14,200		20,400	
Net current assets		9,700		10,600
		86,000		109,000
Loans (due for repayment 1999)		(60,000)		(60,000)
		26,000		49,000
Called up share capital		6,000		10,000
Share premium account		1,000		3,000
Revaluation reserve		-		8,000
Profit and loss account		19,000		28,000
		26,000		49,000

The stock at 31 December 1994 was £10,000,000.

The summarised profit and loss accounts for the company for the years ended 31 December 1995 and 1996 were:

	Year ended 31 December	
	1995	*1996*
	£'000	£'000
Sales	64,000	108,000
Cost of sales	40,000	75,600
Gross profit	24,000	32,400
Expenses	10,000	12,400
Net profit before tax	14,000	20,000

Required:

(a)   Calculate the following accounting ratios for both years:

   (i)   The gross profit percentage
   (ii)   The current ratio and the quick ratio (or acid test)
   (iii)   Debtors collection period in days
   (iv)   Trade creditors' payment period in days (based on purchases figures which are to be calculated)
   (v)   Gearing ratio.

   Show full workings.

(10 marks)

(b)   Explain what you can deduce from the ratios as at 31 December 1996 and from comparing them with those for 1995.

(5 marks)

(c)   State two points which could cause the movement in the gross profit percentages between the two years and explain how they could bring the change about.

(2 marks)

(d)   State the extent to which you agree or disagree with the following and give brief reasons for your answers.

   (i)   The current ratio and the quick ratio help to assess whether a company is able to meet its debts as they fall due. Therefore the higher these ratios are the better placed the company is.

   (ii)   A high gearing ratio is advantageous to shareholders, because they benefit from the income produced by investing the money borrowed.

(3 marks)
(Total: 20 marks)

4   The treasurer of the Ace Sports Club has prepared a summary of the club's receipts and payments for the year ended 31 December 1995, based on the club's bank account.

She wishes to present an income and expenditure account and balance sheet to the members and has asked for your assistance in preparing them.

The receipts and payments summary is as follows:

Receipts	£	*Payments*	£
Balance at 1 January 1995	660	Rent of field and pavilion	6,000
Subscriptions	13,720	Wages of groundsman	10,800
Sales of sports equipment (Note 1)	23,440	Purchase of sports equipment for sale	18,260
Receipts for hire of sports equipment	8,640	Purchase of sports equipment for hire to members	11,200
Sale of tickets for annual dinner	2,800	Costs for annual dinner	1,680
Income from investments	410	Sundry expenses	3,140
Balance at 31 December 1995	1,410		
	£51,080		£51,080

Note 1. All sales of sports equipment were from the stock of items for sale. There were no sales of items held for hire to members.

The following additional information is also available:

	As at 1 January 1995 £	As at 31 December 1995 £
Sports equipment for hire (net book value) (Accumulated depreciation as at 1 January 1995 was £6,200. The club charges depreciation at 25% (reducing balance basis) with a full year's charge in the year of acquisition.)	18,600	to be ascertained
Sports equipment - stock of new items for sale	4,950	5,180
Subscriptions paid in advance	450	800
Subscriptions in arrears (all received shortly after the end of the year for which they were due)	290	360
Investments at cost	10,500	10,500
Amounts due for payment for sundry expenses	450	580

Required:

(a)   Prepare the club's income and expenditure account for the year ended 31 December 1995, showing the surplus arising on sales of sports equipment and on the annual dinner, and a balance sheet as at that date. Ignore taxation.

(16 marks)

(b)   Provide an explanation, for presentation to the members of the club, of why an income and expenditure account and balance sheet can give them a better understanding of the club's affairs than a receipts and payments account.

(4 marks)
(Total: 20 marks)

5   SSAP 17 Accounting for post balance sheet events defines the treatment to be given to events arising after the balance sheet date but before the financial statements are approved by the Board of Directors.

Required:

(a)   Define the terms 'adjusting events' and 'non-adjusting events' as they are used in SSAP 17.

(4 marks)

(b)   Consider each of the following four post balance sheet events.

If you think the event is an adjusting one, show exactly how items in the accounts should be changed to allow for the event.

If you think the event is non-adjusting, write a suitable disclosure note, including such details as you think fit.

You may assume that all the amounts are material but that none is large enough to jeopardise the going concern status of the company.

(i)   The company makes an issue of 100,000 shares which raises £180,000 shortly after the balance sheet date.

(ii)   A legal action brought against the company for breach of contract is decided, shortly after the balance sheet date, and as a result the company will have to pay costs and damages totalling £50,000. No provision has currently been made for this event. The breach of contract concerned occurred before the balance sheet date.

(iii)   Stock included in the accounts at cost £28,000 was subsequently sold for £18,000.

(iv)   A factory in use at the balance sheet date and valued at £250,000 was completely destroyed by fire. Only half of the value was covered by insurance. The insurance company has agreed to pay £125,000 under the company's policy.

(16 marks)
(Total: 20 marks)

6   The objective of financial statements is to provide information about the financial position, performance and financial adaptability of an enterprise that is useful to a wide range of users for assessing the stewardship of management and for making economic decisions. (Draft Statement of Principles for Financial Reporting, issued by the UK Accounting Standards Board in November 1995).

Required:

(a)   State five potential users of company published financial statements, briefly explaining for each one their likely information needs from those statements.

(10 marks)

(b)   Briefly discuss whether you think that UK company published financial statements achieve the objective stated above, giving your reasons.

Include in your answer two ways in which you think the quality of the information disclosed in financial statements could be improved.

(10 marks)
(Total: 20 marks)

UK FOUNDATION PILOT PAPER 1
ACCOUNTING FRAMEWORK

ANSWERS

1   (a)

Harmonica Limited
Profit and Loss Account for the year ended 31 December 1995

	£'000
Sales	28,600
Cost of sales (Working 1)	(17,450)
Gross profit	11,150
Distribution costs (Working 1)	(5,060)
Administrative expenses (Working 1)	(4,800)
Profit on ordinary activities before interest	1,290
Interest paid	(100)
Profit for year	1,190
Dividends: Interim paid	(40)
Final proposed	(180)
Retained profit for the financial year	970

Harmonica Limited Balance Sheet as at 31 December 1995

	£'000	£'000
Fixed assets - cost		17,000
aggregate depreciation		(4,700)
		12,300
Current assets		
Stock	5,000	
Debtors (6,900 - 400 - 130)	6,370	
Prepayments	110	
	11,480	
Creditors: amounts falling due within one year		
Trade creditors	(3,800)	
Overdraft at bank	(2,080)	
Accruals	(230)	
Proposed dividend	(180)	
	(6,290)	
Net current assets		5,190
Total assets less current liabilities		17,490
Creditors: amounts falling due after more than one year		
10% debentures		(1,000)
		16,490
Called up share capital (4,000 + 500)		4,500
Share premium account (1,300 + 1,000)		2,300
Profit and loss account (8,720 + 970)		9,690
		16,490

Working 1 Expenses

	Cost of Sales £'000	Distribution £'000	Administration £'000
Purchases	18,000		
Opening stock	4,500		
Warehouse wages		850	
Salespersons' salaries and commission		1,850	
Administrative salaries			3,070
General administrative expenses			580
General distribution expenses		490	
Directors' remuneration		300	570
Depreciation		1,190	510
Profit on sale of fixed assets (150 - 100)	(50)		
Closing stock	(5,000)		
Accruals and prepayments (net)		50	70
Bad debts written off		400	
Reduction in bad debt provision		(70)	
	17,450	5,060	4,800

Working 2 Fixed Assets and Aggregate Depreciation

	Fixed Assets cost £'000	Aggregate Depreciation £'000
Per trial balance	18,000	3,900
Elimination for sale	(1,000)	(900)
	17,000	3,000
Depreciation for year		1,700
Per balance sheet	17,000	4,700

(b) (i) Authorised share capital is the amount of share capital a company takes power to issue on formation or subsequently. The issued share capital is that part of the authorised capital which has actually been issued to members.

The expression 'called up' refers to the extent to which the cash due to pay for shares issued has actually been demanded from the members.

On the issue of shares, members are usually required to pay the full amount due immediately, and the shares are 'fully called up' on issue. In other cases, the money due may be payable in instalments and the shares are 'partly called up' until the final payment is demanded.

(ii) A capital reserve is not available for distribution as dividend, while a revenue reserve is.
Examples:
Capital reserve: Revaluation reserve
Revenue reserve: Profit and loss account balance

(iii) A rights issue is an issue of shares to existing members, usually at a price somewhat below the current market price of the shares, to raise capital for the company.

A bonus issue is also an issue of shares to existing members, but without cost to them. A bonus issue is made by converting reserves into share capital. No cash is raised, and the object is to reduce the unit price of the shares.

2   Upright, Year Ended 31 October 1995

(a)   Adjustments to profit

'000	+ £	- £
Profit per draft accounts	48,200	
(a) Insurance: opening balance omitted		1,305
(b) Profit on sale of vehicle	1,600	
Reduction in sales figure		6,000
(c) Depreciation: Reduction 20% × £22,000	4,400	
(d) Insurance paid in advance omitted	1,500	
(e) Rent receivable understated	400	
	56,100	7,305
	7,305	
Revised profit	£48,795	

(b)

Suspense Account

	£			£
Balance	1,175	(a)	Insurance account (opening balance omitted)	1,305
(e) Rent receivable	400			
		(f)	Purchases ledger account	270
	1,575			1,575

3   (a)

		1995	1996
(i)	Gross profit percentages		
	24,000/64,000 × 100	37.5%	
	32,400/108,000 × 100		30%
(ii)	Current ratio		
	23,900/14,200	1.68:1	
	31,000/20,400		1.52:1
	Quick ratio		
	11,900/14,200	0.84: 1	
	16,000/20,400		0.78:1
(iii)	Debtors' collection period		
	10,500/64,000 × 365	60 days	
	14,000/108,000 × 365		47 days

(iv)   Creditors' payment period
           (See working 1)

           6,800/42,000 × 365   59 days
           9,400178,600 × 365   44 days

(v)   Gearing ratio
           60,000/(60,000 + 26,000)   70%
           60 000/(60,000 + 49,000)   55%

Working 1

Calculation of purchases

	1995 £'000	1996 £'000
Cost of sales	40,000	75,600
Add: closing stock	12,000	15,000
	52,000	90,600
Less: opening stock	10,000	12,000
Purchases	42,000	78,600

(b)   (i)   The gross profit percentage is considerably reduced from 37.5% to 30%. This is a strong indication of the need for an investigation to discover the reasons. If there has been no change in pricing policy and/or sales mix to explain it, the reason could be fraud or error. Possible explanations are given in (c) below.

        (ii)   The current ratios and quick ratios both show a small fall between 1995 and 1996. However, the company appears to be able to pay its creditors promptly (ratio (iv)), and £11,000,000 out of the total of £20,400,000 of current liability is not due for payment immediately. The company appears to be able to operate successfully with these levels of current assets and current liabilities.

        (iii)   Debtors' collection period. This shows a decrease from 60 days to 47 days - from a good level to an exceptionally good level if all-sales are on normal credit terms. Further investigation would be necessary to establish the extent, if any, to which the sales include cash sales or sales with special short credit terms, or whether the ratios are distorted by seasonal factors.

        (iv)   Creditors' payment period
                The company appears to pay its creditors promptly and to be shortening the interval between purchase and payment. Similar special factors to those indicated in (iii) above could be distorting the ratios.

        (v)   Gearing ratio
                The level of gearing is very high at 70%. The company's retention of £9,000,000 of profits and the impact of the revaluation have operated to reduce the level somewhat, but 55% is still high in relation to an average figure for most trading companies of about 30%. The company could reduce its risk by reducing the gearing further (see (d) below).

(c) The gross profit percentage is down from 37.5% to 30%, a substantial movement.

Possible explanations are:

- an error in stock-taking. If closing stock had been understated by £8,100, that could account for the difference because the correction of the error would increase profit to £40,500, or 37.5% of £108,000.

- acceptance of a contract at an unusually low price. If sales included a contract attracting less than the normal gross profit percentage, the overall gross profit percentage would be reduced.

- an increase in the price of goods purchased, not passed on to customers in increased sale prices. Such an increase will increase purchases and thus reduce the overall gross profit percentage.

(d) (i) I agree that the current ratio and quick ratio help to assess whether a company is able to meet its debts as they fall due, but disagree that the higher their values are the better, because high current ratios and quick ratios mean that stock, debtors and cash are high in relation to current liabilities. Resources tied up in current assets do not produce profits as fixed assets normally do. A company should therefore try to keep the levels of current assets as low as possible, consistent with maintaining sufficient stocks to support production and sales, and sufficient cash flow to pay creditors as they fall due.

(ii) I think this statement is partly true. Shareholders can benefit from the investment of borrowed money, as long as the percentage return obtained is greater than the percentage rate of interest being paid on the borrowings.

However. if the rate of return on the investment falls below the rate of interest being paid, the shareholders lose.

Thus in good times the shareholders benefit, but in bad times they can lose. The risk of the operation is increased.

4   (a)

Ace Sports Club
Income and expenditure account
for the year ended 31 December 1995

	1995 £	1996 £
Income		
Subscriptions (working 1)		13,440
Surplus on sales of equipment (working 2)		5,410
Hire charges for sports equipment		8,640
Annual dinner:		
Ticket sales	2,800	
Costs	(1,680)	
Surplus		1,120
Income from investments		410
		29,020
Less:		
Expenses		
Rent of field and pavilion	6,000	
Wages of groundsman	10,800	
Depreciation of equipment for hire	7,450	
Sundry expenses (3,140 - 450 + 580)	3,270	
		27,520
Surplus for year		£1,500

Ace Sports Club
Balance sheet as at 31 December 1995

	£	£	£
Fixed assets			
Sports equipment for hire - cost		36,000	
Less: aggregate depreciation		(13,650)	22,350
Current assets			
Stock		5,180	
Subscriptions in arrears		360	
Investments		10,500	
		16,040	
Less:			
Current liabilities			
Subscriptions in advance	800		
Sundry creditors	580		
Bank overdraft	1,410	2,790	13,250
			£35,600
Club fund account			
As at 1 January 1995 (working 3)			34,100
Add: Surplus for year to date			1,500
			£35,600

Workings

1   Subscriptions

Subscriptions

	£		£
Opening arrears	290	Opening in advance	450
Subscriptions for year	13,440	Cash received	13,720
Closing in advance	800	Closing arrears	360
	£14,530		14,530

2   Surplus on sales of equipment

		£	£
Sales			23,440
Less:	cost of sales		
	opening stock	4,950	
	purchases	18,260	
		23,210	
	closing stock	5,180	
			18,030
	Surplus		5,410

3   Club fund account as at 1 January 1995

		£	£
Assets:	Sports equipment for hire		18,600
	Sports equipment for sale		4,950
	Subscriptions in arrears		290
	Investments		10,500
	Cash at bank		660
			35,000
Less:	Liabilities		
	Subscriptions in advance	450	
	Sundry expenses	450	
			900
			£34,100

(b)   The main advantages to members are:

(i)   the income and expenditure account allows for accrued expenses and for subscriptions in advance and in arrear whereas the receipts and payments account does not. Members thus have a clearer idea of the surplus or deficit for each period.

(ii)   the balance sheet details assets and liabilities other than the balance at bank. Members thus have a clearer idea of the club's position at the end of a period.

(Tutorial note:
The balance sheet includes the investments as a current asset. Alternative presentations showing the investments as a fixed asset would also be acceptable.)

5   (a)   Adjusting events are post balance sheet events which provide evidence of conditions existing at the balance sheet date.

            Non-adjusting events are post balance sheet events which concern conditions that did not exist at the balance sheet date.

    (b)   (i)   (Non-adjusting)

                    The company issued 100,000 50p ordinary shares at £1.80 per share on 10 March 1996. The purpose of the issue was to raise money for the rebuilding of the company's factory

           (ii)   (Adjusting)

                    The £50,000 should be included as an expense in the calculation of operating profit, with disclosure of the details by note. The £50,000 will also appear in the balance sheet as a creditor due within one year.

           (iii)   (Adjusting)

                    Assuming that the loss in value is not due to post balance sheet damage, the stock at the balance sheet date should be reduced by £10,000, thus reducing operating profit and the balance sheet stock figure by this amount.

           (iv)   (Non-adjusting)

                    A fire on 1 February 1996 completely destroyed one of the company's factories valued at £250,000. Half of this sum was covered by insurance, and the insurance company has agreed to pay £125,000 under the policy.

6   (a)

User	Information Needs
(1) Investors and their advisers	- performance of management in achieving profit growth while ensuring the continued solvency of the company - the risk inherent in the company's operations.
(2) Employees	- stability and survival of the company - ability of the company to provide remuneration, employment opportunities and retirement benefits.

(3)	Lenders	- the solvency of the company - profitability, to ensure payment of interest when due - asset values.
(4)	Suppliers and other creditors	- information as to the solvency of the company and its ability to pay, probably over a shorter period than lenders.
(5)	Customers	- information about the continuance of the company, especially if they have a long-term involvement with it.

(b)   Users of financial statements are interested in three main areas in their use of company financial statements:

- profitability
- solvency/liquidity
- the risk of the operation

The profit and loss account provides a measure of profitability, more useful since FRS 3 increased the quality and quantity of information disclosed. However, the use of historical cost accounting means that the profit is often overstated as depreciation is often based on historical cost of assets.

The balance sheet details of current assets and liabilities enable users to form a reasonable assessment of a company's solvency, because they are reasonably reliably valued. Lack of information about the dates of payments to sundry creditors or receipts from sundry debtors could affect the position.

The gearing ratio (the percentage of total long-term capital provided from loan capital) provides a reasonably reliable assessment of the financial risk of the company's operation.

Two ways in which the quality of information disclosed in financial statements could be improved:

- requiring regular revaluation of fixed assets
- reducing the number of alternative accounting treatments allowed by accounting standards.

UK Foundation Pilot Paper 1
Accounting Framework

Marking Scheme

Marks

1	(a)	Profit and loss account		4
		Working 1		6
		Balance sheet		6
		Layout and style		3
			Available	19
			Maximum	16
	(b)	2 marks per item 3 × 2	Available	6
			Maximum	6
			Total available	25
			Maximum	**22**
2	(a)	2 marks per item in statement: 6 × 2	Available	12
			Maximum	12
	(b)	2 marks per entry 3 × 2	Available	6
			Maximum	6
			Total available	18
			Maximum	**18**
3	(a)	2 marks per pair of ratios 5 × 2	Available	10
	(b)	1 marks for comment on each of five ratios	Available	5
	(c)	1 mark per point	Available	2
	(d)	2 marks per statement 2 × 2	Available	4
			Maximum	3
			Total available	21
			Maximum	**20**

Marks

4	(a)	Income and expenditure account		
		Subscriptions		3
		Surplus on sales of equipment		2
		Annual dinner		1
		Depreciation		1
		Sundry expenses		1
		Other items		1
		Balance sheet		
		Fixed assets		3
		Current assets		2
		Current liabilities other than overdraft		1
		Overdraft		1
		Club fund account		3
			Available	19
			Maximum	**16**
	(b)	Explanation		
		Better idea of surplus or deficit		2
		Details of assets other than cash or bank		2
			Available	4
			Maximum	4
			Total available	23
			Maximum	**20**
5	(a)	Definition of: events requiring adjustment		2
		events not requiring adjustment		2
			Available	4
			Maximum	4
	(b)	4 marks per item 4 × 4		16
		Additional marks for fullness of answer		2
			Available	18
			Maximum	16
			Total available	22
			Maximum	**20**

				Marks
6	(a)	5×2		10
		Additional marks for fullness of answer		2
			Available	12
			Maximum	10
	(b)	Discussion		8
		2 improvements 2×2		4
			Available	12
			Maximum	10
			Total available	24
			Maximum	**20**

2 ANALYSIS OF PAST PAPERS

Topics	J94		D94		J95		D95		J96		D96	
Limited company accounts	1	O					2	O			3	●
Accounting for stocks	2	O										
Accounting principles and concepts	3	●	3	O					2	O	2	●
The balance sheet	3	●					1	●	1	O	1	●
Accounting for fixed assets	3	●			1	O						
Partnership accounts			1	O			1	O				
SSAP 2			2	O							2	●
The cash flow statement					2	O	3	●				
Interpretation of accounts					2	●			3	O	3	●
Control account reconciliations					3	O					1	●
Journal entries					3	O						
The audit					4	O	3	●				
FRS 3							2	●				
The profit and loss account							3	●	1	●	1	●
Income and expenditure account									1	O		

Key

The number refers to the number of the question where this topic was examined in the exam.

O   This topic formed the whole or a substantial part of the question.
●   This topic formed a non-substantial part of a question.

3 GENERAL REVISION GUIDANCE

PLANNING YOUR REVISION

What is revision?

Revision is the process by which you remind yourself of the material you have studied during your course, clarify any problem areas and bring your knowledge to a state where you can retrieve it and present it in a way that will satisfy the Examiners.

Revision is not a substitute for hard work earlier in the course. The syllabus for this paper is too large to be hastily 'crammed' a week or so before the examination. You should think of your revision as the final stage in your study of any topic. It can only be effective if you have already completed earlier stages.

Ideally, you should begin your revision shortly after you begin an examination course. At the end of every week and at the end of every month, you should review the topics you have covered. If you constantly consolidate your work and integrate revision into your normal pattern of study, you should find that the final period of revision - and the examination itself - are much less daunting.

If you are reading this revision text while you are still working through your course, we strongly suggest that you begin now to review the earlier work you did for this paper. Remember, the more times you return to a topic, the more confident you will become with it.

The main purpose of this book, however, is to help you to make the best use of the last few weeks before the examination. In this section we offer some suggestions for effective planning of your final revision and discuss some revision techniques which you may find helpful.

Planning your time

Most candidates find themselves in the position where they have less time than they would like to revise, particularly if they are taking several papers at one diet. The majority of people must balance their study with conflicting demands from work, family or other commitments.

It is impossible to give hard and fast rules about the amount of revision you should do. You should aim to start your final revision at least four weeks before your examination. If you finish your course work earlier than this, you would be well advised to take full advantage of the extra time available to you. The number of hours you spend revising each week will depend on many factors, including the number of papers you are sitting. You should probably aim to do a minimum of about six to eight hours a week for each paper.

In order to make best use of the revision time that you have, it is worth spending a little of it at the planning stage. We suggest that you begin by asking yourself two questions:

- How much time do I have available for revision?
- What do I need to cover during my revision?

Once you have answered these questions, you should be able to draw up a detailed timetable. We will now consider these questions in more detail.

How much time do I have available for revision?

Many people find it helpful to work out a regular weekly pattern for their revision. We suggest you use the time planning chart provided to do this. Your aim should be to construct a timetable that is sustainable over a period of several weeks.

Time planning chart

	Monday	Tuesday	Wednesday	Thursday	Friday	Saturday	Sunday
00.00							
01.00							
02.00							
03.00							
04.00							
05.00							
06.00							
07.00							
08.00							
09.00							
10.00							
11.00							
12.00							
13.00							
14.00							
15.00							
16.00							
17.00							
18.00							
19.00							
20.00							
21.00							
22.00							
23.00							

1   First, block out all the time that is **definitely unavailable** for revision. This will include the hours when you normally sleep, the time you are at work and any other regular and clear commitments.

2   Think about **other people's claims on your time**. If you have a family, or friends whom you see regularly, you may want to discuss your plans with them. People are likely to be flexible in the demands they make on you in the run-up to your examinations, especially if they are aware that you have considered their needs as well as your own. If you consult the individuals who are affected by your plans, you may find that they are surprisingly supportive, instead of being resentful of the extra time you are spending studying.

3   Next, give some thought to the times of day when you **work most effectively**. This differs very much from individual to individual. Some people can concentrate first thing in the morning. Others work best in the early evening, or last thing at night. Some people find their day-to-day work so demanding that they are unable to do anything extra during the week, but must concentrate their study time at weekends. Mark the times when you feel you could do your best work on the

timetable. It is extremely important to acknowledge your personal preferences here. If you ignore them, you may devise a timetable that is completely unrealistic and which you will not be able to adhere to.

4   Consider your **other commitments**. Everybody has certain tasks, from doing the washing to walking the dog, that must be performed on a regular basis. These tasks may not have to be done at a particular time, but you should take them into consideration when planning your schedule. You may be able to find more convenient times to get these jobs done, or be able to persuade other people to help you with them.

5   Now mark some time for **relaxation**. If your timetable is to be sustainable, it must include some time for you to build up your reserves. If your normal week does not include any regular physical activity, make sure that you include some in your revision timetable. A couple of hours spent in a sports centre or swimming pool each week will probably enhance your ability to concentrate.

6   Your timetable should now be taking shape. You can probably see obvious study sessions emerging. It is not advisable to work for too long at any one session. Most people find that they can only really concentrate for one or two hours at a time. If your study sessions are longer than this, you should split them up.

What do I need to cover during my revision?

Most candidates are more confident about some parts of the syllabus than others. Before you begin your revision, it is important to have an overview of where your strengths and weaknesses lie.

One way to do this is to take a sheet of paper and divide it into three columns. Mark the columns:

OK   Marginal   Not OK

or use similar headings to indicate how confident you are with a topic. Then go through the syllabus (reprinted in Section 1) and list the topics under the appropriate headings. Alternatively, you could use the list of key topics in Section 5 of this book to compile your overview. You might also find it useful to skim through the introductions or summaries to the textbook or workbooks you have used in your course. These should remind you of parts of the course that you found particularly easy or difficult at the time. You could also use some of the exercises and questions in the workbooks or textbooks, or some of the questions in this book, as a diagnostic aid to discover the areas where you need to work hardest.

It is also important to be aware which areas of the syllabus are so central to the subject that they are likely to be examined in every diet, and which are more obscure, and not likely to come up so frequently. Your textbooks, workbooks and lecture notes will help you here, and section 2 of this book contains an analysis of past papers. Remember, the Examiner will be looking for broad coverage of the syllabus. There is no point in knowing one or two topics in exhaustive detail if you do so at the expense of the rest of the course.

Writing your revision timetable

You now have the information you need to write your timetable. You know how many weeks you have available, and the approximate amount of time that is available in each week.

You should stop all serious revision 48 hours before your examination. After this point, you may want to look back at your notes to refresh your memory, but you should not attempt to revise any new topics. A clear and rested brain is worth more than any extra facts you could memorise in this period.

Make one copy of this chart for each week you have available for revision.

Using your time planning chart, write in the times of your various study sessions during the week.

In the lower part of the chart, write in the topics that you will cover in each of these sessions.

Example of a revision timetable

Revision timetable Week beginning:	Monday	Tuesday	Wednesday	Thursday	Friday	Saturday	Sunday
Study sessions							
Topics							

Some revision techniques

There should be two elements in your revision. You must **look back** to the work you have covered in the course and **look forward** to the examination. The techniques you use should reflect these two aspects of revision.

Revision should not be boring. It is useful to try a variety of techniques. You probably already have some revision techniques of your own and you may also like to try some of the techniques suggested here, if they are new to you. However, don't waste time with methods of revision which are not effective for you.

- Go through your lecture notes, textbook or workbooks and use a highlighter pen to mark important points.

- Produce a new set of summarised notes. This can be a useful way of re-absorbing information, but you must be careful to keep your notes concise, or you may find that you are simply reproducing work you have done before. It is helpful to use a different format for your notes.

- Make a collection of key words which remind you of the essential concepts of a topic.

- Reduce your notes to a set of key facts and definitions which you must memorise. Write them on cards which you can keep with you all the time.

- When you come across areas which you were unsure about first time around, rework relevant questions in your course materials, then study the answers in great detail.

- If there are isolated topics which you feel are completely beyond you, identify exactly what it is that you cannot understand and find someone (such as a lecturer or recent graduate) who can explain these points to you.

- Practise as many exam standard questions as you can. The best way to do this is to work to time, under exam conditions. You should always resist looking at the answer until you have finished.

- If you have come to rely on a word processor in your day-to-day work, you may have got out of the habit of writing at speed. It is well worth reviving this skill before you sit down in the examination hall: it is something you will need.

- If you have a plentiful supply of relevant questions, you could use them to practise planning answers, and then compare your notes with the answers provided. This is not a substitute for writing full answers, but can be helpful additional practice.

- Go back to questions you have already worked on during the course. This time, complete them under exam conditions, paying special attention to the layout and organisation of your answers. Then compare them in detail with the suggested answers and think about the ways in which your answer differs. This is a useful way of 'fine tuning' your technique.

- During your revision period, do make a conscious effort to identify situations which illustrate concepts and ideas that may arise in the examination. These situations could come from your own work, or from reading the business pages of the quality press. This technique will give you a new perspective on your studies and could also provide material which you can use in the examination.

4 EXAMINATION TECHNIQUES

THE EXAMINATION

This section is divided into two parts. The first part considers the practicalities of sitting the examination. If you have taken other ACCA examinations recently, you may find that everything here is familiar to you. The second part discusses some examination techniques which you may find useful.

The practicalities

What to take with you

You should make sure that you have:

- your ACCA registration card
- your ACCA registration docket.

You may also take to your desk:

- pens and pencils
- a ruler and slide rule
- a calculator
- charting template and geometrical instruments
- eraser and correction fluid.

You are not allowed to take rough paper into the examination.

If you take any last-minute notes with you to the examination hall, make sure these are not on your person. You should keep notes or books in your bag or briefcase, which you will be asked to leave at the side of the examination hall.

Although most examination halls will have a clock, it is advisable to wear a watch, just in case your view is obscured.

If your calculator is solar-powered, make sure it works in artificial light. Some examination halls are not particularly well-lit. If you use a battery-powered calculator, take some spare batteries with you. For obvious reasons, you may not use a calculator which has a graphic/word display memory. Calculators with printout facilities are not allowed because they could disturb other candidates

Getting there

You should arrange to arrive at the examination hall at least half an hour before the examination is due to start. If the hall is a large one, the invigilator will start filling the hall half an hour before the starting time.

Make absolutely sure that you know how to get to the examination hall and how long it will take you. Check on parking or public transport. Leave yourself enough time so that you will not be anxious if the journey takes a little longer than you anticipated. Many people like to make a practice trip the day before their first examination.

At the examination hall

Examination halls differ greatly in size. Some only hold about ten candidates. Others can sit many hundreds of people. You may find that more than one examination is being taken at the hall at the same time, so don't panic if you hear people discussing a completely different subject from the one you have revised.

While you are waiting to go in, don't be put off by other people talking about how well, or badly, they have prepared for the examination.

You will be told when to come in to the examination hall. The desks are numbered. (Your number will be on your examination docket.) You will be asked to leave any bags at the side of the hall.

Inside the hall, the atmosphere will be extremely formal. The invigilator has certain things which he or she must tell candidates, often using a particular form of words. Listen carefully, in case there are any unexpected changes to the arrangements.

On your desk you will see a question paper and an answer booklet in which to write your answers. You will be told when to turn over the paper.

During the examination

You will have to leave your examination paper and answer booklet in the hall at the end of the examination. It is quite acceptable to write on your examination paper if it helps you to think about the questions. However, all workings should be in your answers. You may write any plans and notes in your answer booklet, as long as you cross them out afterwards.

If you require a new answer booklet, put your hand up and a supervisor will come and bring you one.

At various times during the examination, you will be told how much time you have left.

You should not need to leave the examination hall until the examination is finished. Put up your hand if you need to go to the toilet, and a supervisor will accompany you. If you feel unwell, put up your hand, and someone will come to your assistance. If you simply get up and walk out of the hall, you will not be allowed to reenter.

Before you finish, you must fill in the required information on the front of your answer booklet.

Examination techniques

Tackling Paper 1

The examination will be in two sections. The first part, which will be worth 40 marks, will consist of 2 compulsory questions. The second part will consist of a choice of 3 out of 4 questions of 20 marks each.

Sometimes, you will be asked to discuss concepts and rationales. There may not be one 'right answer' to these questions, so do not be afraid to put forward your own arguments. The Examiners will be looking for evidence that you have really understood the subject and can apply your knowledge in new situations. You will not be expected to repeat facts.

One question may be based on information which is provided as supplementary text within the question.

Your general strategy

You should spend the first ten minutes of the examination reading the paper. Where you have a choice of question, decide which questions you will do. You must divide the time you spend on questions in proportion to the marks on offer. Don't be tempted to spend more time on a question you know a lot about, or one which you find particularly difficult. If a question has more than one part, you must complete each part.

On every question, the first marks are the easiest to gain. Even if things go wrong with your timing and you don't have time to complete a question properly, you will probably gain some marks by making a start.

Spend the last five minutes reading through your answers and making any additions or corrections.

You may answer written questions in any order you like. Some people start with their best question, to help them relax. Another strategy is to begin with your second best question, so that you are working even more effectively when you reach the question you are most confident about.

Once you have embarked on a question, you should try to stay with it, and not let your mind stray to other questions on the paper. You can only concentrate on one thing at once. However, if you get completely stuck with a question, leave space in your answer book and return to it later.

Answering the question

All Examiners say that the most frequent reason for failure in examinations, apart from basic lack of knowledge, is candidates' unwillingness to answer the question that the Examiner has asked. A great many people include every scrap of knowledge they have on a topic, just in case it is relevant. Stick to the question and tailor your answer to what you are asked. Pay particular attention to the verbs in the question.

You should be particularly wary if you come across a question which appears to be almost identical to one which you have practised during your revision. It probably isn't! Wishful thinking makes many people see the question they would like to see on the paper, not the one that is actually there. Read a question at least twice before you begin your answer. Underline key words on the question paper, if it helps focus your mind on what is required.

If you don't understand what a question is asking, state your assumptions. Even if you do not answer in precisely the way the Examiner hoped, you may be given some credit, if your assumptions are reasonable.

Presentation

You should do everything you can to make things easy for the marker. Although you will not be marked on your handwriting, the marker will find it easier to identify the points you have made if your answers are legible. The same applies to spelling and grammar. Use blue or black ink. The marker will be using red or green.

Use the margin to clearly identify which question, or part of a question, you are answering.

Start each answer on a new page. The order in which you answer the questions does not matter, but if a question has several parts, these parts should appear in the correct order in your answer book.

If there is the slightest doubt when an answer continues on another page, indicate to the marker that he or she must turn over. It is irritating for a marker to think he or she has reached the end of an answer, only to turn the page and find that the answer continues.

Use columnar layouts for computations. This will help you to avoid mistakes, and is easier to follow.

Use headings and numbered sentences if they help to show the structure of your answer. However, don't write your answers in one-word note form.

If your answers include diagrams, don't waste time making them great works of art. Keep them clear, neat and simple. Use your rule and any templates or geometric instruments you have with you. Remember to label the axes of graphs properly. Make reference to any diagrams in the body of your text so that they form an integral part of your answer.

It is a good idea to make a rough plan of an answer before you begin to write. Do this in your answer booklet, but make sure you cross it out neatly afterwards. The marker needs to be clear whether he or she is looking at your rough notes, or the answer itself.

Computations

Before you begin a computation, you may find it helpful to jot down the stages you will go through. Cross out these notes afterwards.

It is essential to include all your workings and to indicate where they fit in to your answer. It is important that the marker can see where you got the figures in your answer from. Even if you make mistakes in your computations, you will be given credit for using a principle correctly, if it is clear from your workings and the structure of your answer.

If you spot an arithmetical error which has implications for figures later in your answer, it may not be worth spending a lot of time reworking your computation.

If you are asked to comment or make recommendations on a computation, you must do so. There are important marks to be gained here. Even if your computation contains mistakes, you may still gain marks if your reasoning is correct.

Use the layouts which you see in the answers given in this booklet and in model answers. A clear layout will help you avoid errors and will impress the marker.

Essay questions

You must plan an essay before you start writing. One technique is to quickly jot down any ideas which you think are relevant. Re-read the question and cross out any points in your notes which are not relevant. Then number your points. Remember to cross out your plan afterwards.

Your essay should have a clear structure. It should contain a brief introduction, a main section and a conclusion. Don't waste time by restating the question at the start of your essay.

Break your essay up into paragraphs. Use sub-headings and numbered sentences if they help show the structure of your answer.

Be concise. It is better to write a little about a lot of different points than a great deal about one or two points.

The Examiner will be looking for evidence that you have understood the syllabus and can apply your knowledge in new situations. You will also be expected to give opinions and make judgements. These should be based on reasoned and logical arguments.

Reports, memos and other documents

Some questions ask you to present your answer in the form of a report or a memo or other document. It is important that you use the correct format - there are easy marks to be gained here. Adopt the format used in sample questions, or use the format you are familiar with in your day-to-day work, as long as it contains all the essential elements.

You should also consider the audience for any document you are writing. How much do they know about the subject? What kind of information and recommendations are required? The Examiner will be looking for evidence that you can present your ideas in an appropriate form.

5 KEY REVISION TOPICS

The aim of this Section is to provide you with a checklist of key information relating to this Paper. You should use it as a reminder of topics to be revised rather than as a summary of all you need to know. Aim to revise as many topics as possible because many of the questions in the exam draw on material from more than one section of the syllabus. You will get more out of this Section if you read through Section 3, *General Revision Guidance* first.

For ease of reference the syllabus has been split into four main areas, and we shall look at each in turn.

1 THE PRINCIPLES OF ACCOUNTING

This area of the syllabus concentrates on the basic principles underlying the preparation of a set of accounts. A student should:

(a) **Be able to identify the users and uses of financial statements and the different types of accounts that can be prepared**

Users:

- Shareholders or owners
- Investors / lenders
- Competitors / suppliers
- Government agencies - tax and VAT
- Managers
- Employees and their representatives.

Uses:

- To measure the result / profit of the business
- To measure the worth of the business
- To help plan and make decisions
- To make comparisons with other businesses
- To understand the financial position of the business
- To safeguard the assets of the business - the stewardship function.

Forms of financial statement

- Balance sheet - shows the assets and liabilities of a business at the end of a financial period

- Trading account - shows the gross profit earned by a business

- Profit and loss account - incorporates the trading account and deducts other expenses to arrive at the net profit

- Cash flow statement - shows where money has come from and gone to during the year

- Budget - forecasts of the future performance of the business.

(b)   **Be able to prepare a profit and loss account and balance sheet for a business**

Note: - the correct format:

Balance sheet:

	£	£	£
Fixed assets			
Land and buildings		80,000	
Plant and machinery		28,000	
Motor vehicles		25,000	
			133,000
Current assets			
Stock in trade	14,000		
Trade debtors	10,000		
Cash	3,000		
		27,000	
Less: **Current liabilities**			
Trade creditors		12,000	
Net current assets (working capital)			15,000
			148,000
Less: **Long-term liabilities**			
Loans			25,000
			123,000
Capital			
Opening capital			102,000
Plus: injections			10,000
Profit			17,000
			129,000
Less: Drawings			6,000
Closing capital			123,000

Profit and loss account

Trading and profit and loss account for the year ended 30 June 19X9

	£	£	£
Sales			x
Less: Returns			x
			x
Less: Opening stock		x	
Purchases	x		
Add: Carriage in	x		
	x		
Less: Returns	x		
		x	
		x	
Less: Closing stock		(x)	
Cost of sales			x
Gross profit			x
Add: Other revenues			
Discounts received		x	
Rent receivable		x	
Interest		x	
		x	
			x
Less: Administration expenses*		x	
Selling expenses*		x	
Finance expenses*		x	
			(x)
Net profit			x

* with relevant detail within these groups.

The purposes of these two primary statements:

The trading and profit and loss account show financial information for a period, ending on a certain date, whereas the balance sheet shows the information relating to that date only. Together they provide a progress report for the year (profit and loss account) and a 'snapshot' of the state of the business at a particular date.

(c)   **Be able to record transactions using the double entry method of bookkeeping in ledger accounts**

Remember that double entry bookkeeping is based upon the principles of:

- Duality
- The accounting equation,

The accounting equation states that: assets = capital + liabilities.

Key revision topics

To ensure that the accounts always balance we apply the principle of duality to the preparation of accounts, as every transaction is recorded on both the debit (left) and the credit (right) side of a ledger account. Practise a few simple bookkeeping entries to remind yourself of the procedures.

Remember that:

A DEBIT is:

1   an *INCREASE IN AN ASSET,* or
2   a *DECREASE IN A LIABILITY,* OR
3   an item of *EXPENSE.*

A CREDIT is:

1   a *DECREASE IN AN ASSET,*
2   an *INCREASE IN A LIABILITY,* or
3   an item of *INCOME.*

(d)   **Know and be able to explain the basic accounting principles that underlie the preparation of financial statements**

The Statement of Principles for Financial Reporting

In November 1995 the ASB published an Exposure Draft of its proposed Statement of Principles, the existence and role of which (excluding Chapter 7, The reporting entity) is examinable in Paper 1. The general issues and ideas inherent in areas covered by the Statement are examinable, however the detailed content of any of the chapters is not examinable.

The purpose of the Statement of Principles is to provide a framework, a set of internally consistent definitions, assumptions and conventions which will underpin and inform accounting practice in general and accounting standards in particular. The six examinable chapters cover:

* the objectives of financial statements
* the qualitative characteristics of financial information
* the elements of financial statements
* recognition in financial statements
* measurement in financial statements
* presentation of financial information

The balance sheet:

As well as understanding the make-up of the figures in the balance sheet, you should be aware of the basic principles that determine its structure; these are:

* The fact that a business is a separate entity from its owner, and therefore the business owes its owner the money he has put into or left in the business. The business owes the owner his capital stake in the business.

* The accounting equation will make the balance sheet balance. The equation is as shown at (c) above.

The profit and loss account:

The statement can be seen to be made up of two parts:

The *trading account* - sales income and the cost of those sales, leading to gross profit.

The *trading and profit and loss account* - incorporates the trading account, adding in non-trading income and deducting non-trading expenses, leading to net profit.

The income and expenses in both parts of the statement should be included on the accruals basis, that is, matching the income that should have been earned in the period being reported on, together with the full expenses incurred to make that income. We ignore income of future periods and include income of the current period even if it has not been received yet. We include expenses of the current period even if they have not been paid yet, but ignore expenses of future periods.

(e)   **Be able to record transactions in journal form as well as in ledger account format**

- A journal is a method of writing out a piece of double entry as a memo to record the entry that has been made in the ledgers. For example a journal to record the purchase of goods for resale for £100 cash would read:

Date	Details	Dr	Cr
xx.xx.xx	Dr Purchases	100	
	Cr Cash		100

   This is a record of purchase of goods for resale on xx.xx.xx for cash. Some examination questions may ask for the double entry for certain transactions to be recorded in journal format.

- The purpose of the journal is usually to provide a list of the entries that have been made to correct accounting errors.

(f)   **State the principal ledgers used in an accounting system and their purpose**

The principal ledgers are:

Cash book - records details of transactions on the cash and bank accounts

Sales ledger - Contains details of the personal accounts of credit customers

Purchase ledger - contains details of the personal accounts of credit suppliers

Nominal ledger - records the details of all other accounts, and includes total figures for debtors and creditors from the sales and purchase ledgers.

(g)   **Be able to prepare and explain the use of control accounts in the accounts preparation process**

Control accounts are used to check the double entry, because they contain total figures for all transactions which have been entered individually in the sales and purchases ledgers. These can then be compared to the sum of the individual balances.

Control accounts can also be used to find missing figures when the accounting records are incomplete as we shall see later.

(h) **Prepare and understand the uses of a trial balance**

A trial balance is a list of all the debit and credit balances in the ledgers. It is prepared to check that the double entry has been correct, before the year-end adjustments are made to the accounting records. If the double entry is correct, then the debit balances extracted from the ledgers should equal the credit balances extracted from the ledgers.

The trial balance will not highlight the following types of mistake.

- Principle - wrong account / wrong type
- Reversal - sides reversed
- Omission - left out
- Commission - wrong account / right type
- Original entry - wrong figure entered on both sides of the double entry
- Compensating - debit errors matched by credit errors.

(i) **Prepare and explain the purpose of bank reconciliations**

Because cash is an asset which can be easily stolen it needs to be checked carefully. One method of checking is to ensure that the balance of the cash at the bank. according to the bank statement, agrees with the balance of cash, according to the cash book.

The cash book and bank statement balances may be different due to timing differences.

- Entries in the cash book but not yet on the bank statement
- Entries on the bank statement, but not yet in the cash book
- Errors, either by the bookkeeper or the bank.

(j) **Have a brief knowledge of how computerised accounting systems function and their advantages**

2   **THE THEORY AND PRACTICE OF ACCOUNTING**

The student should be able to do the following:

(a) **Define fixed assets and depreciation and explain what the depreciation of such assets entails (SSAP 12)**

Fixed assets: 'those assets which are intended for use on a continuing basis in the enterprise's activities.'

Depreciation: 'the measure of wearing out, consumption or other reduction in the useful economic life of a fixed asset whether arising from use, effluxion of time or obsolescence through technological change'.

Depreciation matches the cost of a fixed asset with the income it helps to generate, by spreading the cost of the asset over the period of time it is in use.

You should also be aware of how to record fixed assets; their depreciation and revaluation in the ledger accounts.

(b)   **Explain the accounting treatment for stock (SSAP 9)**

- Know what items can be classified as stock.

- Stock should be valued at the lower of cost and net realisable value:

    Cost - purchase cost, conversion costs, transport costs etc.
    Net realisable value - actual or estimated selling price less all further costs to be incurred before sale.

- Be able to value stock using common valuation methods: for example, FIFO; LIFO; weighted average.

(c)   **Account for debtors and cash**

- *Debtors* are those who owe us for goods and services supplied to them on credit terms.

- A *bad debt* is a debt which will definitely not be paid and so is a definite deduction from the value of debtors for inclusion in the accounts.

- A *doubtful debt* is a debt which may yet be paid but over which there is some doubt. No specific deduction is made from debtors for a doubtful debt, but a provision can be set up which, when set against the full value of debtors in the balance sheet, will deduct the amount of the debtors that are doubtful.

Make sure that you are aware of the accounting centres required for bad and doubtful debts, and bank and cash balances

(d)   **Explain and understand accounting for accruals and prepayments**

An *accrual* is an amount included in the financial statements because an amount is owed to or by the business at the accounting period end.

A *prepayment* is an amount excluded from the profit and loss account and included as a debtor (expense) or creditor (income), because expenditure or income from a future period has been paid/received early.

Accounting for accruals and prepayments ensures that the accounts follow the *matching* process: that income is matched with the expenditure incurred to make that income.

Ensure that you know how to deal with accruals and prepayments in the accounts of a business.

- Profit and loss account:
    ADD - CLOSING ACCRUAL
    DEDUCT - OPENING ACCRUAL
    ADD - OPENING PREPAYMENT
    DEDUCT - CLOSING PREPAYMENT

- Balance sheet:
    Accrued expenses / prepaid income = CREDITORS
    Accrued income / prepaid expenses = DEBTORS

(e) **Define and illustrate accounting for goodwill**

- Goodwill is 'the difference between the value of a business as a whole and the aggregate of the fair values of its separable net assets'.

- Purchased goodwill should be included in the accounts; it can be written off immediately on acquisition against reserves, or it can be valued as an intangible fixed asset and amortised like any other asset over its useful life to the profit and loss account.

- Non-purchased goodwill should not be included in the balance sheet (prudence).

Be aware of the valuation methods for goodwill.

(f) **Define and explain accounting for research and development costs (SSAP 13)**

Be aware of the definitions of research and development expenditure.

If development expenditure satisfies five criteria:

(i)   clearly defined product
(ii)   separately identifiable expenditure
(iii)   outcome technically feasible and commercially viable
(iv)   total development and sales costs less than total sales revenue
(v)   adequate resources to see the development through,

then, the development expenditure *may* be capitalised instead of being expensed in the profit and loss account. This development expenditure asset must then be amortised over the production life of the product, commencing when production commences.

(g) **Define, explain and illustrate accounting for contingencies (SSAP 18)**

- A contingency is a condition which exists at the balance sheet date, where the outcome will be confirmed on the occurrence or non-occurrence of one or more uncertain future events.

Accounting treatment:

Likelihood of outcome	Potential gain	Potential loss
1 Probable	Disclose by way of note	Accrue
2 Possible	Do not disclose	Disclose by way of note
3 Remote	Do not disclose	Do not disclose

Be able to give examples of these types of transactions. Accounting for contingencies is a good example of the concept of prudence prevailing over the accruals concept.

(h) **Define, explain and illustrate accounting for post balance sheet events (SSAP 17)**

- Post balance sheet events are those events, both favourable and unfavourable, which occur between the balance sheet date and the date on which the financial statements are approved by the board of directors.

- Adjusting events are those which provide additional evidence of conditions existing at the balance sheet date.

- Non-adjusting events are post balance sheet events which concern conditions which did not exist at the balance sheet date.

Be able to give examples of both adjusting and non-adjusting events.

Accounting treatment:

- Adjusting events - alter the figures in the financial statements in line with the event if it is material.

- Non-adjusting events - do not alter the figures in the accounts, but disclose the event if non-disclosure would affect the ability of the users of the accounts to understand the financial position of the company.

(i) **Understand, define and explain accounting conventions and accounting policies**

Accounting conventions are the broad assumptions underlying the preparation of accounts for businesses. There are four conventions detailed in SSAP 2:

- *Going concern* - The business will continue in operation for the foreseeable future.

- *Accruals* - Revenue and costs are recognised as they are earned or incurred and matched together in the profit and loss account of the period to which they relate.

- *Prudence* - Revenue and profits are not anticipated but are recognised only when realised in the form of cash or other assets, whereas provision is made for all known liabilities.

- *Consistency* - The accounting treatment of like items within each accounting period and from one accounting period to another is consistent.

Be able to apply these conventions to the preparation of accounts and give examples of their application.

The Companies Act 1985 also mentions another convention:

- *Separate valuation* - which means that assets and liabilities should not be netted off against one another to produce a single figure.

SSAP 2 also defines accounting bases and policies:

Accounting bases are the methods which have been developed for applying the accounting conventions to financial transactions.

Accounting policies are the specific accounting bases judged by enterprises to be appropriate to their circumstances.

Students should also be able to give examples of accounting bases and policies.

3 **THE PREPARATION OF FINANCIAL STATEMENTS FOR DIFFERENT KINDS OF BUSINESS ENTITY**

(a) **The preparation of accounts for limited companies**
   - Be able to explain terms relating to limited companies
   - Know the prescribed formats for the preparation of company accounts as contained in the Companies Acts.

Profit & loss account - format 1

		£	£
1.	Turnover		X
2.	Cost of sales		(X)
			—
3.	Gross profit or loss		X
4.	Distribution costs		(X)
5.	Administrative expenses		(X)
6.	Other operating income		X
			—
			X
7.	Income from shares in group companies	X	
8.	Income from participating interests	X	
9.	Income from other fixed asset investments	X	
10.	Other interest receivable and similar income	X	
		—	X
			—
			X
11.	Amount written off investments		(X)
12.	Interest payable and similar charges		(X)
			—
	Profit or loss on ordinary activities before taxation		X
13.	Tax on profit or loss on ordinary activities		(X)
			—
14.	Profit or loss on ordinary activities after taxation		X
15.	Extraordinary income	X	
16.	Extraordinary charges	(X)	
		—	
17.	Extraordinary profit or loss	X	
18.	Tax on extraordinary profit or loss	(X)	
		—	X
19.	Other taxes not shown under the above items		(X)
			—
20.	Profit or loss for the financial year		X
	Dividends	(X)	
	Transfers to/from reserves	X	
		—	
			(X)
			—
			X
	Profit & Loss account b/f		X
			—
	Profit & Loss account c/f		X
			—

Balance sheet

A	Called-up share capital not paid		X
B	Fixed assets		
I	Intangible assets		
	1 Development costs	X	
	2 Concessions, patents, licences, trade marks and similar rights and assets	X	
	3 Goodwill	X	
	4 Payment on account	X	
		—	

   X

II Tangible assets
1. Land and buildings — X
2. Plant and machinery — X
3. Fixtures, fittings, tools and equipment — X
4. Payments on account and assets in course of construction — X

                   X

III Investments
1. Shares in group companies — X
2. Loans to group companies — X
3. Shares in related companies — X
4. Loans to related companies — X
5. Other investments other than loans — X
6. Other loans — X
7. Own shares — X

          X

Total B — X

C Current assets

I Stocks
1. Raw materials and consumables — X
2. Work in progress — X
3. Finished goods and goods for resale — X
4. Payments on account — X

   X

II Debtors
1. Trade debtors — X
2. Amounts owed by group companies — X
3. Amounts owed by related companies — X
4. Other debtors — X
5. Called-up share capital not paid — X
6. Prepayments and accrued income — X

   X

III Investments
1. Shares in group companies — X
2. Own shares — X
3. Other investments — X

   X

IV Cash at bank and in hand — X

Total C — X

D Prepayments and accrued income — X

Total C and D		X	

E	Creditors: amounts falling due within one year		
	1 Debenture loans	X	
	2 Bank loans and overdrafts	X	
	3 Payments received on account	X	
	4 Trade creditors	X	
	5 Bills of exchange payable	X	
	6 Amounts owed to group companies	X	
	7 Amounts owed to related companies	X	
	8 Other creditors including taxation and social security	X	
	9 Accruals and deferred income	X	

Total E   X

F Net current assets (liabilities) (**C + D**) - **E**   X

G Total assets less current liabilities (**A + B**) - **F**   X

H	Creditors: amounts falling due after more than one year		
	1 Debenture loans	X	
	2 Bank loans and overdrafts	X	
	3 Payments received on account	X	
	4 Trade creditors	X	
	5 Bills of exchange payable	X	
	6 Amounts owed to group companies	X	
	7 Amounts owed to related companies	X	
	8 Other creditors including taxation and social security	X	
	9 Accruals and deferred income	X	

Total H   X

I	Provisions for liabilities and charges	X	
	1 Pensions and similar obligations	X	
	2 Taxation, including deferred taxation	X	
	3 Other provisions	X	

Total I   X

J Accruals and deferred income   X

G - (H + I + J)   XX

K	Capital and reserves			
	I Called-up share capital			X
	II Share premium account			X
	III Revaluation reserve			X
	IV Other reserves			
	1 Capital redemption reserve		X	
	2 Reserve for own shares		X	
	3 Reserves provided for by the articles of association		X	
	4 Other reserves		X	
			—	
				X
	V Profit & loss account			X
				—
				XX
				—

Any balance sheet item identified in the Companies Act format by an Arabic number can be shown either on the face of the balance or by way of a note.

Remember, it is likely that an *aide-mémoire* will be provided if you are required to produce Companies Act accounts in the Paper 1 exam.

- Be aware of the regulation of the preparation of company accounts.

(b) **The preparation of partnership accounts**

- The principles of law and accounting for partnerships

- The effect of admissions, retirements (of partners), amalgamations and dissolutions (of partnerships) on partnership accounts.

Note: The provisions of the **Partnership Act 1890** state that in the absence of a formal partnership agreement profits are to be split as follows:

1 No salary or interest on capital

2 Profits split equally

3 Interest at 5% per annum can be given on capital introduced by partners that is greater than the fixed capital requirements of the partnership.

If the Examiners want you to apply these rules in a question they will usually remind you of them first.

(c) **The preparation of accounts for clubs and societies**

- The preparation of a receipts and payments account and how to convert it into an income and expenditure account.

(d)   **The preparation of accounts from incomplete accounting records**

Learn how to compensate for the lack of accounting information by:

- using the accounting equation to balance accounts
- using control accounts to find missing information
- using cost structures to find missing information in the trading account.

4   INTERPRETATION OF FINANCIAL STATEMENTS

(a)   **Cash flow statements**

(i)   The uses and users of cash flow statements

(ii)   The contents of FRS1 and the preparation of a cash flow statement.

The original FRS1 was issued in September 1991. In October 1996 a revised version of FRS1 was issued, which is examinable in 1997. The key points of FRS1 (revised) are explained in the Updating Notes in the next section of this book.

(b)   **Ratio analysis**

(i)   The calculation of profitability, liquidity and financing ratios. The more frequently used ratios are shown below:

I   *Profitability*

(a)   Return on capital employed

$$= \frac{\text{Profit before interest and tax}}{\text{Capital employed}}$$

Where capital employed = Total assets less current liabilities

(b)   Profit margin on sales

$$= \frac{\text{Profit before interest and tax}}{\text{Sales}}$$

(c)   Asset turnover

$$= \frac{\text{Sales}}{\text{Capital employed}}$$

(d)   Fixed asset turnover

$$= \frac{\text{Sales}}{\text{Fixed assets}}$$

(e)   Working capital turnover

$$= \frac{\text{Sales}}{\text{Net current assets}}$$

II *Liquidity*

    (a)   Current ratio

$$= \frac{\text{Current assets}}{\text{Current liabilities}}$$

    (b)   Quick ratio

$$= \frac{\text{Current assets - stock}}{\text{Current liabilities}}$$

    (c)   Stock turnover

$$= \frac{\text{Cost of sales}}{\text{Stock}}$$

    (d)   Collection period   or   Debtor turnover

$$= \frac{\text{Debtors}}{\text{Credit sales per day}} \qquad = \frac{\text{Credit sales}}{\text{Debtors}}$$

III *Gearing*

    (a)   Debt/Equity

        (i)   Long term

$$= \frac{\text{Long term debt}}{\text{Equity shareholders' funds}}$$

        (ii)   Total

$$= \frac{\text{Total debt}}{\text{Equity shareholders' funds}}$$

    (b)   Interest cover

$$= \frac{\text{Profit before interest and tax}}{\text{Interest payable}}$$

IV *Investors' ratios*

    (a)   Dividend yield

$$= \frac{\text{Net dividend per share + Tax credit}}{\text{Current market price per share}}$$

    (b)   Dividend cover

$$= \frac{\text{Earnings per share}}{\text{Net dividend per share}}$$

(c)   Price/earnings ratio

$$= \frac{\text{Current market price per share}}{\text{Earnings per share}}$$

(d)   Net assets per share

$$= \frac{\text{Net assets}}{\text{Number of shares}}$$

(e)   Earnings per share

$$= \frac{\text{Net profit available to ordinary shareholders}}{\text{Total number of issued ordinary shares}}$$

(ii)   The explanation of the results produced by the ratios.

(iii)   The users and uses of ratio analysis.

6 UPDATES

INTRODUCTION

Examinable documents

Every six months (on 1 July and 1 December) the ACCA publish a list of 'examinable documents' which form the basis of the legislation and accounting regulations that will be examinable at the following diet.

The ACCA Official Textbooks published in June 1996 were fully up-to-date for the examinable documents published by the Association on 1 July 1996 and this section gives details of additional examinable documents listed by the ACCA at 1 December 1996.

In addition we include further details of the new examination format, the new examiner and the syllabus modification.

1 NEW EXAMINABLE DOCUMENT

REVISION TO FRS 1 'CASH FLOW STATEMENTS'

Introduction

Following five years practical experience in operating the original FRS 1, the ASB issued a revised FRS1 'Cash flow statements' in October 1996. This is examinable in the ACCA examinations in 1997.

Key changes in the revised FRS 1

The following changes are made from the original FRS 1:

(i)   the concept of cash equivalents has been dropped. The cash flow statement now shows movements in cash only ie, movements in cash in hand and deposits repayable on demand less overdrafts repayable on demand.

(ii)   a cash flow statement should now list its cash flows for the period under eight standard headings:

- operating activities
- returns on investments and servicing of finance
- taxation
- capital expenditure and financial investment
- acquisitions and disposals (of businesses)
- equity dividends paid
- management of liquid resources
- financing

(iii)   a new reconciliation is required between the movement in cash in the period and the movement in net debt. This is in addition to the reconciliation required between operating profit and the net cash flow from operating activities.

Example

The following example shows a cash flow statement prepared in accordance with FRS 1 (revised).

XYZ Ltd
Cash flow statement for the year ended 31 December 19X6

	Note	£'000
Net cash inflow from operating activities		6,889
Returns on investments and servicing of finance	1	2,999
Taxation		(2,922)
Capital expenditure	1	(1,525)
		5,441
Equity dividends paid		(2,417)
		3,024
Management of liquid resources	1	(450)
Financing	1	57
Increase in cash		2,631

Reconciliation of operating profit to net cash inflow from operating activities

	£'000
Operating profit	6,022
Depreciation charges	899
Increase in stocks	(194)
Increase in debtors	(72)
Increase in creditors	234
Net cash inflow from operating activities	6,889

Reconciliation of net cash flow to movement in net debt

	£'000
Increase in cash in the period	2,631
Cash used to repurchase debenture	149
Cash used to increase liquid resource	450
Change in net debt	3,230
Net debt at 1 Jan 19X6	(2,903)
Net funds at 31 Dec 19X6	327

Note 1: Gross cash flows

		£'000
Return on investments and servicing of finance		
Interest received		3,011
Interest paid		(12)
		2,999
Capital expenditure		
Payments to acquire tangible fixed assets		(1,567)
Receipts from sales of tangible fixed assets		42
		(1,525)
Management of liquid resources		
Purchase of Treasury Bills		(650)
Sale of Treasury Bills		200
		(450)
Financing		
Issue of ordinary share capital		211
Repurchase of debenture loan		(149)
Expenses paid on share issues		(5)
		57

Conclusion

By requiring cash flow statements to show movements in cash only, rather than movements in the aggregate of cash and cash equivalents, the ASB have simplified matters. The former cash equivalents are now to be shown on the face of the cash flow statement under a new heading 'management of liquid resources'.

The reconciliation required between cash movement in the period and the movement in net debt should give valuable new information to users of accounts, concerning the entity's liquidity, solvency and financial adaptability.

2 CHANGE TO EXAMINATION FORMAT

With effect from June 1997, the format of the examination is to change. Multiple choice questions will no longer be set and the format of the exam will be as follows.

		No of marks
Section A	2 compulsory questions	40
Section B	3 (out of 4) questions of 20 marks each	60

It has previously been the case that a Supplement may be used in paper 1. With effect from June 1997, a Supplement will not be provided. However the Examiner may decide to provide supplementary information within the text of the question, for example an extract from an Accounting Standard.

The pilot paper for the new structure is set out in section 1 of this book, on page xii.

3 NEW EXAMINER

From June 1997, Paper 1 will have a new examiner. He recently issued the following comments on his approach to the paper.

Approach to the paper

The objective of the Accounting Framework paper is there to ensure that candidates can only progress to the Certificate Stage if they demonstrate two main skills:

(a)   the ability to prepare simple financial statements and the underlying accounting records;

(b)   an understanding of the principles on which accounting is based, including the ability to criticise existing practice. Other supporting skills are also desirable.

The paper will normally consist of 50% to 70% computational questions and 30% to 50% non-computational questions.

Questions requiring large-scale recording of routine trading transactions will not be set, but double entry skills will be tested by questions on the following topics among others:

(a)   correction of errors;

(b)   journal entries;

(c)   fixed asset accounting;

(d)   ledger control accounts.

Interpretation of the syllabus

All five parts of the syllabus are important. The end product of accounting is the production of meaningful accounting statements (part 4) and their interpretation (part 5). However, these statements do not exist in a vacuum and must be based on theory - accounting principles - and the practical recording of transactions.

Questions dealing with the preparation of financial statements can test aspects of candidates' ability to record transactions and to understand accounting principles, either within a computation or in a non-computational requirement added to the main part of a question. It thus seems logical to emphasise this section of the syllabus in devising a paper - it would be a strange foundation accounting examination paper which did not contain a question requiring the preparation of a profit and loss account and balance sheet for one of three types of entity - sole traders, partnerships and companies.

Part 5 of the syllabus includes the preparation of cash flow statements and interpretation, two important topics. A paper could include questions on both of them.

4 SYLLABUS REVISIONS

There will be some minor amendments to the syllabus with effect from the December 1997 examination. **You should note that these changes do not affect the June 1997 sitting.**

1   Ethics and independence of the accounting and auditing profession

This is to be deleted from the paper 1 syllabus but will remain in the later accounting and auditing papers.

2   Dissolution of Partnerships

This is currently examinable in Paper 10, but from December 1997 will be introduced into the Paper 1 syllabus under Section 4c.

We set out below some notes on dissolution of partnerships.

THE DISSOLUTION OF A PARTNERSHIP

Order of repayment

On a dissolution the partnership assets are disposed of and the proceeds applied in the following order:

(a)   outside third party creditors;
(b)   partners' advances or loans;
(c)   partners' capitals;
(d)   any profits on realisation would be distributed in profit-sharing ratios.

Realisation account

The accounting treatment involves a realisation account, which acts as a profit and loss account for the disposals. The assets are transferred at book values to the debit of this account, and the realisation proceeds or agreed take-over values are credited. The balance remaining then represents the profit or loss on disposal, which is transferred to the partners' accounts in profit sharing ratio. The books are finally closed by the settlement of cash between the partners, which will eliminate the remaining balance.

Example

A, B and C share profits 4 : 3 : 3. They agree to dissolve their partnership at the end of the financial year, when the balance sheet appeared as follows:

	£	£
Fixed assets, at cost less depreciation:		
Freehold		4,000
Plant and machinery		1,500
Motor vehicles (three cars)		1,600
		7,100
Current assets:		
Stock	5,000	
Debtors	2,500	
Cash	1,500	
	9,000	
Current liabilities	2,100	
		6,900
Loan account - D		(2,000)
		12,000

	A £	B £	C £	
Partners' accounts:				
Capital	4,000	3,000	2,000	9,000
Current	1,500	1,000	500	3,000
	5,500	4,000	2,500	12,000

The following are sold for cash:

	£
Freehold, for	8,000
Plant and machinery, for	1,300
Stock, for	4,300
	13,600

The creditors are settled for £2,000.

C takes over the debtors at an agreed value of £2,200.

A takes over D's loan at its book value.

A, B and C take over the cars at the following valuations:

A	£600
B	£800
C	£400

Realisation expenses are £200.

You are required to prepare the ledger accounts to show the closing of the partnership books.

Solution

Numbers in brackets refer to sequence of entries

Realisation account

Book value of assets		£	£	Sale or disposal proceeds:		£
Realisation expenses				(i) Cash - sold		
To partners - profit on realisation in PSR				(ii) Partners' accounts - assets taken over		
(1) Freehold account			4,000	(2) Cash - sale proceeds		13,600
(1) Plant and machinery account			1,500	(4) Discount received on creditors		100
(1) Motor vehicles account			1,600	Partners' accounts - assets taken over:		
(1) Stock account			5,000	(5) C debtors		2,200
(1) Debtors account			2,500	(5) A motor car		600
(7) Cash - realisation expenses			200	(5) B motor car		800
Partners' accounts - profit on realisation:				(5) C motor car		400
A 40%		1,160				
B 30%		870				
C 30%		870				
			2,900			
			17,700			17,700

Partners' accounts

		A	B	C			A	B	C
		£	£	£			£	£	£
(5)	Debtors taken over			2,200		Balances b/d: Capital accounts	4,000	3,000	2,000
(5)	Motor cars taken over	600	800	400		Current accounts	1,500	1,000	500
(8)	Cash to settle	8,060	4,070	770			5,500	4,000	2,500
					(6)	D's loan account	2,000		
						Realisation account - profit	1,160	870	870
		8,660	4,870	3,370			8,660	4,870	3,370

Creditors' account

		£		£
(3)	Cash	2,000	Balance b/d	2,100
(4)	Realisation account - discount received on settlement	100		
		2,100		2,100

D's loan account

		£		£
(6)	A's partner account	2,000	Balance b/d	2,000

Cash account

		£	£			£	£
	Balance b/d		1,500	(3)	Creditors		2,000
	Sale proceeds to realisation account:			(7)	Realisation expenses		200
					Partners' accounts to settle:		
(2)	Freehold	8,000		(8)	A	8,060	
(2)	Plant and machinery	1,300		(8)	B	4,070	
(2)	Stock	4,300		(8)	C	770	
			13,600				12,900
			15,100				15,100

Important points

(a) The capital and current accounts are combined since, in the context of the dissolution, the distinction between distributable and retained assets is irrelevant.

(b) A partner with a deficiency on his account, after giving effect to realisation, must pay cash into the firm's bank account to clear his debit balance.

(c) If the partner with the deficiency is bankrupt and cannot pay in, a loss (rather like a bad debt) has arisen, and this loss must be borne by the remaining partners.

It was decided in Garner v Murray (1904) that the remaining partners should bear this loss in CAPITAL SHARING RATIO. The capital figures to be taken will be based on the last normal balance sheet of the firm.

The double entry is:

>Dr   Remaining partners in capital sharing ratio
>   Cr   Insolvent partner with any deficiency

Activity

Smart and Swift were in partnership as hotel proprietors sharing profits and losses: Smart three-fifths, Swift two-fifths. No interest was charged on drawings or credited on capital.

The following was a summary of their trial balances as at 31 December 19X8:

Debits	£	£	Credits	£	£
Debtors		600	Bank overdraft		4,590
Fittings and fixtures		1,800	Loan - Smart at 6%		3,000
Foodstuffs - stock			Partners' capital accounts:		
at 31 December 19X7		420	Smart	3,000	
Foodstuffs purchased		2,600	Swift	500	
Freehold premises		6,000			3,500
General expenses		810	Sundry creditors		210
Partners' drawings:			Takings		5,100
Smart	520				
Swift	750				
		1,270			
Motor vehicle		700			
Wages		2,200			
		16,400			16,400

For the purpose of accounts as on 31 December 19X8 the stock of foodstuffs was valued at £300, and £200 was to be written off the book value of the motor vehicle and £100 off fittings and fixtures. A provision of £60 was required for accrued general expenses and Smart was to be credited with a year's interest on his loan account.

The partnership was dissolved on 31 December 19X8, it being agreed that:

(a)   Smart should take over the stock of foodstuffs for £250 and part of the fittings and fixtures for £600.

(b)   Swift should take over the motor vehicle for £400.

(c)   Interest on Smart's loan should cease as on 31 December 19X8.

During January 19X9:

(a)   The freehold premises were sold, realising a net amount of £6,800.

(b)   £480 was collected from debtors (the balance proving irrecoverable).

(c)   The net proceeds from an auction of the balance of fittings and fixtures were received amounting to £1,400. It was agreed that the few unsold items should be taken over partly by Smart for £40 and the rest by Swift for £20.

(d)   Creditors were paid in full together with incidental realisation and dissolution expenses of £120.

(e)   All amounts receivable or payable by Smart and Swift were settled.

You are required:

(a) to prepare the profit and loss account for the year ended 31 December 19X8 excluding any profit or loss arising on dissolution;

(b) to prepare the realisation account;

(c) to prepare the cash account for January 19X9; and

(d) to prepare partners' capital accounts (in columnar form) showing the final settlement on dissolution.

Activity solution

(a)

Profit and loss account for the year ended 31 December 19X8

	£	£	£
Hotel receipts			5,100
Catering and hotel expenses:			
Foodstuffs (stocks adjusted)	2,720		
Wages	2,200		
General expenses	870		
		5,790	
Depreciation:			
Motor vehicle	200		
Fittings	100		
		300	
Loan interest		180	
			6,270
Net loss for the year			1,170
Allocated:			
Smart (three-fifths)			702
Swift (two-fifths)			468
			1,170

(b)

Realisation account

	£	£		£	£
Sundry assets:			Assets taken over:		
Debtors		600	Smart:		
Fittings and fixtures		1,700	Stock of foodstuffs	250	
Stocks of foodstuffs		300	Fittings and fixtures		
Freehold premises		6,000	(part)	600	
Motor vehicle		500	Sundry items	40	
Dissolution expenses		120		——	890
Profit on realisation:			Swift:		
Smart (three-fifths)	462		Motor vehicle	400	
Swift (two-fifths)	308		Sundry items	20	
	——	770		——	420
			Assets realised:		
			Freehold		6,800
			Debtors		480
			Fittings and fixtures		1,400
		9,990			9,990

(c)

Cash account for January 19X9

	£		£
Proceeds of:		Balance b/d	4,590
Freehold	6,800	Dissolution, etc expenses	120
Debtors	480	Sundry creditors £(210 + 60)	270
Fittings and fixtures	1,400	Loan - Smart	3,000
Cash paid in by Swift	830	Cash withdrawn by Smart	1,530
	9,510		9,510

(d)

Capital accounts

	Smart £	Swift £		Smart £	Swift £
Drawings	520	750	Balances b/d	3,000	500
Net loss for 19X8	702	468	Loan interest	180	
Assets taken over	890	420	Profit on realisation	462	308
Cash withdrawn	1,530		Cash paid in		830
	3,642	1,638		3,642	1,638

7 PRACTICE QUESTIONS

1	SEMA PLC

Sema plc, a company in the heavy engineering industry, carried out an expansion programme in the 19X6 financial year, in order to meet a permanent increase in contracts.

The company selected a suitable site and commissioned a survey and valuation report, for which the fee was £1,500. On the basis of the report the site was acquired for £90,000. Solicitors' fees for drawing up the contract and conveyancing were £3,000.

Fees of £8,700 were paid to the architects for preparing the building plans and overseeing the building work. This was carried out partly by the company's own workforce (at a wages cost of £11,600), using company building materials (cost £76,800) and partly by sub-contractors who charged £69,400, of which £4,700 related to the demolition of an existing building on the same site.

The completed building housed two hydraulic presses.

The cost of Press A was £97,000 (ex works), payable in a single lump sum two months after installation. Sema was given a trade discount of 10% and a cash discount for prompt payment of 2%. Hire of a transporter to collect the press and to convey it to the new building was £2,900. Installation costs were £2,310, including hire of lifting gear, £1,400.

Press B would have cost £105,800 (delivered) if it had been paid in one lump sum. However, Sema opted to pay three equal annual instalments of £40,000, starting on the date of acquisition. Installation costs were £2,550, including hire of lifting gear, £1,750.

The whole of the above expenditure was financed by the issue of £500,000 7% debentures (on which the annual interest payable was £35,000).

Before the above acquisitions were taken into account, the balances (at cost) on the fixed asset accounts for premises and plant were £521,100 and £407,500 respectively.

You are required:

(a)   using such of the above information as is relevant, to post and balance the premises and plant accounts for the 19X6 financial year;

(12 marks)

(b)   to state, with reasons, which of the given information you have not used in your answer to (a) above.

(4 marks)
(Total: 16 marks)
(ACCA Dec 86)

2   FULLER LTD

The bank account of Fuller Ltd, prepared by the company's bookkeeper, was as shown below for the month of October 19X6:

Bank account

19X6 Oct		£	19X6 Oct		Cheque No.	£
1	Balance b/d	91.40	2	Petty cash	062313	36.15
3	McIntosh & Co	260.11	3	Freda's Fashions		
3	Malcolm Brothers	112.83			062314	141.17
3	Cash sales	407.54	6	Basford Ltd	062315	38.04
14	Rodney Photographic	361.02	8	Hansler Agencies		
17	Puccini's Cold Store Ltd	72.54			062316	59.32
20	Eastern Divisional Gas Board rebate (Aug. direct credit)	63.40	9	Duncan's Storage	062317	106.75
			9	Aubrey plc	062318	18.10
22	Grainger's Garage	93.62	10	Secretarial Services Ltd	062319	28.42
29	Cash sales	235.39				
31	Balance c/d	221.52	14	Trevor's Auto Repairs	062320	11.75
			15	Wages cash	062321	115.52
			16	Towers Hotel	062322	44.09
			17	Bank charges (Sep.)		12.36
			20	Broxcliffe Borough Council	SO	504.22
			21	Eastern Area Electricity Board	DD	196.83
			24	Eastern Divisional Gas Board	DD	108.64
			28	Petty cash	062323	41.20
			30	Wages cash	062324	119.07
			31	Salaries transfers		337.74
		1,919.37				1,919.37
			Nov 1	Balance b/d		221.52

In early November the company's bank sent a statement of account which is reproduced below:

Statement of account with Lowland Bank plc
Account: Fuller Ltd current account no. 10501191
Date of issue: 1 November 19X6

19X6 October	Description	Debit £	Credit £	Balance £
1	BCE			90.45
2	CR		175.02	265.47
2	062310	111.34		154.13
3	062312	9.18		144.95
3	062309	15.41		129.54
3	CR		780.48	910.02
7	062313	36.15		873.87
10	ADJ		12.90	886.77
15	062315	38.04		848.73
16	062314	141.17		707.56
17	CR		443.56	1,151.12
20	SO	504.22		646.90
21	062317	106.75		540.15
21	DD	196.83		343.32
21	062320	11.75		331.57
22	141981	212.81		118.76
22	ADJ	10.00		108.76
22	062319	28.42		80.34
22	062320	11.75		68.59
22	CR		93.62	162.21
24	ADJ		212.81	375.02
27	INT (loan account)	26.35		348.67
27	062321	115.52		233.15
28	062322	44.09		189.06
28	DD	108.64		80.42
30	CGS	9.14		71.28
31	ADJ		11.75	83.03

Abbreviations: BCE = Balance; CR = Credit; ADJ = Adjustment;
SO = Standing order; DD = Direct debit; INT = Interest;
CGS = Charges. Balances are credit unless marked OD.

You are required to prepare the company's bank reconciliation statement as at 31 October 19X6.

(16 marks)
(ACCA Dec 86)

3   ARISTOCRATIC AUTOS

Duke and Earl are in partnership operating a garage business named Aristocratic Autos.

In addition to selling petrol and oil, the garage has a workshop where car repairs and maintenance are carried out and also a small showroom from which new and second-hand cars are sold.

For accounting purposes each of these three activities is treated as a separate department.

At 30 September 19X6 balances extracted from the ledgers of Aristocratic Autos comprised:

	£
Cash sales:	
Workshop (repair charges)	32,125
Petrol and oil	32,964
Showroom (car sales)	8,500
Credit sales:	
Workshop (repair charges)	65,892
Petrol and oil	41,252
Showroom (car sales)	81,914
Stocks (at 1 Oct. 19X5):	
Workshop (repair materials)	1,932
Petrol and oil	3,018
Showroom (cars)	20,720
Credit purchases:	
Workshop (repair materials)	23,860
Petrol and oil	41,805
Showroom (cars)	52,100
Fixed assets (at 1 Oct. 19X5) (at cost):	
Freehold buildings ('Freehold' = held in perpetuity):	
Workshop	12,600
Petrol and oil	14,200
Showroom	38,000
Plant, equipment and vehicles:	
Workshop	65,180
Petrol and oil	22,900
Showroom	17,450
Provisions for depreciation (at 1 Oct. 19X5):	
Freehold buildings:	
Workshop	5,060
Petrol and oil	7,100
Showroom	19,390
Plant, equipment and vehicles:	
Workshop	48,254
Petrol and oil	17,077
Showroom	9,451
Fixed asset acquisitions during year (at cost):	
Plant and equipment:	
Workshop	26,210
Petrol and oil	4,520
Showroom	1,060
Fixed asset disposal proceeds during year (see note (3)):	
Plant and equipment:	
Workshop	5,200
Salaries:	
Showroom	10,200
Rates	26,738
Electricity	9,453
General expenses	10,692

	£
Wages:	
Direct:	
Workshop	34,050
Petrol and oil	5,602
Indirect:	
Workshop	6,810
Showroom	4,160
Creditors:	
Workshop	4,225
Petrol and oil	5,602
Showroom	15,250
Bank/cash:	
Workshop	316
Petrol and oil	1,605
Showroom	30,470
Debtors:	
Workshop	1,365
Petrol and oil	537
Drawings:	
Duke	12,190
Earl	9,740
Current accounts (at 1 Oct 19X5) (credit balances):	
Duke	9,750
Earl	10,477
Capital accounts:	
Duke	50,000
Earl	40,000

Notes at 30 September 19X6:

(1)   Stocks at 30 September 19X6:

	£
Workshop	2,752
Petrol and oil	2,976
Showroom	25,310

(2)   Depreciation is calculated using the straight line method (assuming no residual value) and is applied to the original cost of the asset at the end of the financial year, using the following rates:

Freehold buildings	20%
Plant, equipment and vehicles	20%

The depreciation charges for the current year have not yet been posted to the accounts.

The freehold buildings are temporary structures with a five year life.

(3)   No entries have yet been made to transfer the cost (£19,500) and accumulated depreciation (£15,633) of the workshop plant sold during the year.

(4)   Accruals at 30 September 19X6:

		£
Wages:		
Direct:		
	Workshop	113
	Petrol and oil	83
Indirect:		
	Workshop	214
	Showroom	231
Electricity		517
General expenses		1,304

(5)   Prepayments at 30 September 19X6:

Rates   £13,300

(6)   Rates and electricity are apportioned over departments on the basis of the original cost of freehold buildings at the end of the current financial year.

(7)   General expenses are apportioned over departments on the basis of turnover for the current year.

(8)   Duke and Earl are credited with interest on their respective capital account balances at the rate of 5% pa.

You are required to prepare, using separate columns for each department and the business as a whole:

(a)   a departmental trading and profit and loss account for Aristocratic Autos for the year ended 30 September 19X6;

(20 marks)

(b)   a departmental balance sheet for Aristocratic Autos as at 30 September 19X6.

(14 marks)
(Total: 34 marks)
(ACCA Dec 86)

Notes:

(1)   Marks will be awarded for workings which are an essential part of the answer.
(2)   All calculations should be correct to the nearest whole £1.

---

4   DOUBTFUL DEBTS

(a)   You are given the following balances at 1 January 19X1:

Debtors	£10,000
Bank overdraft	£5,000
Provision for doubtful debts	£400

You ascertain the following information:

	£
Sales for the year 19X1 (all on credit)	100,000
Sales returns for the year 19X1	1,000
Receipts from customers during 19X1	90,000
Bad debts written off during 19X1	500
Discounts allowed during 19X1	400

At the end of 19X1 the provision for doubtful debts is required to be 5% of debtors, after making a specific provision for a debt of £200 from a customer who has gone bankrupt.

	£
Sales for the year 19X2 (90% on credit)	100,000
Sales returns for the year 19X2 (90% relating to credit customers)	2,000
Receipts from credit customers during 19X2	95,000
Debtor balances settled by contra against creditor balances during 19X2	3,000
Bad debts written off during 19X2 (including 50% of the debt due from the customer who had gone bankrupt, the other 50% having been received in cash during 19X2)	1,500
Discounts allowed during 19X2	500

At the end of 19X2 the provision for doubtful debts is still required to be 5% of debtors.

You are required to write up the debtors and provision for doubtful debts accounts for 19X1 and 19X2, bringing down the balances at the end of each year and showing in those accounts the double entry for each item.

(14 marks)

(b)   The normal accounting approach with credit sales, as illustrated in part (a) above, is to recognise revenue on the sale when it is made, and then to allow for the possibility of some bad debts.

You are required to outline, by reference to appropriate accounting conventions, the justification for this approach.

(6 marks)
(Total: 20 marks)
(ACCA June 88)

5   LEDGER ACCOUNTS AND TRIAL BALANCE

The following information is to be recorded:

(1)   Opening balances are cash £50 and bank overdraft £100

(2)   Cash sales   £500

(3)   Credit purchases from P   £400

(4)   Wages paid in cash   £100

(5)   Bankings   £200

(6)   Credit sales to Q   £300

(7)   Paid P £250 less 10% discount, by cheque.

(8)   Received cash from Q, £200 less 5% discount.

(9)   Send goods to R on approval (ie, on sale or return), cost £60 and selling price £135.

(10)   Wages paid by cheque   £100

(11)   R returns one-third of the goods he was sent on approval, accepts one-third and delays a decision on the remaining one-third.

(12)   Bank charges notified of   £30

(13)   Receive balance due from Q, less discount of 4%, in cash.

You are required:

(a)   to open all necessary accounts, including a three-column cash book or otherwise, and record this information. Include any closing entries you consider necessary in relation to the transactions with R. Close off the accounts and prepare partial trial balance. Entries may be cross-referenced by the number of the transaction rather than by narrative.

(16 marks)

(b)   Why do you think it is necessary to continue to study exercises such as (a) above, given the increasing availability of computerised bookkeeping packages?

(4 marks)
(Total: 20 marks)
(ACCA June 91)

---

6   YOUNG AND INEXPERIENCED

A young and inexperienced bookkeeper is having great difficulty in producing a bank reconciliation statement at 31 December. He gives you his attempt to produce a summarised cash book, and also the bank statement received for the month of December. These are shown below. You may assume that the bank statement is correct. You may also assume that the trial balance at 1 January did indeed show a bank overdraft of £7,000.12.

Cash book summary - draft

	£	£	£		
Jan 1					
Opening overdraft		7,000.12	35,000.34	payments Jan-Nov	
Jan-Nov receipts	39,500.54				
Add: Discounts	500.02				
		40,000.56	12,000.34	balance Nov 30	
		47,000.68	47,000.68		
Dec 1		12,000.34		payments Dec	Cheque No.
Dec receipts	178.19		37.14		7654
	121.27		192.79		7655
	14.92		5,000.00		7656
	16.88		123.45		7657
		329.26	678.90		7658
			1.47		7659
Dec receipts	3,100.00		19.84		7660
	171.23		10.66		7661
	1,198.17				
		4,469.40	10,734.75	Balance c/d	
		16,799.00	16,799.00		
Dec 31 balance		10,734.75			

Bank statement - December 31

	Withdrawals £	Deposits £		Balance £
			1 December	800.00
7650	300.00	178.19		
7653	191.91	121.27		
7654	37.14	14.92		
7651	1,111.11	16.88		
7656	5,000.00	3,100.00		
7655	129.79	171.23		
7658	678.90	1,198.17		
		117.98		
Standing order	50.00			
7659	1.47			
7661	10.66			
Bank charges	80.00		31 December	3,472.34

You are required:

(a) to prepare a corrected cash book and a reconciliation of the balance on this revised summary with the bank statement balance as at 31 December, as far as you are able.

(20 marks)

(b) to prepare a brief note as to the likely cause of any remaining difference.

(2 marks)
(Total: 22 marks)
(ACCA Dec 89)

---

7 OBS

You are given the following information about a sole trader.

Trial Balance at 31 December 19X8

	£'000	£'000
Bank	53	
Capital		300
Land and Buildings	320	
Plant and machinery: Cost	200	
Depreciation		80
Closing stock	100	
Sales		1,000
Cost of sales	600	
Operating expenses (including depreciation of 20)	140	
Bad debt written off	2	
Debtors	100	
Accruals		5
Creditors		130
	1,515	1,515

Cash Receipts - year to 31 December 19X8

Sales	950

Cash Payments - year to 31 December 19X8

Purchases	560
Plant (1 January 19X8)	90
Operating items	130
Drawings	20

The creditors figure has doubled since 1 January 19X8.

Required

Open appropriate T accounts to enable you to calculate the items in the OPENING balance sheet at 1 January 19X8. Submit the summarised 1 January 19X8 balance sheet and all workings.

(ACCA June 89)

---

8   SPREADSHEETS

'The increasing use of spreadsheets will make accounting out of date'

Required

Briefly explain the usefulness of spreadsheets to accountants, and comment on the above statement.

(10 marks)
(ACCA Dec 91)

---

9   ETHELRED

The machinery register of Ethelred Engineering Plc on 1 January 1991 contained the following items:

	Cost	Year of Purchase
	£	
Machine A	10,000	1980
Machine B	12,000	1984
Machine C	15,000	1986
Machine D	16,000	1989
Machine E	20,000	1990

Depreciation policies are as follows:

Machines A and B on straight-line basis assuming zero scrap value, over 10 years.

Machine C on reducing balance basis at 20% p.a. assuming scrap value of £1,000.

Machines D and E on straight-line basis assuming scrap value equal to 10% of the original cost, over 5 years.

All machines receive a full year's depreciation in the year of purchase.

Relevant transactions during the year to 31 December 1991 are as follows:

(a)   Machine B is taken on part exchange by the supplier of machine F. The invoice for machine F reads as follows:

	£	£
New machine - list price	25,000	
trade discount	1,000	
		24,000
Allowance on your old machine		2,000
		22,000
Delivery of new machine	1,500	
Collection of old machine	1,000	
		2,500
Total due		24,500

(b)   The motor in machine E is discovered to be inadequate. By agreement it is replaced by a more powerful motor. The new motor costs £6,000 as compared with £4,000 for the original motor. The old inadequate motor is taken back by the supplier and full credit of the original £4,000 is given against the £6,000 cost of the new motor. This change is not expected to increase the life of the machine and it is agreed to treat this as a correction of the original cost.

The depreciation policy for the new machine F is the same as for machines D and E.

Required

(a)   Prepare a table showing for each machine: cost, depreciation to date and net balance sheet figure, and the profit and loss account entries for the year 1991.

                                                                        (19 marks)

A loan of £20,000, at 15% interest, has been taken out especially to help finance the purchase of machine F. The managing director of Ethelred Engineering suggests that the interest payable on the loan in 1991 should be regarded as part of the cost of the machine.

Required

(b)   Comment briefly on the managing director's proposal, supporting your opinion by reference to accounting conventions.

                                                                        (5 marks)
                                                              (Total: 24 marks)
                                                                (ACCA June 91)

---

10   DYNOSAUR PLC

As auditor of Dynosaur plc you are presented with the following trial balance by the bookkeeper, who tells you that:

(a)   he did not know where to post certain debits and credits so he posted one side of the entry to a suspense account; and that

(b)   for some inexplicable reason the trial balance did not balance, so he put the difference into a trial balance difference account.

Trial balance as at 30 September 19X3

	Dr £	Cr £
Ordinary share capital (50p shares)		100,000
Share premium account		20,000
Plant and machinery:		
Cost	136,000	
Depreciation		35,000
Freehold land and buildings:		
Cost	562,553	
Depreciation		137,652
Stock as at 1 October 19X2	113,137	
Sales ledger control account	51,737	
Provision for bad debts		2,657
Bank balance	37,123	
Purchase ledger control account		37,986
10% debentures (repayable 19X10)		70,000
Sales		1,123,456
Purchases	762,234	
Rent and rates	34,267	
Electricity	25,386	
Debenture interest	7,000	
Sundry expenses	21,417	
Trial balance difference		796
Suspense		74,000
Profit and loss account		149,307
	1,750,854	1,750,854

You discover the following:

(1)   The suspense account consists of:

	Dr £	Cr £
Proceeds of issue of 50,000 ordinary shares @ 60p		30,000
Proceeds of sale of freehold buildings (cost £100,000, accumulated depreciation £49,000)		52,000
Bad debt written off	8,000	
Balance c/d	74,000	
	82,000	82,000

(2)   Depreciation has not been provided and is to be so on cost at the year end as follows:

Freehold land	Nil
Freehold buildings	2%
Plant and machinery	10%

There were no additions to land or buildings during the period and as at 1 October 19X2 the land owned by the company cost £236,000.

(3)   The bad debt provision should have been amended (per company policy) to 5% of the closing debtors.

(4)   Rent and rates prepaid amount to £3,637, electricity accrued to £1,967.

(5)   On posting the total of the sales book for March 19X3 the bookkeeper correctly posted £363,727 to sales ledger but posted £363,772 to sales.

(6)   Closing stock was originally valued at £52,557. However, upon enquiry you discover that stock that cost £3,637 has a net realisable value of £1,856.

(7)   Bank charges of £3,637 have to be provided for.

(8)   The total of the cash book purchase ledger payments column had been overcast by £841. The total payments column was correctly totalled.

You are required:

(a)   to provide journal entries to amend the trial balance as a result of your discoveries above (narrative is required).

(16 marks)

(b)   to prepare a trading and profit and loss account for the year ended 30 September 19X3 and a balance sheet for the year then ended for Dynosaur plc in a form suitable for consideration by the directors.

(12 marks)
(Total: 28 marks)

11   JETELECTRONICS PLC

Most of the work carried out by Jetelectronics plc is under government contracts granted by the Ministry of Defence. The Ministry employs a dual system of payments for contract work, consisting of a pre-agreed sum for the work performed plus a percentage addition for the simple average amount of net assets employed by the company during the accounting year. For this purpose net assets employed are defined as the aggregate of tangible fixed assets and working capital before accounting for the amount due from the Ministry under the contract.

For the year ended 31 March 19X4 the amount due from the Ministry for work performed is £6,426,792 of which £6,375,000 has already been received. An additional amount is now due representing 5% of the simple average net assets employed (as defined above) in excess of the sum of £4,000,000. The relevant net assets employed figures to be used for calculating the simple average (above), but excluding all amounts from the Ministry, are:

	£	
At 1 April 19X3 (opening)	4,268,490	(confirmed)
At 31 March 19X4 (closing)	4,999,650	(provisional)

It has now been discovered that in arriving at the closing figure:

(1)   During the year the company sold on credit for £16,000 plant which had originally cost £76,000 and on which £51,000 depreciation had been provided to 31 March 19X3. (For the company's depreciation policy refer to note 5 below.) None of these figures has been reflected in the closing net assets employed figure.

(2)   The accountant had transferred all the overhead expenses to profit and loss account including

£26,910 attributable to work-in-progress.

(3)   Included in the company's ledger were the following two accounts for Minuscule Ltd.

Debtors ledger	£4,941 (debit balance)
Creditors ledger	£19,606 (credit balance)

The account in the debtors ledger had been the subject of a contra settlement on 31 March 19X4 but no entries have as yet been made for this transaction.

(4)   During the year the company had acquired an additional warehouse at an annual rent of £6,000 payable quarterly in advance. Payments had been made as follows:

	£	
30 June 19X3	1,500	(first payment)
30 September 19X3	1,500	
31 December 19X3	1,500	
31 March 19X4	1,500	

A junior member of staff had wrongly treated this as capital expenditure and had included the total payments made during the year in fixed assets - premises.

(5)   The depreciation charge for the year (£306,800) has been wrongly calculated by the same junior member of staff who had applied the reducing balance method. The company's policy is to use the straight line method at 10% on cost and to charge a full year's amount in the year of acquisition but none in the year of disposal.

At 1 April 19X3 fixed asset balances totalled £2,582,500 at cost. Disposals during the year are stated in note 1 above. There were no additions.

(6)   Prepaid insurances of £1,618 had been wrongly accounted for as accruals and accrued power charges of £5,042 had been wrongly accounted for as prepayments.

(7)   The amount included for bank balance in the closing net assets employed figure was the closing balance taken directly from the company's bank account. Subsequently the Eastmid Bank plc, the company's bank, had returned cheques from credit customers totalling £973 and marked 'Refer to drawer - insufficient funds', has received a direct debit of £8,480 from the Loamshire Borough Council for rates for the period 1 April 19X4 to 30 September 19X4 and has charged overdraft interest of £570 and bank charges of £122. Each of these transactions arose before 31 March 19X4 and has not been accounted for by the company.

You are required:

(a)   to journalise such of the transactions (including bank and cash) contained in notes 1 to 7 above as are relevant to finalising the company's accounts for the year ended 31 March 19X4.

(11 marks)

(b)   to prepare a statement amending the closing net assets employed figure for the matters contained in notes 1 to 7 above.

(6 marks)

(c)   to prepare a statement of the final claim to be submitted to the Ministry for the year ended 31 March 19X4.

(3 marks)

All workings must be shown.

(Total: 20 marks)

(ACCA Dec 84)

12 SUSPENSE ACCOUNT AND PROVISION FOR DOUBTFUL DEBTS

(a) A trial balance has an excess of debits over credits of £14,000 and a suspense account has been opened to make it balance. It is later discovered that:

(i) the discounts allowed balance of £3,000 and the discounts received balance of £7,000 have both been entered on the wrong side of the trial balance;

(ii) the creditors control account balance of £233,786 had been included in the trial balance as £237,386;

(iii) an item of £500 had been omitted from the sales records (ie, from the sales day book);

(iv) the balance on the current account with the senior partner's wife had been omitted from the trial balance. This item when corrected removes the suspense account altogether.

You are required to open the suspense account and record the necessary corrections in it. Show in the account the double entry for each item entered.

(8 marks)

(b) The following transactions are to be recorded. At the beginning of year 1 a provision for doubtful debts account is to be opened. It should show a provision of 2% against debtors of £50,000. During the year bad debts of £2,345 are to be charged to the provision account. At the end of year 1 the bad debt provision is required to be 2% against debtors of £60,000.

In year 2 bad debts of £37 are to be charged against the account. At the end of year 2 a provision of 1% against debtors of £70,000 is required.

You are required to prepare a provision for doubtful debts account for the two years. Show in the account the double entry for each item, and carry down the balance at the end of each year.

(9 marks)
(Total: 17 marks)
(ACCA June 90)

13 REASONS FOR CONTROL ACCOUNTS

(a) Why are many accounting systems designed with a purchase ledger (creditors ledger) control account, as well as with a purchase ledger (creditors ledger)?

(4 marks)

(b) The following errors have been discovered:

(i) An invoice for £654 has been entered in the purchase day book as £456.

(ii) A prompt payment discount of £100 from a creditor had been completely omitted from the accounting records.

(iii) Purchases of £250 had been entered on the wrong side of a supplier's account in the purchase ledger.

(iv) No entry had been made to record an agreement to contra an amount owed to X of £600 against an amount owed by X of £400.

(v)   A credit note for £60 had been entered as if it was an invoice.

State the numerical effect on the purchase ledger control account balance of correcting each of these items (treating each item separately).

(8 marks)

(c)   Information technology and computerised systems are rapidly increasing in importance in data recording.

Do you consider that this trend will eventually remove the need for control accounts to be incorporated in the design of accounting systems? Explain your answer briefly.

(4 marks)
(Total: 16 marks)
(ACCA Dec 88)

---

14   C LTD

The sales ledger control account of C Ltd is shown below:

Sales ledger control

	Dr £		Cr £
Balance b/d	70,814.16	Balance b/d	1,198.73
Sales	54,738.36	Sales returns	2,344.39
Dishonoured cheque	607.15	Payments received	68,708.27
Debt collection fees	108.81	Contra	378.82
		Bad debts written off	474.16
Balance c/d	1,194.26	Balance c/d	54,358.37
	127,462.74		127,462.74

A listing of the individual customer balances in the sales ledger gives the following totals:

Debits   £55,136.65   Credits   £1,194.26
(used above)

The following facts have been discovered:

(1)   No entries have been made in the sales ledger for the debt collection charges or bad debts written off.

(2)   A credit balance of £673.46 has been taken as a debit balance in the listing of the customer balances.

(3)   The sales day-book has been over-added by £500.00.

(4)   The account of the customer who settled by contra was debited with £378.82.

(5)   A balance on a customer's account of debit £347.58 has been entered on the listing of balances as debit £374.85.

(6)   The sales returns day-book had been under-added by £10.00.

(7)   The dishonoured cheque had been entered in the sales ledger as credit £601.75.

You are required:

(a)   to correct the sales ledger control account (commencing with the closing balances given) and reconcile the listing of the individual balances to the new sales ledger control account balances;

(12 marks)

(b)   to explain the purposes of control accounts.

(3 marks)
(Total: 15 marks)

---

15   IN SUSPENSE

The trial balance of MLN plc was extracted on 30 September 19X9 and showed the following totals:

Debit   £1,605,668   Credit   £1,603,623

A suspense account was opened and used to record the difference until it could be investigated but the company continued its draft accounts by applying the prudence concept to the treatment of the suspense account balance.

After investigation the following facts emerged:

(1)   Discounts allowed of £1,248 had not been entered in the sales ledger control account.

(2)   A credit sale of £857 to SEC Ltd had not been entered in the sales day-book.

(3)   A contra entry between the sales and purchase ledgers had been entered in the control accounts as:

Debit sales ledger control	£731
Credit purchase ledger control	£731

(4)   A telephone bill of £54 for telephones had been entered in the telephone expense account as £45 but was correctly entered in the creditor's account.

(5)   Bank charges of £66 had been correctly entered in the expense account but had not been entered in the cash book.

(6)   One of the pages of the purchase day-book had been incorrectly totalled as £11,269 instead of £11,629.

(7)   During the year a fixed asset was sold for £740. Its original cost was £3,600 and its net book value at the date of disposal was £800. The only entry made was to debit the proceeds of sale to the bank account.

You are required:

(a)   to record in the suspense account the effects of correcting (1) to (7) above;

(5 marks)

(b)   to reconcile the difference between the balance on the sales ledger control account in the original trial balance and the sum of the individual customer balances in the sales ledger. The original control account balance was £327,762;

(5 marks)

(c)   to prepare a statement of adjusted net profit showing both the original net profit of £412,967 as given by the draft accounts and the net profit after correcting items (1) to (7) above.

(5 marks)

(Total: 15 marks)

---

16   WHOLESALERS PLC

(a)   On 1 January 1991 the accounting records of Wholesalers plc included the following balances. All figures are in £000.

			£
Sales ledger control account			50
Provision for doubtful debts			2
Individual sales ledger memorandum balances - positive	A		10
"	B		20
"	C		8
"	D		9
"	E		6
negative	F		2
"	G		1

The following unaudited information is presented to you concerning the year 1991.

Sales day book			*Cash book receipts*		
Customer	*Amount*		*Customer*	*Amount*	*Discount*
				£	£
A	30		A	35	2
B	35		B	30	
D	18		C	5	
E	9		D	20	
F	8		E	12	
G	7		F	5	1
			G	4	
	—			—	—
	117			111	3
	—			—	—

Sales return book			*Bad debts written off*	
Customer	*Amount*		*Customer*	*Amount*
	£			£
A	2		C	2
F	3			
	—			—
	5			2
	—			—

Contra with creditors ledger	
Customer	*Amount*
	£
E	2
G	4
	—
	6
	—

The closing balance on the provision for doubtful debts account is required to be 4% of debtors, plus provision in full for any obviously doubtful specific debts.

You are required to prepare sales ledger control account, provision for doubtful debts account, and memorandum sales ledger accounts for each customer, for the year 1991. Carry down year-end balances and prove that the sales ledger control balance reconciles with the memorandum balances. **The ledger** accounts may be presented in any summarised form you find convenient provided all entries are clear.   **(18 marks)**

(b)   State TWO advantages of preparing both memorandum and control records   **(2 marks)**

(Total: 20 marks)

(ACCA Dec 91)

---

17   A NEW CLERK

(a)   A new clerk takes over responsibility for some of the sales records on 1 January 1992. The summary figures he receives from his predecessor are as follows (£s at 1 January 1992):

	£
Sales ledger control account	10,000
Sales ledgers - total of debit balances	10,483
Sales ledgers - total of credit balances	497

At 31 December 1992, after his first year of responsibility, the clerk arrives at the following summary figures:

	£
Sales ledger control account	16,600
Sales ledgers - total of debit balances	15,547
Sales ledgers - total of credit balances	551

On investigation, you find the following facts, all of which relate to between 1 January 1992 and 31 December 1992

(i)   The June sales total had been added as £9,876 when it should have been correctly added as £8,967.

(ii)   A sales invoice which should have been charged to A's ledger account with an amount of £642 had actually been charged to B's ledger account with an amount of £426.

(iii)   A credit note of customer D of £123 had been incorrectly treated as a sales invoice in her ledger account. (Customer D's account had a large debit balance at 31 December 1992.)

(iv)   Contra entries of £800, correctly entered in the separate ledger accounts, had been omitted from the control accounts.

(v)   Cash discounts given of £74 have been completely ignored by the clerk.

Required:

(i)   Calculate, with necessary workings, the adjusted figures at 31 December 1992 for sales ledger control account, total of sales ledger debit balances and total of sales ledger credit balances.

(ii)   Produce a clear statement of the net amount of the remaining errors which the clerk appears to have made during the year 1992 which have not yet been discovered.   **(10 marks)**

(b)   The balance on the provision for doubtful debts account on 1 January 1991 was £1,000, equal to 5% of debtors at that date.

In the 12 months to 31 December 1991 sales are £90,000, cash receipts from sales are £80,000 and bad debts (charged to the provision account) are £600. The doubtful debts provision balance at close of business on 31 December 1991 is required to be 5% of debtors.

In the 12 months to 31 December 1992 sales are £100,000, cash receipts from sales are £110,000 and bad debts (charged directly to expenses) are £400. The doubtful debts provision balance at close of business on 31 December 1992 is required to be 5% of debtors. (The change in treatment of bad debts in the second year does not imply an adjustment or correction should be made in relation to the first year.)

Required:

Prepare the provision for doubtful debts account for the period 1 January 1991 to 1 January 1993, clearly bringing down the balance at the end of each year, and indicating the double entry for each item in the account. Submit necessary workings in a convenient form.   **(7 marks)**

(c)   Is the balance on the provision for doubtful debts account a liability? Explain your answer briefly but clearly.   **(5 marks)**
(Total: 22 marks)
(ACCA Dec 93)

18   ACCOUNTING CONCEPTS

(a)   Explain clearly, in terms which a non-accountant would understand, the following accounting terms:

(i)   Historic cost;
(ii)   Historic cost accounting;
(iii)   Objectivity;
(iv)   Prudence.   **(9 marks)**

(b)   To what extent is historic cost accounting objective and prudent?   **(9 marks)**
(Total: 18 marks)
(ACCA Dec 87)

19   ACCOUNTING TERMS

Explain clearly **four** of the following terms as an accountant would understand them:

(a)   Financial accounting.   **(5 marks)**
(b)   Realisation.   **(5 marks)**
(c)   Matching.   **(5 marks)**
(d)   Materiality.   **(5 marks)**
(e)   Inflation.   **(5 marks)**
(Total: 20 marks)
(ACCA Dec 88)

20   COST CONCEPTS

'The historical cost convention looks backwards but the going concern convention looks forwards.'

You are required:

(a)   to explain clearly what is meant by:

    (i)   the historical cost convention;
    (ii)   the going concern convention.

(6 marks)

(b)   Does traditional financial accounting, using the historical cost convention, make the going concern convention unnecessary? Explain your answer fully.

(8 marks)

(c)   Which do you think a shareholder is likely to find more useful - a report on the past or an estimate of the future? Why?

(4 marks)
(Total: 18 marks)
(ACCA Dec 90)

21   AUDITED ACCOUNTS

The following letter has been received from a client. 'I gave my bank manager those audited accounts you prepared for last year. But he says he needs more information before he will agree to increase my overdraft. What could he possibly want to know that he can't get from those accounts? If they are not good enough why bother to prepare them?'

You are required to outline the major points which should be included in a reply to this letter.

(12 marks)
(ACCA June 91)

22   RESEARCH AND DEVELOPMENT

Discuss how the fundamental accounting concepts of matching, prudence and going concern apply to the treatment of research and development costs in an organisation's financial statements.

(15 marks)

23   GOODWILL

Prepare a report for the owner of the business for which you work explaining the concept of goodwill.

Your report should:

(1)   explain how the goodwill of a business is created;

(2)   distinguish between purchased goodwill and inherent goodwill;

(3)   explain the recommended accounting treatment for each type of goodwill and the reasons for that treatment.

(15 marks)

---

24   FINANCIAL REPORTING

(a)   What is the fundamental objective of financial reporting?

(3 marks)

(b)   To whom should information contained in a financial report be communicated?

(4 marks)

(c)   What are the desirable characteristics of information which will satisfy the fundamental objective of financial reporting?

(4 marks)

(d)   Describe **briefly** the kind of information needed by **two** of the groups of people you mentioned in (b).

(4 marks)
(Total: 15 marks)

---

25   REGULATORY INFLUENCES

Required

State three different regulatory influences on the preparation of the published accounts of quoted companies and briefly explain the role of each one. Comment briefly on the effectiveness of this regulatory system.

(10 marks)
(ACCA Dec 89)

---

26   REVENUE

A firm produces a standard manufactured product. The stages of production and sale of the product may be summarised as follows:

Stage	A	B	C	D
Activity	Raw material	WIP-1	WIP-11	Finished Product
	£	£	£	£
Costs to date	100	120	150	170
Net realisable value	80	130	190	300

Stage	E	F	G	H
Activity	For sale	Sale agreed	Delivered	Paid for
	£	£	£	£
Costs to date	170	170	180	180
Net realisable value	300	300	300	300

Required

(a)   What general rule do accountants apply when deciding when to recognise revenue on any particular transaction?

(4 marks)

(b)   Apply this rule to the above situation. State and explain the stage at which you think revenue will be recognised by accountants.

(4 marks)

(c)   How much would the gross profit on a unit of this product be? Why?

(4 marks)

(d)   Suggest arguments in favour of delaying the recognition of revenue until stage H.

(4 marks)

(e)   Suggest arguments in favour of recognising revenue in appropriate successive amounts at stages B, C and D.

(4 marks)
(Total 20 marks)
(ACCA June 90)

27   FOLLOWING TERMS

(a)   Explain the following terms as used by accountants:

(i)   asset
(ii)   fixed asset
(iii)   current asset
(iv)   depreciation.

(9 marks)

(b)   Do you regard each of the following as an asset of a business for accounting purposes? Explain your answers.

(i)   a screwdriver bought in 1987
(ii)   a machine hired by the business
(iii)   the good reputation of the business with its customers.

(6 marks)

(c)   The fixed assets in the balance sheet of a company have been summarised as follows:

		£m
Land at valuation		3
Buildings at cost		1
Plant and equipment - cost	2	
- depreciation	1.5	0.5
		4.5

Required

Explain the meaning of this £4.5m figure to one of the company's shareholders, and comment on its relevance from a shareholder's point of view.

(4 marks)
(Total: 25 marks)
(ACCA June 92)

28   EXPLAIN THE TERMS

(a)   Explain clearly the following accounting terms in a manner which an intelligent non-accountant could understand in the context of a profit-oriented organisation:

    (i)   expense
    (ii)   matching
    (iii)   prudence
    (iv)   objectivity.   **(10 marks)**

(b)   Your client has received the following invoice, and has come to you for advice.

From: Marketing Services plc

Due for our services for the three months 1 October to 31 December 1992.

	£
Agreed monthly fee for general advice three months at £1,000 per month	3,000
Supply of new colour photocopier on 1.10.92, with five-year guarantee, for use by your marketing department	10,000
Deposit paid by us on your behalf for television advertising time in February 1993	5,000
Full cost of advertising campaign in newspaper, from 1 November to 30 November 1992	50,000

Payable in total by 31.1.93.

Required:

Write a letter to your client suggesting, for each of the four items on the invoice, how each item is likely to affect the expenses figure for the accounting year ended 31 December 1992. You should explain your suggestions, and justify them by reference to accounting conventions.

                        (13 marks)
                (Total: 23 marks)
                    (ACCA Dec 92)

29   ACCOUNTING INFORMATION

It is frequently suggested that accounting information and accounting reports should attempt to be relevant and reliable. These terms could be explained as follows.

'Information has the quality of relevance when it influences the economic decisions of users by helping them evaluate past, present or future events or by confirming, or correcting, their past evaluations.

'Information has the quality of reliability when it is free from material error and bias and can be depended on by users to represent faithfully in terms of valid description that which it either purports to represent or could reasonably be expected to represent.'

Required:

(a)   Explain what accountants mean by the convention of objectivity.

(3 marks)

(b)   Why do shareholders need to read published accounts of companies in which they own shares?

(3 marks)

(c)   'From the viewpoint of shareholders, objectivity will tend to lead to accounts being more reliable, but less relevant.' Do you agree?

(4 marks)
(Total: 10 marks)
(ACCA June 93)

---

30   LEGAL CASES

Your managing director is having a polite disagreement with the auditors on the subject of accounting for contingencies. Since the finance director is absent on sick leave he has come to you for advice. The auditor has given him the text of Part 3 of SSAP 18, and this is attached as Appendix A.

It appears that your firm is involved in four unrelated legal cases, P, Q, R and S. In case P the firm is suing for £10,000, in case Q the firm is suing for £20,000, in case R the firm is being sued for £30,000 and in case S the firm is being sued for £40,000. The firm has been advised by its expert and expensive lawyers that the chances of the firm winning each case are as follows:

Case	Percentage likelihood of winning
P	8
Q	92
R	8
S	92

You are required to write a memorandum to the managing director which

(a)   explains why SSAP 18 is relevant to these situations;
(b)   states the required accounting treatment for each of the four cases in the published accounts;
(c)   gives journal entries for any necessary adjustments in the double-entry records;
(d)   suggests the contents of any Notes to the Accounts that are required by the SSAP;
(e)   briefly discusses whether SSAP 18 leads to a satisfactory representation of the position.

(16 marks)
(Pilot Paper)

Appendix A

Part 3 - Standard accounting practice

15   In addition to amounts accrued under the fundamental concept of prudence in SSAP 2 **Disclosure of accounting policies,** a material contingent loss should be accrued in financial statements where it is probable that a future event will confirm a loss which can be estimated with reasonable accuracy at the date on which the financial statements are approved by the board of directors.

16   A material contingent loss not accrued under paragraph 15 above should be disclosed except where the possibility of loss is remote.

17   Contingent gains should not be accrued in financial statements. A material contingent gain should be disclosed in financial statements only if it is probable that the gain will be realised.

18   In respect of each contingency which is required to be disclosed under paragraphs 16 and 17 above, the following information should be stated by way of notes in financial statements:

(a)   the nature of the contingency;

(b)   the uncertainties which are expected to affect the ultimate outcome; and

(c)   a prudent estimate of the financial effect, made at the date on which the financial statements are approved by the board of directors; or a statement that it is not practicable to make such an estimate.

19   Where there is disclosure of an estimate of the financial effect of a contingency, the amount disclosed should be the potential financial effect. In the case of a contingent loss, this should be reduced by:

(a)   any amounts accrued; and
(b)   the amounts of any components where the possibility of loss is remote.

The net amount only need be disclosed.

20   The estimate of the financial effect should be disclosed before taking account of taxation, and the taxation implications of a contingency crystallising should be explained where necessary for a proper understanding of the financial position.

21   Where both the nature of, and the uncertainties which affect, a contingency in respect of an individual transaction are common to a large number of similar transactions, the financial effect of the contingency need not be individually estimated but may be based on a group of similar transactions. In these circumstances the separate contingencies need not be individually disclosed.

Date from which effective

22   The accounting practices set out in this statement should be adopted as soon as possible and regarded as standard in respect of financial statements relating to accounting periods beginning on or after 1 September 1980.

31   EXPLANATIONS

(a)   Explain the following terms used in financial accounting.

Matching
Prudence
Inflation
Price changes
Going concern
Objectivity.   **(15 marks)**

(b)   Should price changes be taken into account during the matching process? Give reasons for your answers.   **(7 marks)**
(Total: 22 marks)
(Pilot Paper)

32   AMATEUR FOOTBALL CLUB

After the draft accounts had been prepared for the financial year ended 31 December 19X3 the treasurer of an amateur football club discovered a batch of vouchers which had fallen down behind his desk, none of which had been processed.

The vouchers related to the following matters:

(1)   an invoice dated 23 January 19X4 from Patchems Medical Supplies for a new first aid kit for the club's trainer. The kit had cost £21.96 and had been supplied on 5 January 19X4;

(2)   an invoice dated 11 January 19X4 from Sports Equipment Ltd for £36.70, being the cost of a new goal net, corner flags and linesmen's flags, delivered to the club on 20 December 19X3;

(3)   a cheque counterfoil, dated 15 December 19X3, for £15, being the match fee for a match away from the home ground to be played on 4 February 19X4;

(4)   a cheque counterfoil, dated 5 January 19X4, for £20, being the match fee for a match away from the home ground to be played on 18 February 19X4;

(5)   an invoice dated 6 January 19X4 for £328.85 for work carried out at the club's home ground during November 19X3 by Plumbing Services. The work consisted of the installation of two extra shower baths in the changing rooms (£268.30) and sundry repairs and renovations (£60.55);

(6)   a cheque counterfoil dated 17 January 19X4 for £32.62 being the wages of the part-time groundsman, £11.21 of which had been earned up to 31 December 19X3.

Other information:

The club depreciates its equipment at the rate of 20% per annum on a straight-line basis on gross cost at the year-end.

You are required:

(a)   to journalise such of the above transactions as affect the 19X3 final accounts.

(11 marks)

(b)   to state the individual items in the draft balance sheet affected by the journal entries in (a) and the respective amounts by which they would increase or decrease.

(5 marks)
(Total: 16 marks)
(ACCA June 84)

33	SPRINGTIME GARDENERS' CLUB

The following receipts and payments account for the year ended 31 December 19X6 for the Springtime Gardeners' Club has been prepared by the club's treasurer:

	£		£
Opening bank balance	876	National Gardening Show:	
Seed sales	1,684	Purchase of tickets and brochures	3,600
National Gardening Show:		Seed purchases	1,900
Ticket sales to non-members	400	Lawn mower purchases	5,400
Lawn mower sales	3,800	Coaches to National Gardening Show	490
Subscriptions received	7,190	Club premises - rent	500
Closing bank overdraft	270	Gardening magazines for members'	
		use	390
		Secretarial expenses	940
		Proposed new club building plans -	
		architect's fees	1,000
	14,220		14,220

The club's executive committee has now decided that members should receive an income and expenditure account for the year ended 31 December 19X6 and a balance sheet as at that date.

Accordingly, the following additional information has been given:

(1)   Club assets and liabilities, other than bank balances or overdrafts:

	As at 1 Jan 19X6 £	As at 31 Dec 19X6 £
Plot of land for proposed new club building, bought 1 Jan 19X0 for £2,000; current market value	5,000	5,500
Stocks of seeds, at cost	250	560
Debtors - lawn mower sales	400	1,370
Membership subscriptions received in advance	240	390
Creditors:		
Lawn mower supplier	800	170
Seed growers	110	340

(2)   The club sells lawn mowers at cost price to members; however, the club never holds any stock of unsold lawn members.

(3)   Membership benefits include a ticket and transport to the National Gardening Show.

You are required:

(a)   to prepare the club's accumulated fund as at 1 January 19X6;

(6 marks)

(b)   to prepare the club's income and expenditure account for the year ended 31 December 19X6;

(10 marks)

(c)   to prepare the club's balance sheet as at 31 December 19X6.

(7 marks)

(Total: 23 marks)

34	HB TENNIS CLUB

The HB tennis club was formed on 1 April 19X0 and has the following receipts and payments account for the six months ended 30 September 19X0:

Receipts	£	*Payments*	£
Subscriptions	12,600	Purchase of equipment	4,080
Tournament fees	465	Groundsman's wages	4,520
Bank interest	43	Rent and business rates	636
Sale of club ties	373	Heating and lighting	674
Life membership fees	4,200	Postage and stationery	41
		Court maintenance	1,000
		Tournament prizes	132
		Purchase of club ties	450
		Balance c/d	6,148
	17,681		17,681

Notes:

(1) The annual subscription fee is £300. On 30 September there were five members who had not paid their subscriptions, but this money was received on 4 October 19X0.

(2) The equipment is expected to be used by the club for five years, after which time it will need to be replaced. Its estimated scrap value at that time is £50.

(3) During the six months, the club purchased 100 ties printed with its own design. Forty of these ties remained unsold at 30 September 19X0.

(4) The club has paid business rates in advance on 30 September 19X0 of £68.

(5) The club treasurer estimates that the following amounts should be accrued for expenses:

	£
Groundsman's wages	40
Postage and stationery	12
Heating and lighting	53

(6) The life membership fees received relate to payments made by four families. The scheme allows families to pay £1,050 which entitles them to membership for life without further payment. It has been agreed that such receipts would be credited to Income and Expenditure in equal instalments over 10 years.

You are required:

(a) to prepare the club's Income and Expenditure account for the six months ended 30 September 19X0;

(8 marks)

(b) to prepare the club's balance sheet at 30 September 19X0.

(7 marks)

(Total: 15 marks)

35   HAPPY TICKERS

The accounting records of the Happy Tickers Sports and Social Club are in a mess. You manage to find the following information to help you prepare the accounts to 31 December 1990.

Summarised balance sheet 31 December 1989

	£
Half-share in motorised roller	600
New sports equipment unsold	1,000
Used sports equipment at valuation	700
Rent (2 months)	200
Subscriptions 1989	60
Cafe stocks	800
Cash and bank	1,210
	4,570

	£
Insurance (3 months)	150
Subscriptions 1990	120
Life subscriptions	1,400
	1,670
Accumulated fund	2,900
	4,570

Receipts in the year to 31 December 1990:

		£
Subscriptions:	1989	40
	1990	1,100
	1991	80
	life	200
From sales of new sports equipment		900
From sales of used sports equipment		14
Cafe takings		4,660
		6,994

Payments in the year to 31 December 1990

	£
Rent (12 months)	1,200
Insurance (18 months)	900
To suppliers of sports equipment	1,000
To cafe suppliers	1,900
Wages of cafe manager	2,000
Total cost of repairing motorised roller	450
	7,450

(i)   Ownership and all expenses of the motorised roller are agreed to be shared equally with the Carefree Conveyancers Sports and Social Club which occupies a nearby site. The roller cost a total of £2,000 on 1 January 1986 and had an estimated life of 10 years.

(ii) Life subscriptions are brought into income equally over 10 years, in a scheme begun in 1985. Since the scheme began the cost of £200 per person has been constant. Prior to 31 December 1989 10 life subscriptions had been received.

(iii) Four more annual subscriptions of £20 had been promised relating to 1990, but not yet received. Annual subscriptions promised but unpaid are carried forward for a maximum of 12 months.

(iv) New sports equipment is sold to members at cost plus 50%. Used equipment is sold off to members at book valuation. Half the sports equipment bought in the year (all from a cash and carry supplier) has been used within the club and half made available for sale, new, to members. The "used equipment at valuation" figure in the 31 December 1990 balance sheet is to remain at £700.

(v) Closing cafe stocks are £850 and £80 is owed to suppliers at 31 December 1990.

You are required

(a) to calculate the profit on cafe operations and profit on sale of sports equipment.

(6 marks)

(b) to prepare a statement of subscription income for 1990.

(4 marks)

(c) to prepare an income and expenditure statement for the year to 31 December 1990 and a balance sheet as at 31 December 1990.

(11 marks)

(d) why do life subscriptions appear as a liability?

(4 marks)
(Total: 25 marks)
(ACCA Dec 90)

---

36 THINGUMMY LTD

The trial balance of Thingummy Ltd at 1 January 19X9 is made up of the following balances:

	£'000
Share capital (£1 ordinary shares)	200
Profit and loss account balance	80
Debtors	100
Bad debt provision	4
Creditors	90
Land and buildings	110
Plant machinery - cost	140
depreciation	50
Prepayments for operating expenses	4
Accruals for operating expenses	10
Stock	100
Bank overdraft	20

At 31 December 19X9 you are given the following information relating to the year 19X9:

	£'000
Sales	500
Cash receipts from debtors	440
Bad debts written off	20
Purchases	300

Payments to suppliers	310
Contra between debtors and creditors	5
Discounts allowed	15
Discounts received	10
Bad debts provision is to be 10% of debtors	?
Shares issued (50,000 £1 ordinary shares)	75
Operating expenses paid	95
Payments for plant and machinery	60
Proceeds on disposal of plant and machinery (depreciated to half its original cost)	15
Profit on disposal of plant and machinery	6
Gain on revaluation of land and buildings	40

You are required to submit a trial balance as at 31 December 19X9 incorporating all the given information. You are **not** required to calculate the profits for the year, or to prepare a profit and loss account or balance sheet. Workings may be in any form you find convenient. All written workings should be clear and legible.

(18 marks)
(ACCA Dec 89)

37   DELTIC

You are approached by a new client, Deltic, who is coming to the end of his first year's trading and is somewhat concerned that he will now have to prepare accounts as a result. He informs you that he has not kept proper books and records but, after discussing matters with him, the following information comes to light about the year ended 30 September 19X4:

(1)   His chance to set up in business came when he won £200,000 from Littlewoods Pools. He invested the money in the bank and set up in business as a retailer of lingerie.

(2)   He banks his takings periodically after payment of the following amounts:

Wages	£75 per week
Cleaning	£10 per week
Sundries	£15 per week
Personal expenses	£25 per week

His cash in hand at the end of the year was £250.

(3) A summary of his bank statements reveals the following:

	£		£
Capital introduced	200,000	Purchase of leasehold	
Bankings	125,750	premises	150,000
		Purchase of van	6,000
		Telephone	896
		Rent and rates	1,682
		Payments to suppliers	86,232
		Wages	15,282
		Repairs	3,637
		Personal expenses	323
		Balance c/d	61,698
	———		———
	325,750		325,750
	———		———

You discover that a cheque for repairs of £385 paid on 28 September 19X4 was not presented at the bank until 5 October 19X4.

(4) Other assets and liabilities were as follows as at 30 September 19X4:

	£
Stock	8,400
Trade debtors	10,350
Trade creditors	29,957
Accrual - telephone	125
Prepayment - rent and rates	258

(5) Depreciation is to be provided on the van at 25% of its cost, whilst the lease on the premises is for fifty years.

(6) Deltic estimates that his gross profit percentage is 25%, and also informs you that he does not keep a record of the goods he took for his own use.

You are required:

(a) to prepare a trading and profit and loss account for the year ended 30 September 19X4;

(b) to prepare a balance sheet as at that date.

(19 marks)

38   I WRIGHT

(a) I Wright is a professional author whose income is derived mainly from royalties, ie, payments from his publisher based on the number of his books sold. He also receives fixed rate fees for articles and features which he writes for magazines and periodicals. Two of his books have been reproduced in instalments by a weekly newspaper which pays serialisation fees to his publisher who then pays Wright a proportion of these fees. Additionally, he derives a small part of his income from publicity activities and from lecturing.

He carries out his writing activities in a purpose-equipped study room at his home. His accounting year ended 31 May 19X2, for which the following information is available:

	£
Royalties received (including advance royalties £900) *(note 8)*	23,650
Fees received for articles and features published	8,000
Serialisation fees received	5,400
Fees received for publicity activities *(note 9)*	2,734
Fees received for lecturing on writers' residential courses	250

Expenses:

	£
Rates *(notes 1 and 2)*	440
Heating and lighting *(notes 1 and 3)*	916
Postages	414
Stationery *(note 4)*	659
Telephone charges *(notes 1 and 5)*	762
Secretarial expenses	6,866
Travelling expenses *(note 9)*	3,427
Photocopying expenses	640
Fees paid to artist (for providing illustrations for inclusion in his books)	715
Insurance *(notes 1 and 6)*	308
Subscriptions:	
Professional societies	70
Writers' periodicals and magazines	226
Miscellaneous expenses *(note 9)*	691

Other information:

	£
Drawings by cheque during year	21,547
Office equipment at 1 June 19X1 (cost £2,200)	1,700
Office furniture at 1 June 19X1 (cost £600)	510
Bank balance at 31 May 19X2	2,265
Cash balance at 31 May 19X2	28
Capital account at 1 June 19X1	2,150

The above items need to be adjusted, where appropriate, to reflect the following:

(1)   When invoices are received which include combined business and private expenses, it is Wright's practice to pay them out of the business bank account and to make the necessary transfers at the end of the accounting year.

(2)   Rates of £480 for the six months 1 April to 30 September 19X2 have not yet been paid. One quarter of the total rates is attributable to his study room.

(3)   An electricity invoice for £60 in respect of the three months ended 31 May 19X2 has been received but not yet paid. One quarter of the total heating and lighting charge is attributable to his study room.

(4)   Items of stationery (typing and duplicating paper, typewriter ribbons and carbons etc,) unused at 31 May 19X2 amount to £123.

(5)   A telephone invoice has been received, but not yet paid, as follows:

	£
Telephone rental (main installation and extensions) (for three months 1 June 19X2 to 31 August 19X2)	24
Telephone calls (for three months 1 February to 30 April 19X2)	270
	294

An estimated one third of all calls have been made for private purposes not connected with Wright's authorship.

(6)   Insurance premiums have been prepaid by £72. One half of the total insurance charge has been incurred for private purposes.

(7)   Depreciation of fixed assets is to be provided on original cost at the following rates:

Office equipment	25%
Office furniture	20%

There were no additions to fixed assets during the year ended 31 May 19X2.

(8)   Advance royalties are a fixed fee paid by publishers to authors when the contract is signed and/or when the draft manuscript is delivered to them. If, for any reason, the author does not fulfil the terms of the contract, they must be repaid. The £900, therefore, remains repayable until publication takes place.

(9)   Publicity fees include a total amount of £456, being reimbursement of travelling expenses (£370) and of miscellaneous expenses (£86) incurred by Wright in carrying out these activities.

You are required to prepare the profit and loss account for Wright for the year ended 31 May 19X2 and his balance sheet at that date.

(27 marks)

(b)   Wright is concerned about the efficiency with which he is operating his professional affairs and has consulted you for your opinion whether his net profit for the year expressed as a percentage of his net assets is a suitable indicator.

You are required to advise Wright on a suitable 'operating' indicator in his particular circumstances.

(5 marks)
(Total: 32 marks)
(ACCA Dec 82)

---

39   BENDS

On 1 January Mr Bends starts business buying and selling motor cars. He gives you a summary of the business receipts and payments account as follows, for the year to 31 December (all figures are in £'000).

Receipts

	£'000
Capital introduced (1 January)	100
From customers (after deducting worthless cheque, see note (iii) below)	400
10% loan from his mother	50
	550

Payments

	£'000
To suppliers of new cars	320
To suppliers of second-hand cars	93
Wages	36
Rent	15
Purchase of furniture	5
Purchase of showroom display equipment	5
Insurance electricity and stationery	7
Bank charges	1
Transfers to private bank account	26
	508

You are informed that:

(a)   Rent payable is £3,000 for each 3-month period.

(b)   Mr Bends has bought a total of 37 new cars at a cost of £10,000 each. One of these was destroyed by fire the day before Mr Bends signed his insurance policy, two were taken into use by Mr. Bends and his senior salesman, and 27 have been sold at a mark-up of 20% on cost (one of which has not yet been paid for).

(c)   Mr Bends had a problem with the very first second-hand car that he sold. He accepted a cheque for £5,000 which proved worthless, and he has been unable to trace the customer. Since then all sales of second-hand cars have been for cash. All purchases of second-hand cars have also been for cash.

(d)   Four second-hand cars remain in stock at 31 December. The cost of these to Mr Bends was £6,000, £6,000, £7,000 and £8,000 respectively.

(e)   All fixed assets are to be depreciated at the rate of 20% for the year.

You are required to prepare in good order:

(a)   Trading account for new cars.
(b)   Trading account for second-hand cars.
(c)   Profit and loss account for the business for the year.
(d)   Balance sheet as at 31 December.

Indicate clearly the calculation of all figures in your solution.

(25 marks)
(ACCA June 90)

---

40   RACKETS UNLIMITED

You have been appointed the bookkeeper of a tennis club called Rackets Unlimited. The club began on 1 July 1989, and no accounts have yet been prepared. The club has three ways of receiving subscriptions,

(i)   £10 per year.

(ii)   If two years' subscriptions are paid at once £1 may be deducted from the second year. If three years' subscriptions are paid at once, £2 may also be deducted from the third year.

(iii)   If 10 years' subscriptions are paid at once no deductions are allowed, but members are regarded as members for life.

You have completed the following table of subscription receipts:

Member	relevant to membership year ended 30.6.90		relevant to membership year ended 30.6.91		relevant to membership year ended 30.6.92	
	date received	amount £	date received	amount £	date received	amount £
A	July '89	10				
B	July '89	10	July '90	10		
C	July '89	10	June '90	10	July '91	10
D	Sept '89	10	Sept '90	27		
E	Oct '89	27				
F	Oct '89	10	July '90	10	June '91	27
G	Oct '89	100				
H	Oct '89	10	June '90	10	June '91	100
I	Oct '89	10	June '90	19		
J			July '91	10		
K			July '90	27		
L	Dec '89	10			June '91	10
M	July '90	19				
N			July '91	100		

The club does not intend to accrue for any income not received by the date of preparation of financial statements

Required:

(a)   To assist in the preparation of some accounts, complete a table with the following headings:

Member	Income year to 30.6.90	Income year to 30.6.91	Balance c/f at 30.6.91	
			Dr.	Cr.

(13 marks)

(b)   State TWO comments about your table which you think might be helpful to the Club committee.

(2 marks)
(Total: 15 marks)
(ACCA June 92)

---

41   ALBERT ZWEISTEIN

Albert Zweistein began business on 1 January 1992 as a manufacturer of clocks. He believes his business is relatively successful but he has failed to keep proper records and is unsure of the real financial position. Unfortunately he seems to have been rather absent-minded, and is only able to give you limited information, as shown below. He wants you to prepare a single profit and loss account for the 18 months to 30 June 1993, and a balance sheet as at 30 June 1993.

Mr Zweistein gives you a summarised cash book as shown together with the following additional information which he thinks could be relevant.

(i)   The stock of clocks at 30 June 1993 has a cost of £20,000. This figure is obtained from the following table.

	Model A	Model B	Total
Cost	£15,000	£5,000	£20,000
Expected selling price	£28,000	£3,000	£31,000

(ii)   All machines and vehicles were bought and put into use on the first day of the relevant six-month period. Depreciation should be calculated pro rata, assuming a five-year life, equal usage in each six-month period, and zero scrap value.

(iii)   Items appearing on the bank statement for the business for the month of June 1993 include the following, none of which was included in the cash book summary given.

Standing order receipt from customer	£3,000
Bank charges	£500
Standing order payment to supplier	£1,000

Albert Zweistein, summarised cash book
January 1992 to June 1993

Cash	Bank	Cash	Bank	
				January–June 1992
	100,000			Capital (1 January)
	120,000			Loan from Russell (1 January)
			10,000	Rent for 12 months
		5,000	25,000	Purchase of material and parts
5,000			5,000	Transfer
		8,000		Factory wages
			3,000	Office wages
			2,000	Business formation costs
			125,000	Purchase of machines and vehicles
		1,000	4,000	Sundry expenses
		1,000	5,000	Personal spending
10,000	30,000			Sales
				July–December 1992
		6,000	26,000	Purchase of materials and parts
		10,000		Factory wages
			4,000	Office wages
			9,000	Purchase of vehicles
		1,500	5,000	Sundry expenses
		1,200	7,000	Personal spending
			12,000	12 month interest to 31 December on loan from Russell
12,000	50,000			Sales
10,000			10,000	Transfers
				January–June 1993
		7,000	30,000	Purchase of material and parts
		12,000		Factory wages
			6,000	Office wages
			8,000	Purchase of machines
	20,000			Additional capital
9,000	60,000			Sales
		800	6,000	Sundry expenses
			8,000	Personal spending
11,000			11,000	Transfer
57,000	380,000	53,500	321,000	

(iv)   Items properly included in the cash book summary, but not recorded on the bank statements up to 30 June 1993, include the following:

Cash deposit	£700
Unpresented cheque	£2,000

(v)   Clocks which had cost £200 and had been sold for a total of £300 had been returned under guarantee and replaced. The returned clocks had been thrown away. The replacements had cost the same as the original ones.

(vi)   Mr Zweistein has produced a pile of papers which suggest that at 30 June 1993 customers owe him £2,000 for clocks already despatched. You notice, however, that the pile making up this £2,000 appears to include two identical photocopies of a document confirming a sale of £300. One of the other sales took place on 14 February 1992, for £200.

(vii)   Mr Zweistein had given a clock, cost £100, normal selling price £200, to a supplier in exchange for clock parts for which he would normally have had to pay £150.

(viii) Mr Zweistein produced invoices from suppliers, unpaid at 30 June 1993, totalling £6,000.

Required:

Prepare profit and loss account for the single period 1 January 1992 to 30 June 1993 and summarised balance sheet as at 30 June 1993. Written workings may be in any form and to any volume you find convenient, but should be clear and legible.

(25 marks)
(ACCA June 93)

42   HEAD, HANDS AND FEET

Head and Hands have been in partnership for some years sharing profits, after providing for interest on capital at 5% pa, in the ratio of 3 : 2.

On 1 April 19X3 Feet was admitted into partnership and the terms of the partnership from that date were to be as follows:

(1)   Head, Hands and Feet to be entitled to annual salaries of £1,500, £1,000 and £1,000 respectively;

(2)   Balance of profits to be shared between Head, Hands and Feet in the ratio of 3 : 2 : 1. No interest would be paid on capital.

On 1 April 19X3 Feet paid £6,000 into the partnership, of which £2,000 was in respect of the goodwill taken over by him. The whole £6,000 was at 1 April 19X3 credited to his capital account; the partnership has not maintained and does not intend to maintain an account for goodwill. Any goodwill adjustment is to be made through the partners' capital accounts.

The following is the trial balance of the partnership at 31 December 19X3:

	£	£
Capital accounts:		
Head		20,000
Hands		10,000
Feet		6,000
Drawings on current accounts:		
Head	4,500	
Hands	3,200	
Feet	1,700	
Creditors		7,400
Debtors	19,000	
Stock at 1 January 19X3	11,000	
Fixtures and fittings at 1 January 19X3:		
At cost	15,000	
Accumulated depreciation		6,000
Sales (£24,000 up to 1 April 19X3)		120,000
Purchases	100,000	
Staff salaries	6,000	
Rent and rates	1,500	
General expenses	2,580	
Cash at bank	4,920	
	169,400	169,400

The following adjustments are to be incorporated into the final accounts:

(1)   depreciation to be provided on fixtures and fittings at 20%, reducing balance;

(2)   stock at 31 December 19X3 of £14,500;

(3)   a bad debt of £110 to be written off in respect of a sale made during June 19X3;

(4)   outstanding at 31 December 19X3 were:

Salaries unpaid	£240
Rates paid in advance	£100

You are required:

(a)   to prepare the trading, profit and loss and appropriation accounts for the year ended 31 December 19X3;

(b)   to prepare the partners' capital accounts showing the goodwill adjustment;

(c)   to prepare the balance sheet as at 31 December 19X3.

Note: apportion gross profit on the basis of sales, and overheads (other than the bad debt) on a time basis.

(24 marks)

---

43   ALPHA AND BETA

Alpha and Beta are in partnership. They share profits equally after Alpha has been allowed a salary of £4,000 pa. No interest is charged on drawings or allowed on current accounts or capital accounts. The trial balance of the partnership at 31 December 19X9 before adjusting for any of the items below, is as follows:

			Dr £'000	Cr £'000
Capital	-	Alpha		30
	-	Beta		25
Current	-	Alpha		3
	-	Beta		4
Drawings	-	Alpha	4	
	-	Beta	5	
Sales				200
Stock 1 Jan 19X9			30	
Purchases			103	
Operating expenses			64	
Loan	-	Beta (10%)		10
	-	Gamma (10%)		20
Land and buildings			60	
Plant and machinery	-	cost	70	
	-	depreciation to 31 December 19X9		40
Debtors and creditors			40	33
Bank				11
			376	376

(i)   Closing stock on hand at 31 December was £24,000.

(ii)   On 31 December Alpha and Beta agree to take their manager, Gamma, into partnership. Gamma's loan account balance is to be transferred to a capital account as at 31 December. It is agreed that in future Alpha, Beta and Gamma will all share profits equally. Alpha will be allowed a salary of £4,000 as before, and Gamma will be allowed a salary of £5,000 pa (half of what he received in 19X9 as manager, included in operating expenses).

The three partners agree that the goodwill of the business at 31 December should be valued at £12,000, but is not to be recorded in the books. It is also agreed that land and buildings are to be revalued to a figure of £84,000 and that this revalued figure is to be retained and recorded in the accounts.

(iii)   Interest on the loan has not been paid.

(iv)   Included in sales are two items sold on 'sale or return' for £3,000 each. Each item had cost the business £1,000. One of these items was in fact returned on 4 January 19X10 and the other one was formally accepted by the customer on 6 January 19X10.

You are required:

(a)   to submit with appropriately labelled headings and subheadings:

(i)   partners' capital accounts in columnar form;
(ii)   partners' current accounts in columnar form;
(iii)   trading, profit and loss and appropriation account for 19X9;
(iv)   balance sheet as at 31 December 19X9.

(20 marks)

(b)   to write a brief note to Gamma, who cannot understand why his capital account balance seems so much less than those of Alpha and Beta.

Explain to him the adjustments you have made.

(5 marks)
(Total: 25 marks)
(ACCA Dec 89)

44   RIVER, STREAM AND POOL

The following trial balance as at 30 September 19X7 has been extracted from the books of River, Stream and Pool who are trading in partnership:

	£	£
Freehold land and buildings - net book value	42,000	
Fixtures and fittings - net book value	16,000	
Stock	9,000	
Debtors	6,000	
Balance at bank	2,000	
Creditors		7,000
Capital accounts as at 1 October 19X6:		
River		30,000
Stream		20,000
Pool		15,000
Current accounts as at 1 October 19X6:		
River		1,000
Stream		700
Pool		-
Drawings:		
River	21,000	
Stream	13,000	
Pool	11,000	
Net profit for the year ended 30 September 19X7 per draft accounts		46,300
	120,000	120,000

Pool joined River and Stream in partnership on 1 October 19X6 under an agreement which included the following terms:

(1)   Pool to introduce £15,000 cash to be credited to his capital account.

(2)   The goodwill of the business of River and Stream as at 1 October 19X6 to be valued at £28,000, but a goodwill account is not to be opened.

(3)   The value of the stock of River and Stream as at 1 October 19X6 to be reduced from £9,000 to £7,000.

(4)   £10,000 is to be transferred on 1 October 19X6 from Rivers' capital account to the credit of a loan account; River to be credited with interest at the rate of 10% per annum on his loan account balance.

(5)   Pool to be credited with a partner's salary of £11,000 per annum.

(6)   Interest at the rate of 5% per annum to be credited to partners in respect of their adjusted capital account balances at 1 October 19X6.

(7)   The balances of profits and losses to be shared between River, Stream and Pool in the ratio 5:3:2 respectively.

It now transpires that effect has not yet been given to the above terms 2 to 7 inclusive in the partnership books.

Up to 30 September 19X6 River and Stream had no formal partnership agreement.

You are required:

(a)   to prepare the partnership profit and loss appropriation account for the year ended 30 September 19X7; and

(8 marks)

(b)   to prepare the partners' capital and current accounts for the year ended 30 September 19X7.

(17 marks)
(Total: 25 marks)
(ACCA Dec 87)

---

45   TIMMY AND LUCY

Timmy and Lucy have been in partnership for some years, sharing profits equally. After the preparation of accounts for the year ended 31 December 1992 their trial balance is as shown below (all figures £s).

		Dr	Cr
Timmy	- capital account		30,000
	- current account		3,000
Lucy	- capital account		40,000
	- current account	4,000	
Land		12,000	
Buildings	- cost	25,000	
	- depreciation		2,000
Machinery	- cost	30,000	
	- depreciation		16,000
Goodwill		10,000	
Net current assets		10,000	
		91,000	91,000

With effect from 1 January 1993, Charlie is admitted into the partnership, and on that day he pays in £20,000 which is entered in his capital account. From that date the partners are to share profits Timmy 40%, Lucy 40%, Charlie 20%.

It is agreed that at 1 January 1993 the land is worth £20,000, the buildings are worth £30,000 and the goodwill is worth £16,000. The necessary adjustments are not to be recorded in the asset accounts, but should be made in the capital accounts.

The operating profit for the year 1993 is £40,000, after charging depreciation of 1% on cost of the buildings and of 10% on cost of the machinery. There have been no sales or purchases of fixed assets in the year.

The partners are allowed 10% per annum interest on capital account balances on a *pro rata* basis. No interest is allowed or charged on current account balances. On 31 December 1993 the partners are advised that the buildings are now worth only £20,000 (though the value of the land is not affected). It is agreed that this revised valuation should be incorporated in the accounts as at 31 December 1993.

Each partner has taken drawings of £4,000 in the year to 31 December 1993.

Required:

(a)   Partners' capital accounts in columnar form for the year 1993.

(6 marks)

(b)   Appropriation account for the year 1993.

(2 marks)

(c)   Partners' current accounts in columnar form for the year 1993.

(2 marks)

(d)   Summary balance sheet as at 31 December 1993, taking net current assets as the balancing figure.

(3 marks)

(e)   A reconciliation of net current assets at 1 January 1993 with net current assets at 31 December 1993.

(5 marks)
(Total: 18 marks)
(ACCA Dec 93)

---

46   A, B AND C PARTNERSHIP

A and B are in partnership, sharing profits equally after taking account of interest on opening balances on capital accounts at 10% pa, and allowing A a management salary of £5,000 pa. No interest is allowed or charged on current accounts or on drawings.

You are presented with the following trial balance as at 31 December 19X1.

	£'000	£'000
Capital account A		50
Capital account B		30
Current account A		12
Current account B		3
Drawings A	7	
Drawings B	6	
Property	90	
Fixtures and fittings, cost and depreciation	40	14
Motor vehicles, cost and depreciation	40	24
Sales		250
Cost of sales	120	
Stocks	20	
Debtors and creditors	40	30
Operating expenses	40	
Goodwill	40	
Bank overdraft		10
Loan from A at 12% pa		15
Loan from D at 12% pa		5
	443	443

The following information is to be taken into account.

(i)   Depreciation on motor vehicles has already been provided for the year 19X1 at 20% pa by the reducing balance method. It is now decided to change this for the year 19X1 to 25% pa by the reducing balance method.

(ii)   It is agreed that a desk included in fixtures and fittings above, at a cost of £3,000, depreciation to date £1,000, is to be transferred to A personally at a valuation of £2,500.

(iii) Interest on the loans from A and D has neither been paid nor provided.

(iv)   From the bank statement for December you discover that:

     (a)   Bank charges of £500 have not been taken account of.

     (b)   A standing order receipt for £1,000 from a customer has been omitted.

     (c)   A cheque for £2,000 from a customer deposited on 29 December has been returned by the bank marked 'refer to drawer'.

     (d)   A cheque for £3,000 sent to a supplier on 25 November is still outstanding.

(v)   C is to join the partnership with effect from the close of business on 31 December 19X1. It is agreed that for the purposes of this admission the property of the partnership is revalued at £120,000, and goodwill at £50,000. However, the property is to remain recorded in the books at the original figure, and goodwill is to be eliminated entirely from the balance sheet. A, B and C are in future to share profits in the ratio of 2:2:1, after taking account of interest on capital accounts at 10%, and allowing both A and C management salaries of £5,000 each. On 31 December C paid £20,000 into a special bank account in the name of the partnership as a capital contribution. This transaction was not accounted for on that date.

You are required:

(a)   to prepare journal entries to take account of item (i) to item (iv) above.

(9 marks)

(b)   to prepare capital and current accounts for A, B and C in columnar form.

(6 marks)

(c)   to prepare profit and loss account, appropriation account, and balance sheet for the partnership in relation to the year 19X1.   **(7 marks)**

(Total: 22 marks)
(Pilot Paper)

---

47   MYDDLETON ACCESSORIES

At 30 September 19X3 the share capital of Myddleton Accessories plc comprised:

Authorised:

500,000 8% preference shares of £1.00 per share.
6,000,000 ordinary shares of £0.50 per share.

(The company's ordinary shares are listed on a recognised UK Stock Exchange. The 8% preference shares are not so listed and have only restricted voting rights.)

Issued and fully paid:

400,000 8% preference shares of £1.00 per share.
4,000,000 ordinary shares of £0.50 per share.

During October 19X3 transactions in the company's shares took place, a selection of which is given below. None of the individuals named is a director of Myddleton Accessories plc.

(1)   Two shareholders, Mr R Dupp and Mr S Kint, sold their entire holdings of 30,000 and 20,000 8% preference shares (respectively) for £1.40 per share (net).

(2)   25,000 8% preference shares were bought for £38,000 by a new shareholder, Mrs Ava Gamble.

(3)   Myddleton Accessories plc issued a further 1,000,000 of its £0.50 ordinary shares at £1.20 per share. Of the shares allotted to new shareholders, the largest single allotment was one of 450,000 shares to Universal Investment Trust plc.

(4)   Some existing shareholders took the opportunity to increase their present holdings. Mr Miles Richer acquired 350,000 of the shares referred to in (3) above. His holding up to this date had been 150,000 of the company's ordinary shares.

You are required:

(a)   to state, giving reasons, in respect of each of the four circumstances listed above, what entries (if any) Myddleton Accessories plc must make in its statutory registers ie, in those registers which it is required by law to maintain.

(*Note:* the relevant entries in the company's ledger accounts are not required.)

(b)   to state to what extent the registers you have identified in answer to part (a) must be available for public inspection.

(16 marks)
(ACCA June 83)

---

48   ANNUAL REPORT

The chairman of a public limited company has written his annual report to the shareholders, extracts of which are quoted below.

Extract 1:

'In May 19X6, in order to provide a basis for more efficient operations, we acquired PAG Warehousing and Transport Ltd. The agreed valuation of the net tangible assets acquired was £1.4 million. The purchase consideration, £1.7 million, was satisfied by an issue of 6.4 million equity shares, of £0.25 per share, to PAG's shareholders. These shares do not rank for dividend until 19X7.'

Extract 2:

'As a measure of confidence in our ability to expand in 19X7 and 19X8, and to provide the necessary financial base, we issued £0.5 million 8% redeemable debenture stock, 19X25/19X32, 20 million 6% £1 redeemable preference shares and 4 million £1 equity shares. The opportunity was also taken to redeem the whole of the 5 million 11% £1 redeemable preference shares.'

You are required to answer the following questions on the above extracts:

(Extract 1)

(a)   What does the difference of £0.3 million between the purchase consideration (£1.7m) and the net tangible assets value (£1.4m) represent?

(b)   What does the difference of £0.1 million between the purchase consideration (£1.7m) and the nominal value of the equity shares (£1.6m) represent?

(c)   What is the meaning of the term 'equity shares'?

(d)   What is the meaning of the phrase 'do not rank for dividend'?

(7 marks)

(Extract 2)

(e)   In the description of the debenture stock issue, what is the significance of:

(i)   8%?
(ii)   19X25/19X32?

(f)   In the description of the preference share issue, what is the significance of:

(i)   6%?
(ii)   redeemable?

(g)   What is the most likely explanation for the company to have redeemed existing preference shares but at the same time to have issued others?

(h)   What effect will these structural changes have had on the gearing of the company?

(j)   Contrast the accounting treatment, in the company's profit and loss accounts, of the interest due on the debentures with dividends proposed on the equity shares.

(k)   Explain the reasons for the different treatments you have outlined in your answer to (j) above.

(9 marks)
(Total: 16 marks)
(ACCA Dec 86)

---

49   FIDDLES PLC

The accountant of Fiddles plc has begun preparing final accounts but the work is not yet complete. At this stage the items included in the trial balance are as follows:

	£'000
Land	100
Buildings	120
Plant and machinery	170
Depreciation provision	120
Share capital	100
Profit and loss balance brought forward	200
Debtors	200
Creditors	110
Stock	190
Operating profit	80

Debentures (16%)	180
Provision for doubtful debts	3
Bank balance (asset)	12
Suspense	1

Notes (i) to (vii) below are to be taken into account:

(i)   The debtors control account figure, which is used in the trial balance, does not agree with the total of the debtors ledger. A contra of £5,000 has been entered correctly in the individual ledger accounts but has been entered on the wrong side of both control accounts.

   A batch total of sales of £12,345 had been entered in the double entry system as £13,345, although individual ledger account entries for these sales were correct. The balance of £4,000 on sales returns account has inadvertently been omitted from the trial balance, though correctly entered in the ledger records.

(ii)   A standing order of receipt from a regular customer for £2,000, and bank charges of £1,000, have been completely omitted from the records.

(iii) A debtor for £1,000 is to be written off. The provision for doubtful debts balance is to be adjusted to 1% of debtors.

(iv)   The opening stock figure had been overstated by £1,000 and the closing stock figure had been understated by £2,000.

(v)   Any remaining balance on suspense account should be treated as purchases if a debit balance and as sales if a credit balance.

(vi)   The debentures were issued three months before the year end. No entries have been made as regards interest.

(vii) A dividend of 10% of share capital is to be proposed.

You are required:

(a)   to prepare journal entries to cover items in notes (i) to (v) above. You are NOT to open any new accounts and may use only those accounts included in the trial balance as given;

(b)   to prepare final accounts for internal use in good order within the limits of the available information. For presentation purposes all the items arising from notes (i) to (vii) above should be regarded as material.

(25 marks)
(ACCA June 91)

50   PARTIZAN PLC

Partizan plc has the following items in its balance sheet at 31 December 19X6:

Capital and reserves

		£
Ordinary shares of 25p each		500,000
10% preference shares of £1 each		100,000
Share premium account		150,000
Profit and loss account		870,000
		1,620,000

The accountant of Partizan plc has prepared a draft profit and loss account for the year ended 31 December 19X7 which shows a net profit before tax of £380,000. You are the financial director of Partizan plc and you discover the following errors which require amendment before the final accounts are produced:

(1)   In arriving at the net profit before taxation the accountant has credited a surplus of £120,000 arising from the revaluation of the company's freehold land and buildings.

(2)   The suspense account has been included in the draft balance sheet as a creditor. It contains a balance of £300,000. You discover that this is the proceeds from the issue of 400,000 ordinary shares of 25p each at a price of 75p per share.

(3)   The corporation tax on the profit for the year is £130,000 and has not yet been included in the draft accounts.

(4)   No dividends were paid during the year. The directors now propose that the annual preference dividend be paid together with an ordinary dividend of 2p per share. The new shares issued during the year carry the right to the full dividend for the year.

(5)   The provision for doubtful debts which was created in year 19X5 is to be reduced by £60,000 this year.

(6)   During the year the company paid £220,000 to redeem its £200,000 of debenture stock. Unfortunately the accountant of Partizan plc has treated the payment as an expense in the draft profit and loss account.

(7)   An accrual for the audit fee of £30,000 is to be provided in the accounts.

You are required:

(a)   to produce journal entries, with narratives, to make the necessary amendments to the draft accounts;

(14 marks)

(b)   to show the Capital and Reserves section of the balance sheet at 31 December 19X7 after the above amendments have been made.

(7 marks)

Ignore taxation other than for entry number 3.   **(Total: 21 marks)**

51   QUEUE PLC

The trial balance of Queue plc at 31 December 19X8, before any of the items noted below, is as follows:

	Dr £	Cr £
Issued share capital (£1 ordinary shares)		30,000
Freehold properties - at cost	40,000	
Motor vehicles:		
At cost	10,000	
Depreciation to 31 December 19X7		4,000
Expenses	11,000	
Stock at 31 December 19X7	12,000	
Purchases	70,000	
Sales		100,000
Debentures (10%)		15,000
Debenture interest	750	
Bank overdraft		1,000
Bank interest	250	
Debtors and creditors	25,000	15,000
Dividend paid	1,500	
Profit and loss balance at 31 December 19X7		5,500
	170,500	170,500

The following notes are to be incorporated as appropriate:

(a)   Closing stock is £10,000.

(b)   The debentures were issued on 1 April 19X8.

(c)   The bank statement received does not agree with the cash book as at 31 December 19X8 because of the following differences:

    (i)   cheque in cash book not on bank statement £600;
    (ii)   standing order included on bank statement but not in cash book £200;
    (iii)   credit transfer from a debtor on bank statement but not in cash book £500.

(d)   All the motor vehicles were purchased in 19X6. Depreciation has been, and is still to be, provided at the rate of 25% per year on cost. On 31 December 19X8 one vehicle, purchased on 1 January 19X6 for £4,500, was sold for £2,750. This sale was accepted in part settlement of the price of £4,000 for a new van. No entries have been made in the books with regard to these transactions, and no money has been paid or received.

(e)   The corporation tax liability for the year to 31 December 19X8 is estimated at £5,000.

(f)   A final dividend of 6p per share on the existing shares is proposed.

(g)   By agreement, 10,000 new £1 ordinary shares are issued at 125p per share and the proceeds transferred immediately to the company bank account.

You are required to prepare final accounts in good order for internal use. Show necessary workings clearly.

(24 marks)

(ACCA Dec 88)

52 TOBY LTD

The trial balance of Toby Ltd at 31 December 19X8 is as follows.

	£	£
Share capital - £1 ordinary shares		10,000
Profit and loss account		19,000
Sales and purchases	61,000	100,000
Sales returns and purchase returns	2,000	4,000
Sales and purchase ledger control a/cs	20,000	7,000
Land and buildings (at cost)	40,000	
Plant (at cost, and depreciation to 1 January 19X8)	50,000	22,000
Debentures (10% pa interest)		30,000
Opening stock	15,000	
Operating expenses	9,000	
Administration expenses	7,000	
Selling expenses	6,000	
Bank		8,000
Suspense account		10,000
	210,000	210,000

Notes

(a)   5,000 new shares were issued during the year at £1.60 per share. The proceeds have been credited to the suspense account.

(b)   Sales returns of £1,000 have been entered in the sales day book as if they were sales.

(c)   The bookkeeper has included the opening provision for doubtful debts of £800 in the selling expenses account in the trial balance. The provision is required to be 5% of debtors.

(d)   A standing order payment of £1,000 for rates paid in December has not been entered. This payment covered the half-year to 31 March 19X9. Any rates account has been included under operating expenses. The balance in the account is £1,500.

(e)   90% of the buildings is factory space: the remainder is offices.

(f)   Closing stock is £18,000.

(g)   No debenture interest has been paid.

(h)   The remaining balance on the suspense account after the above represents the sales proceeds of a fully depreciated item of plant, costing £10,000. No other entries (except bank) have been made concerning this disposal.

(i)   Depreciation at 10% on cost should be provided on the plant.

(j)   A tax charge of £3,000 is to be provided.

Required:

Prepare the trading, profit and loss account for the year, and balance sheet as at 31 December 19X8, to comply with the requirements of the CA 1985, taking account of the above notes.

(20 marks)

The profit and loss account can be produced using either format 1 or format 2.

(5 marks)
(Total 25 marks)
(ACCA Accounting June 89 adapted)

---

53   PERCIVAL PLC

The opening balances in the accounts of Percival plc at 1 January 1991 are given below. All monetary figures are in £000.

Share capital	400
Share premium	100
Revaluation reserves	100
Retained profits	200
Debentures (15%)	200
Land at valuation	350
Property - cost	200
- depreciation	24
Plant - cost	450
- depreciation	180
Stock	225
Trade debtors	200
Provision for doubtful debts	20
Trade creditors	220
Expense accruals	11
Expense prepayments	10
Bank (positive balance)	20

You are given the following information in relation to the year 1991.

Cash sales	100
Credit sales	1,500
Purchases on credit	900
Discounts allowed	20
Discounts received	30
Purchases of plant	120
Proceeds of disposal of plant	30
Original cost of plant disposed of	90
Profit on disposal of plant	20
Cost of stock damaged by fire	40
Scrap proceeds of fire-damaged stock	10
Contras between debtors and creditors	15
Bad debts written off	25
Debenture interest paid	30
Interim dividend paid	20
Final dividend proposed	20
Bank charges	8

Cheques outstanding at 31.12 per bank reconciliation	35
Banking of receipts from credit sales	1,450
Trade creditors at 31.12	280
Depreciation rate on closing cost balances:	
property	2%
plant	10%
Wages and salaries paid	250
Operating expenses paid	240
Expense accruals 31.12	12
Expense prepayments 31.12	14
Provision for doubtful debts required	10% of debtors
Closing stock	170

Required:

Prepare trading, profit and loss account and closing balance sheet, for the year 1991. Workings may be in any form, and to any level of detail, you find convenient, but should be logically and clearly presented.

(25 marks)
(ACCA June 92)

---

54   LINCOLN PLC

You are presented with the following trial balances of Lincoln plc as at 31 December 1992.

	£'000	
		£'000
Share capital, 50p ordinary shares		1,000
Share premium		500
15% Debentures		800
Profit and loss balance 1 January		200
Purchases and sales	2,400	5,000
Purchase returns and sales returns	100	150
Sales and purchase ledger control balances	1,000	400
Property - cost	800	
- depreciation to 1.1.92		200
Land - at valuation on 1.1.83	900	
Machinery - cost	1,600	
- depreciation to 1.1.92		500
Discounts for prompt payment	20	10
Operating expenses	1,300	
Interim dividends paid	100	
Debenture interest paid to 1.7.92	60	
Bank		30
Suspense account	210	
Stock at 1.1.92	300	
	8,790	8,790

The book-keeper has not recorded certain items, and seems to have only partially recorded others. Details are given below.

(i)   Half of the debentures had been redeemed on 1 July 1992 at a cost of £380,000. Only one entry, in the bank account, had been made.

(ii)   During the year 1992, 200,000 more ordinary shares, identical to those already in issue, had been issued at 110 pence per share. Again only one entry, in the bank account, had been made.

(iii)   The managing director has taken £10,000 of the purchases for his own use and no entries have been made for this.

(iv)   The land is to be revalued, as at 31 December 1992, at £1,500,000.

(v)   Depreciation of 2% p.a. on cost needs to be provided on the property.

(vi)   One tenth of the cost of machinery figure represents items which were fully depreciated down to their estimated scrap value of £10,000 prior to 1 January 1992. There have been no purchases or disposals of machinery during 1992. Depreciation of 10% p.a. on the reducing balance basis needs to be provided on the machinery, as appropriate.

(vii)   An amount of £50,000 had been paid during the year 1992 to a customer because of personal injury he had suffered as a result of a fault in the goods delivered to him. Only one entry, in the cash book, had been made.

(viii) A final dividend of 5 pence per share, on all the shares in issue on 31 December 1992, is to be proposed.

(ix)   Closing stock at 31 December 1992 is £400,000. Half of this figure represents purchases still included in the purchase ledger control account balance at 31 December 1992.

(x)   Any balance on the suspense account should be shown in the profit and loss account as a separate item.

Required:

Prepare a profit and loss account, and the balance sheet of Lincoln plc, in good order, as at 31 December 1992. Your layout and use of headings and sub-totals should be designed to give the maximum of helpful information to the reader. All necessary workings should be clearly shown.   **(25 marks)**
(ACCA Dec 92)

55   NANTRED TRADING CO LTD

The outline balance sheets of the Nantred Trading Co Ltd were as shown below:

Balance sheets as at 30 September

19X5				19X6	
£	£			£	£
		Fixed assets (at written down values):			
40,000		Premises	98,000		
65,000		Plant and equipment	162,000		
	105,000				260,000
		Current assets:			
31,200		Stock	95,300		
19,700		Trade debtors	30,700		
15,600		Bank and cash	26,500		
66,500			152,500		
		Current liabilities:			
23,900		Trade creditors	55,800		
11,400		Corporation tax	13,100		
17,000		Proposed dividends	17,000		
52,300			85,900		
	14,200	Working capital			66,600
	119,200	Net assets employed			326,600
		Financed by:			
100,000		Ordinary share capital	200,000		
19,200		Reserves	26,600		
	119,200	Shareholders' funds			226,600
	-	7% debentures			100,000
	119,200				326,600

The only other information available is that the turnover for the years ended 30 September 19X5 and 19X6 was £202,900 and £490,700, respectively, and that on 30 September 19X4 reserves were £26,100.

You are required:

(a)   to calculate, for each of the two years, six suitable ratios to highlight the financial stability, liquidity and profitability of the company;

(9 marks)

(b)   to comment on the situation revealed by the figures you have calculated in your answer to (a) above.

(8 marks)
(Total: 17 marks)
(ACCA Dec 86)

56   GRAVELEA HAULAGE CO PLC

The Gravelea Haulage Co plc is an established company which intends to expand its activities from 19X2 onwards.

In the opinion of the directors, the only feasible means of financing the expansion programme is by obtaining funds from outside sources.

Over a period of weeks the directors have been considering alternative ways of raising the £500,000 needed.

They have now narrowed down the choice to one of three possibilities:

Scheme:

(A)   an issue of £500,000 7% redeemable debentures 19X10/19X17, at par;

(B)   an issue of 500,000 10% redeemable preference shares of £1.00 per share, at par;

(C)   an issue of 400,000 ordinary shares of £1.00 per share, at a premium of £0.25 per share, on which it is hoped to pay an annual dividend of 15% currently paid on existing ordinary shares.

Currently the company's issued share capital consists of 3,000,000 ordinary shares of £1.00 per share, fully paid.

The chief accountant has estimated that the company's profit before interest and tax (without taking account of the additional profit from the expansion programme) is likely to remain static at £574,000 for the next five years. Interest payable on bank overdraft for each of these years has been estimated at £4,000.

It has also been estimated that, after it has been implemented, the programme will produce an annual amount of £130,000 profit before interest and tax, additional to the figure shown above.

Corporation tax has been estimated as an effective rate of 40% on the company's total profit after interest and before tax.

Without taking the expansion programme into account, the company's earnings per share is estimated to be 11.4p, arrived at as follows:

	£
Profit before interest and tax	574,000
Less: Interest	4,000
Profit after interest before tax	570,000
Less: Corporation tax (40% × £570,000)	228,000
Profit after tax	342,000
Less: Preference dividends	Nil
Earnings (attributable to ordinary shareholders)	342,000
Number of ordinary shares in issue and ranking for dividend	*No.* 3,000,000
Earnings per share (EPS) (as above) ((342,000 × 100)/3,000,000)	11.4p

You are required to write notes, or produce calculations, as appropriate, to answer the following questions which have been raised:

(a)   In Schemes A and B, what is the significance of the term 'redeemable'?

(1 mark)

(b)   For what reasons might the company wish to redeem its shares or debentures?

(2 marks)

(c)   What is the significance of the date 19X10/19X17 in Scheme A?

(2 marks)

(d)   In Scheme C will the dividend of 15% be calculated on the nominal value (£400,000) of the additional ordinary shares or on the issue value (£500,000)? What is the alternative way in which the dividend could be expressed?

(1 mark)

(e)   What will be the company's annual earnings per share on the basis that:

(i)   Scheme A is adopted;
(ii)   Scheme B is adopted;
(iii)   Scheme C is adopted?

(Earnings per share (EPS) is defined as the profit in pence attributable to each ordinary share after tax.)

(9 marks)

(f)   What will be the company's capital gearing in a full year after implementation, separately for each of the schemes?

(3 marks)
(Total: 18 marks)
(ACCA June 83)

57   ANTIPODEAN ENTERPRISES

The balance sheets of Antipodean Enterprises at the end of two consecutive financial years were:

Balance sheets as at

31 December 19X2			31 December 19X3	
£	£		£	£
		Fixed assets (at written down values):		
38,000		Premises	37,000	
17,600		Equipment	45,800	
4,080		Cars	18,930	
	59,680			101,730
	17,000	Investments (long-term)		25,000
		Current assets:		
27,500		Stocks	19,670	
14,410		Debtors and prepayments	11,960	
3,600		Short-term investments	4,800	
1,800		Cash and bank balances	700	
	47,310			37,130
		Current liabilities:		
20,950		Creditors and accruals	32,050	
-		Bank overdraft	28,200	
	(20,950)			(60,250)
	103,040	Net assets employed		103,610

31 December 19X2			31 December 19X3	
£	£		£	£
		Financed by:		
67,940		Opening capital	75,040	
4,000		Capital introduced/(withdrawn)	(6,500)	
15,300		Profit/(loss) for year	25,200	
(12,200)		Drawings	(15,130)	
	75,040	Closing capital		78,610
	28,000	Long-term liability - Business development loan		25,000
	103,040			103,610

Profit for the year ended 31 December 19X3 (£25,200) is after accounting for:

	£
Depreciation:	
Premises	1,000
Equipment	3,000
Cars	3,000
Profit on disposal of equipment	430
Loss on disposal of cars	740
Interest payable	3,000

The written down value of the assets at date of disposal was:

	£
Equipment	5,200
Cars	2,010

Interest accrued at 31 December 19X3 is £400.

You are required:

(a)   to prepare a cash flow statement for Antipodean Enterprises for the year ended 31 December 19X3 in accordance with FRS 1 (revised) together with a note reconciling operating profit to net cash inflow from operating activities;

(14 marks)

(b)   to comment on the financial position of the business as revealed by your answer to (a) above and by the balance sheet as at 31 December 19X3.   **(7 marks)**

(Total: 21 marks)

(ACCA June 84)

---

58   CASH FLOW PLC

The summarised balance sheet of Cash Flow plc at 31 December 19X3 is as follows (all figures are in £'000).

	£'000	£'000	£'000
Fixed assets			
Cost	200		
Depreciation	40		
	—	160	
Current assets			
Stock	45		
Debtors	37		
Bank	18		
	—	100	
		—	260
Represented by:			
£1 ordinary shares		50	
Profit and loss balance		70	
10% debentures		100	
Creditors		30	
Dividends		10	
		—	260

In June 19X4 the directors are concerned about the progress of the business and prepare an estimated cash flow statement, as shown, for the year to 31 December 19X4. The 10% debentures have to be redeemed in four equal instalments in the years 19X4 to 19X7 inclusive.

Cash Flow plc
Estimated statement for the year to 31 December 19X4

	£'000
Profit	20
Add: Depreciation	30
Change in stock	(9)
Change in debtors	23
Change in creditors	25
Net cash inflow from operations	89
Issue of 30,000 £1 ordinary shares	40
Issue of 15% debentures	100
Dividends paid	(33)
Fixed assets purchased	(190)
10% debentures redeemed	(30)
Change in liquidity	(24)

You are required:

(a)   to prepare a summarised, estimated balance sheet as at 31 December 19X4, within the limits of the available information, clearly explaining the movement on the profit and loss balance;

(12 marks)

(b)   to prepare a report on the strengths and weaknesses of the company's position and progress. (*Note: the calculation of ratios is **NOT** required.*)

(10 marks)
(Total: 22 marks)
(ACCA June 90)

---

59   AIDA PLC

You are given summarised balance sheets for Aida plc as shown below:

	31 December 19X0		*31 December 19X1*	
	£'000	£'000	£'000	£'000
Ordinary shares		20		25
Share premium		4		9
Property revaluation reserve		5		8
Profit and loss balance		16		16
Debentures				
10%		40		20
15%		0		40
		——		——
		85		118
		——		——
Property		25		45
Plant:				
Cost	30		46	
Depreciation	15		24	
	——	15	——	22
Stock		46		44
Debtors		17		33
Bank		7		0
		——		——
		110		144
Trade creditors	20		13	
Dividends	5		9	
Bank	0		4	
	——	25	——	26
		——		——
		85		118
		——		——

Note: any issues and redemptions of shares or debentures occurred on 1 January 19X1.

All debenture interest is paid within the accounting year in which it is charged.

Only one dividend is declared each year. Dividends are always paid early in the year following that to which they relate. No sales of fixed assets have occurred during the relevant period.

You are required:

(a)   to prepare a statement to show the net cash flow derived from trading operations in the year to 31 December 19X1;

(12 marks)

(b)   to prepare a cash flow statement complying with FRS 1 (revised) to highlight the change in the bank balance during the year to 31 December 19X1.

(8 marks)
(Total: 20 marks)
(ACCA Dec 91 amended)

---

60   FRED PLC

You are given the attached information about Fred plc, comprising summarised profit and loss accounts, summarised balance sheets, and some suggested ratio calculations. You should note that there may be alternative ways of calculating some of these ratios. The holder of a small number of the ordinary shares in the business has come to you for help and advice. There are a number of things he does not properly understand, and a friend of his who is an accountancy student has suggested to him that some of the ratios show a distinctly unsatisfactory position, and that he should sell his shares as quickly as possible.

Required:

(a)   Write a report to the shareholder commenting on the apparent position and prospects of Fred plc, as far as the information permits. Your report should include reference to liquidity and profitability aspects, and should advise whether, in your view, the shares should indeed be sold as soon as possible.

(12 marks)

(b)   Explain the following issues to the shareholder:

(i)   What is the loan redemption fund, and how has it been created?

(3 marks)

(ii)   How on earth can there be £49m of assets on the balance sheet 'not yet in use'? Surely if it is not in use it is not an asset. What are assets anyway? And coming back to that £49m, the depreciation on these items will be artificially reducing the reported profit, won't it?

(6 marks)

(iii)   What is all this about interest being capitalised? What does it mean, and why are they doing it?

(4 marks)
(Total: 25 marks)

Fred plc
Summarised balance sheets at year end (£m)

		1992			1991	
Fixed assets						
Tangible - not yet in use		49			41	
- in use		295			237	
		344			278	
Investments		1			1	
Loan redemption fund		1			1	
			346			280
Current assets						
Stocks		42			41	
Debtors - trade	4			4		
- other	4			4		
	8			8		
Bank		2			5	
Cash		2			2	
		54			56	
Creditors due within one year						
- trade	60			60		
- other	87			112		
	147			172		
Net current liabilities			93			116
Total assets less current liabilities			253			164
Creditors due between one and five years			61			1
Provision for liabilities and charges			4			3
			188			160
Capital and reserves						
Ordinary shares of 10p each			19			19
Preference shares of £1 each			46			46
Share premium			1			1
Profit and loss account			122			94
			188			160

Fred plc
Summarised profit and loss accounts for the year (£m)

	1992		1991	
Sales		910		775
Raw materials and consumables		730		633
		180		142
Staff costs	77		64	
Depreciation of tangible fixed assets	12		10	
Other operating charges	38		30	
		127		104
		53		38
Other operating income		4		3
		57		41
Net interest payable		5		4
		52		37
Profit sharing - employees		2		1
		50		36
Taxation		17		12
		33		24
Preference dividends		2		2
		31		22
Ordinary dividends		3		2
		28		20

Note

Net interest payable:		
interest payable	12	9
interest receivable	(1)	(1)
interest capitalised	(6)	(4)
	5	4

Fred plc

Some possible ratio calculations (which can be taken as arithmetically correct).

	1992	1991
Current ratio	$\frac{54}{147}$ = 36.7%	$\frac{56}{172}$ = 32.6%
Acid test ratio	$\frac{12}{147}$ = 8.2%	$\frac{15}{172}$ = 8.7%

	1992		*1991*	
ROCE	$\frac{57}{249}$	= 22.9%	$\frac{41}{161}$	= 25.5%
ROOE	$\frac{33}{188}$	= 17.5%	$\frac{24}{160}$	= 15.0%
EPS	$\frac{31}{190}$	= 16.3 pence	$\frac{22}{190}$	= 11.6 pence
Trade debtors turnover	$\frac{4}{910}$	× 365 = 2 days	$\frac{4}{775}$	× 365 = 2 days
Trade creditors turnover	$\frac{60}{730}$	× 365 = 30 days	$\frac{60}{633}$	× 365 = 35 days
Gross profit %	$\frac{180}{910}$	= 19.8%	$\frac{142}{775}$	= 18.3%
Operating profit %	$\frac{57}{910}$	= 6.3%	$\frac{41}{775}$	= 5.3%
Stock turnover	$\frac{42}{730}$	× 365 = 21 days	$\frac{41}{633}$	× 365 = 24 days
Gearing	$\frac{61}{188}$	= 32.4%	$\frac{1}{160}$	= 0.6%

(ACCA June 93)

61   LIMITED COMPANIES

(a)   In the context of limited companies explain the following terms. Avoid using further technical expressions as far as possible, and explain any that you do not have to use.

(i)   Shares (do not discuss different types of share)
(ii)   Reserves
(iii)   Debentures
(iv)   Shareholders' equity
(v)   Capital employed.

(12 marks)

(b)   Define return on capital employed, and explain (without numerical illustration) how 'return' is calculated for this purpose. To whom is this ratio likely to give useful information, and why?

(8 marks)
(Total: 20 marks)
(ACCA Dec 93)

8 ANSWERS TO PRACTICE QUESTIONS

1	SEMA PLC

(a)

Premises account

	£		£
Balance b/d	521,100		
Bank or creditors:			
Survey fees	1,500		
Conveyancing fees	3,000		
Vendors	90,000		
Architects	8,700		
Subcontractors	69,400		
Wages	11,600		
Purchases	76,800	Balance c/d	782,100
	782,100		782,100

Plant account

	£		£
Balance b/d	407,500		
Bank or creditors:			
Supplier (Press A)			
(90% × £97,000)	87,300		
Transport	2,900		
Installation	2,310		
Supplier (Press B)	105,800		
Installation	2,550	Balance c/d	608,360
	608,360		608,360

(b) Press B has been capitalised at its cash cost. The difference between the cash cost (£105,800) and the instalment cost (£120,000) is effectively interest. Interest is normally regarded as an expense of running a business rather than a cost of acquisition of a specific item.

For similar reasons the annual interest on the debenture finance is not capitalised, but charged against profit and loss account each year.

The cash discount is a financial item equivalent to interest received. Therefore the discount will be income in 19X6 rather than a reduction in the asset cost.

(Tutorial note:

Demolition costs have been included in the premises account on the basis that they represent preparation of the site. It would be acceptable to write off these costs.)

2   FULLER LTD

(Tutorial note: because of the number of transactions given, the question paper must be used as a working paper, agreeing the entries common to the bank account and the bank statement.

The important points about presentation of the reconciliation statement are:

(i)   date the statement;
(ii)   start with the balance per the bank statement.

The question does not state that the adjustments to the company's 'bank account' were required but the examiner did require them to be shown.

The bank statement contains a large number of errors. The 'Adjustments' are mainly corrections to earlier entries made by the bank incorrectly. All the adjustments can be tied up with earlier figures except the entry on 10 October: £12.90. Presumably this relates to an incorrect entry made by the bank in September and would have been identified in the bank reconciliation statement as at 30 September.)

Bank reconciliation statement as at 31 October 19X6

			£	£
Balance per statement				83.03
Add: Outstanding deposits				235.39
				318.42
Less: Unpresented cheques:				
	Date	No.		
	8.10	062316	59.32	
	9.10	062318	18.10	
	28.10	062323	41.20	
	30.10	062324	119.07	
	31.10	Salaries	337.74	
				575.43
Balance per bank account (overdrawn)				(257.01)

Bank account

		£			£
			31.10.X6	Balance b/d	221.52
			31.10.X6	Interest account	26.35
31.10.X6	Balance c/d	257.01	31.10.X6	Bank charges account	9.14
		257.01			257.01

3   ARISTOCRATIC AUTOS

(a)

**Trading and profit and loss account
for year ended 30 September 19X6**

	Work-shop £	Petrol/oil £	Show-room £	Total £
Sales:				
Cash	32,125	32,964	8,500	73,589
Credit	65,892	41,252	81,914	189,058
	98,017	74,216	90,414	262,647
Opening stock	1,932	3,018	20,720	25,670
Purchases	23,860	41,805	52,100	117,765
	25,792	44,823	72,820	143,435
Closing stock	(2,752)	(2,976)	(25,310)	(31,038)
	23,040	41,847	47,510	112,397
Direct wages (W2)	34,163	5,685	-	39,848
Cost of sales	57,203	47,532	47,510	152,245
Gross profit	40,814	26,684	42,904	110,402
Profit on sale of plant (W1)	1,333	-	-	1,333
	42,147	26,684	42,904	111,735

	Work-shop £	Petrol/oil £	Show-room £	Total £
Indirect wages (W3)	7,024		4,391	11,415
Salaries			10,200	10,200
Rates (W5)	2,613	2,945	7,880	13,438
Electricity (W4)	1,939	2,185	5,846	9,970
General expenses (W6)	4,477	3,389	4,130	11,996
Depreciation:				
Buildings (N1)	2,520	2,840	7,600	12,960
Plant (N1)	14,378	5,484	3,702	23,564
	32,951	16,843	43,749	93,543
Net profit	9,196	9,841	(845)	18,192

	Duke £	Earl £	£
Net profit			18,192
Interest on capitals:			
5% × 50,000 : 40,000	2,500	2,000	(4,500)
			13,692
PSR [Equal division required by Partnership Act if no specific provision]	6,846	6,846	(13,692)
	9,346	8,846	

(b)

Balance sheet as at 30 September 19X6

	Work- shop £	Petrol/ oil £	Show- room £	Total £
Fixed assets:				
Freehold buildings	5,020	4,260	11,010	20,290
Plant (N1)	24,891	4,859	5,357	35,107
	29,911	9,119	16,367	55,397
Current assets:				
Stocks	2,752	2,976	25,310	31,038
Debtors	1,365	537	-	1,902
Prepayments (W8)	2,586	2,915	7,799	13,300
Bank and cash	316	1,605	30,470	32,391
	7,019	8,033	63,579	78,631
Current liabilities:				
Creditors	4,225	5,602	15,250	25,077
Accruals (W7)	915	564	983	2,462
	5,140	6,166	16,233	27,539
Net current assets	1,879	1,867	47,346	51,092
Net assets	31,790	10,986	63,713	106,489

	£	£
Capital accounts:		
Duke	50,000	
Earl	40,000	
		90,000
Current accounts (N2):		
Duke	6,906	
Earl	9,583	
		16,489
		106,489

Notes to the accounts:

(1)   **Fixed assets**

	Work-shop £	Petrol/oil £	Show-room £
Buildings:			
Cost b/d and c/d	12,600	14,200	38,000
Depreciation b/d	5,060	7,100	19,390
Charge for year	2,520	2,840	7,600
	7,580	9,940	26,990
NBV	5,020	4,260	11,010
Plant:			
Cost b/d	65,180	22,900	17,450
Additions	26,210	4,520	1,060
Disposals	(19,500)		
Balance c/d	71,890	27,420	18,510
Depreciation b/d	48,254	17,077	9,451
Disposals	(15,633)		
Charge for year	14,378	5,484	3,702
	46,999	22,561	13,153
NBV	24,891	4,859	5,357

(2)   **Partners' current accounts**

	Duke £	Earl £
Balance b/d	9,750	10,477
Interest	2,500	2,000
Balance of profits	6,846	6,846
Drawings	(12,190)	(9,740)
Balance c/d	6,906	9,583

(Tutorial note:

Approach to question

As there is so much information to insert on the face of the final accounts, workings should be put on a subsidiary schedule to show how the totals have been arrived at. It is helpful to you (and the examiner) if the workings are numbered. The working number can then be transferred to the final accounts at the same time as transferring the accounting figure.

Some 'workings', however, may be able to be presented as notes to the accounts. Put these on a separate page - the page can subsequently be headed up as workings or notes as appropriate. Fixed assets are a good example of a working schedule that doubles up as notes to the accounts.)

WORKINGS

(W1)

Disposal account

	£			£
Cost	19,500	Depreciation		15,633
Profit	1,333	Proceeds		5,200
	20,833			20,833

		Work-shop £	Petrol/oil £	Show-room £	Total £
(W2)	**Direct wages**				
	Per list	34,050	5,602		
	Accrual	113	83		
		34,163	5,685		
(W3)	**Indirect wages**				
	Per list	6,810		4,160	
	Accrual	214		231	
		7,024		4,391	

		Work-shop £	Petrol/oil £	Show-room £	Total £
(W4)	**Electricity**				
	Per list				9,453
	Accrual				517
	Split 12.6 : 14.2 : 38.0	1,939	2,185	5,846	9,970

(Tutorial note: it is important to find the proper expense for the whole business first before apportioning ie, the accrual is also therefore apportioned.)

		Work-shop £	Petrol/oil £	Show-room £	Total £
(W5)	**Rates**				
	Per list				26,738
	Prepayment				(13,300)
	Split as per W4	2,613	2,945	7,880	13,438
(W6)	**General expenses**				
	Per list				10,692
	Accrual				1,304
	Split 98,017 : 74,216 : 90,414	4,477	3,389	4,130	11,996

(W7)   **Accruals**

	W2	113	83	
	W3	214		231
	W4 Split 517	101	113	303
	W6 Split 1,304	487	368	449
		915	564	983

(Tutorial note: as separate balance sheets are required, separate accrual figures are required. These are split in the same ratios as the expense.)

(W8)   **Prepayments**

		Work-shop £	Petrol/oil £	Show-room £
	W5 Split 13,300	2,586	2,915	7,799

4   DOUBTFUL DEBTS

(a)

Debtors

		£			£
1.1.19X1	Balance b/d	10,000		Sales returns	1,000
	Sales	100,000		Bank	90,000
				Bad debts	500
				Discounts allowed	400
			31.12.19X1	Balance c/d	18,100
		110,000			110,000
1.1.19X2	Balance b/d	18,100		Sales returns	1,800
	Sales	90,000		Bank	95,000
				Creditors	3,000
				Bad debts	1,500
				Discounts allowed	500
			31.12.19X2	Balance c/d	6,300
		108,100			108,100
1.1.19X3	Balance b/d	6,300			

Provision for doubtful debts

	£			£
31.12.19X1 Balance c/d:		1.1.19X1	Balance b/d	400
Specific	200		Bad debts	695
General				
5% ×				
(18,100 - 200)	895			
	———			———
	1,095			1,095
	———			———
Bad debts	780	1.1.19X2	Balance b/d	1,095
31.12.19X2 Balance c/d				
(5% × 6,300)	315			
	———			———
	1,095			1,095
	———			———

(b)   The prudence concept in SSAP 2 states that revenues and profits are not anticipated but are recognised in the profit and loss account only when realised in the form of cash or of other assets, the ultimate cash realisation of which can be assessed with reasonable certainty. A credit sale normally involves the creation of a legally binding agreement and the physical transfer of the goods. These two factors will tend to result in the subsequent cash receipt.

Bad debts are another aspect of the prudence concept. Provision should be made for all losses as soon as they are anticipated. Past trading experience of the trader will lead him to expect that some debts will go bad. Provision should therefore be made at each year-end.

5   LEDGER ACCOUNTS AND TRIAL BALANCE

(a)

Cash book

Transaction no.	Discounts allowed	Cash	Bank	Transaction no.	Discounts received	Cash	Bank
	£	£	£		£	£	£
(1)		50		(1)			100
(2)		500		(4)		100	
(5)			200	(5)		200	
(8) (W2)	10	190		(7) (W1)	25		225
(13) (W3)	4	96		(10)			100
Balance c/d			255	(12)			30
				Balance c/d		536	
	—	—	—		—	—	—
	14	836	455		25	836	455
	—	—	—		—	—	—
Balance b/d		536		Balance b/d			255

(Tutorial note: the above cash book is really two ledger accounts in one; a cash ledger and a bank ledger. The discounts columns are memorandum; the actual double entry being for discounts allowed:

Dr   Discounts allowed
Cr   Personal debtor accounts)

Discounts allowed

Transaction no.	£	Transaction no.	£
(8) and (13)	14		

Discounts received

Transaction no.	£	Transaction no.	£
		(7)	25

Sales

Transaction no.	£	Transaction no.	£
		(2)	500
Balance c/d	845	(6)	300
		(11) $(135 \times \frac{1}{3})$	45
	——		——
	845		845
	——		——
		Balance b/d	845

Purchases

Transaction no.	£	Transaction no.	£
(3)	400		

P

Transaction no.	£	Transaction no.	£
(7)	225	(3)	400
(7)	25		
Balance c/d	150		
	——		——
	400		400
	——		——
		Balance b/d	150

Wages

Transaction no.	£	Transaction no.	£
(4)	100	Balance c/d	200
(10)	100		
	——		——
	200		200
	——		——
Balance b/d	200		

Q

Transaction no.	£	Transaction no.	£
(6)	300	(8)	190
		(8)	10
		(13)	96
		(13)	4
	——		——
	300		300
	——		——

R

Transaction no.	£	Transaction no.	£
(11)	45		

Bank charges

Transaction no.	£	Transaction no.	£
(12)	30		

WORKINGS

(W1)	Discount received	=	£250 × 10%	=	£25	
	Hence cash paid	=	£(250 − 25)	=	£225	
(W2)	Discount allowed	=	£200 × 5%	=	£10	
	Hence cash received	=	£(200 − 10)	=	£190	
(W3)	Discount allowed	=	£100 × 4%	=	£4	
	Hence cash received	=	£(100 − 4)	=	£96	

Partial trial balance

Details	*Dr* £	*Cr* £
Cash	536	
Bank		255
Discounts allowed	14	
Discounts received		25
Sales		845
Purchases	400	
P		150
Wages	200	
R	45	
Bank charges	30	
	1,225	1,275

(Tutorial notes:

(i)   The partial trial balance has an excess of credits over debits of £50, as in the given opening balances.

(ii)   With regard to the goods on approval, the essential point is that no revenue can be recognised until the goods are accepted. Until this time, the items concerned remain the property of the retailer. In accounting terms, no transaction has thus taken place if goods are sent out on approval. In practice, a memorandum record would be made of the location of the stock in the potential customer's hands.)

(b)   Reasons for studying such exercises include:

(i)   a thorough understanding of the underlying principles of double entry in an easily practised and demonstrated format;

(ii)   easy to understand and visualise by going through the exercises manually and step by step;

(iii)   has practical applications in simple situations, where computerisation may not be appropriate;

(iv)   an understanding of underlying principles is essential in designing and improving IT-based applications.

6 YOUNG AND INEXPERIENCED

(a) (*Tutorial note:*

The normal approach to a bank reconciliation statement is to adjust the existing cash book balance for any expenses not yet entered and/or errors discovered in the cash book.

In this question the cash book is a draft summary which implies a more detailed record actually exists in the double entry system. In addition the summary seems hopelessly prepared and thus it is easier to write it out again.

However, the question does not state that this should be done. Showing adjustments to the 31 December balance of £10,734.75 could have been done as an alternative.)

Revised cash book summary

		£			£
Jan-Nov	Receipts	39,500.54	1 Jan	Balance b/d	7,000.12
Dec	Receipts	4,918.64	Jan-Nov	Payments	35,000.34
	(per bank statement)		Dec	Payments	
				- cheques	
31 Dec	Balance c/d	3,712.53		7654 to 7661	6,001.25
				Standing order	50.00
				Bank charges	80.00
		_____			_____
		48,131.71			48,131.71

Bank reconciliation as at 31 December

		£	
Balance per bank statement		3,472.34	Overdraft
Add: Cheques not presented	7660	19.84	
	7657	123.45	
		_____	
		3,615.63	
		_____	
Balance per cash book summary		3,712.53	
Balance per bank reconciliation		3,615.63	
		_____	
Unexplained difference		96.90	
		_____	

(*Tutorial note:*

This may be regarded as an unfair question as there is an unexplained difference. However, looking ahead to part (b) there is a reference to a 'remaining difference'. So hopefully time has not been spent looking for the difference!)

(b) The difference has the cash book overdraft exceeding the bank overdraft by £96.90. This may be a cheque drawn in November which has not been presented. The cheque numbers on the bank statement do not include 7652 for example.

7   OBS

Plant and machinery

19X8	£	19X8	£
Cash payment	90	Closing balance	200
Opening balance	110		
	——		——
	200		200
	——		——

Depreciation of plant and machinery

19X8	£	19X8	£
Closing balance	80	Charge for the year	20
		Opening balance	60
	——		——
	80		80
	——		——

Creditors

19X8	£	19X8	£
Closing balance	130	Opening balance (130 × 50%)	65
Cash payments	560	Purchases (bal. fig.)	625
	——		——
	690		690
	——		——

Cost of sales

19X8	£	19X8	£
Purchases (from creditors account)	625	Cost of sales	600
Opening stock (bal. fig.)	75	Closing stock	100
	——		——
	700		700
	——		——

Debtors

19X8	£	19X8	£
Sales	1,000	Closing balance	100
Opening balance	52	Cash receipts	950
		Bad debt written off	2
	——		——
	1,052		1,052
	——		——

Bank

19X8	£	19X8	£
Sales	950	Closing balance	53
		Purchases	560
		Plant	90
		Operating items	130
		Drawings	20
		Opening balance	97
	950		950

Operating expenses

19X8	£	19X8	£
Closing balance	5	Profit and loss (140 – 20)	120
Cash payment	130	Opening balance	15
	135		135

Balance sheet as at 1 January 19X8

	£'000	£'000	£'000
Fixed assets:			
Land and buildings	320	-	320
Plant and machinery	110	60	50
	430	60	370
Current assets:			
Stock		75	
Debtors		52	
		127	
Creditors: amounts falling due within one year			
Creditors	65		
Accruals	15		
Bank overdraft	97		
		177	
Net current liabilities			50
			320
Represented by:			
Capital			320

8   SPREADSHEETS

Answer Plan

Rows and columns; uses; budgeting; double entry; need for accountancy skills.

A spreadsheet is simply a computing device which is made up of a number of rows and columns so as to form cells. Each row and each column has a code and therefore each cell on the matrix has a unique description or code. A spreadsheet will tend to appear to the user as a large sheet of analysis paper.

Spreadsheets can be used in many accounting applications to speed up calculations and perform analysis that would be tedious and time consuming in a manual system. In particular by using suitable formulae or computer programme the effect of varying one or more of a complicated set of variables can be examined and the effect on other figures and the overall result analysed.

For example spreadsheets can be used for budgeting purposes where each column represents an accounting period and each row a cost or revenue. The basic data will be keyed in and formulae would then be used to provide detailed information on expected costs and revenues in future periods. When the budget has been set up the effect of altering one or more of the variables can then be examined with relative ease.

Another example of an application might be where columns equate to credits and rows equate to debits. Each individual cell will then be a complete double entry.

Although such computer techniques as spreadsheets can speed up and ease the calculations that might once have been performed by an accountant they do not make accounting out of date. In most spreadsheet applications it will be necessary for the user to understand the fundamentals of the accounting that is being performed by the computer and of course accountancy knowledge will be necessary to interpret the results given by the computer programme.

Equally the design of computer packages will need the input of accountancy knowledge in order to be of use for the purposes intended.

9   ETHELRED

(a)

	Cost	Depr'n to 31 Dec 1991	Net	Profit and loss charge for 1991
	£	£	£	£
Machine A	10,000	10,000	-	-
Machine B (W1)	-	-	-	2,600
Machine C (W2)	15,000	11,068	3,932	983
Machine D (W3)	16,000	8,640	7,360	2,880
Machine E (W4)	22,000	7,920	14,080	4,320
Machine F (W5)	25,500	4,590	20,910	4,590

WORKINGS

(W1)   Machine B

	£
Original cost	12,000
Depreciation to 31 Dec 1990 (1,200 × 7 years)	8,400
Net book value	3,600
Trade in value (2,000 – 1,000)	1,000
Loss on disposal	2,600

(W2)   Machine C

		£
Original cost		15,000
Depr'n 1986 (15,000 × 20%)		3,000
Net book value		12,000
Depr'n 1987 (12,000 × 20%)		2,400
Net book value		9,600
Depr'n 1988 (9,600 × 20%)		1,920
Net book value		7,680
Depr'n 1989 (7,680 × 20%)		1,536
Net book value		6,144
Depr'n 1990 (6,144 × 20%)		1,229
Net book value		4,915
Depr'n 1991 (4,915 × 20%)		983
Net book value		3,932

(W3)   Depreciation charge = 16,000 – 1,600 = £14,400 over 5 years = £2,880 per annum.

Machine D has been owned for 3 years therefore depreciation to date is 3 × £2,880 = £8,640.

(W4)   Machine E

	£
Original cost	20,000
Depreciation for 1990 ((20,000 - 2,000) ÷ 5)	3,600
Net book value at 1 Jan 1991	16,400
New cost including engine	22,000
New depreciation for 1990 ((22,000 - 2,200) ÷5)	3,960
Depreciation for 1991	3,960
Net book value at 31 Dec 1991	14,080
Charge to the profit and loss account (3,960 + (3,960 - 3,600))	4,320

(W5)   Machine F

	£
Cost (24,000 + 1,500)	25,500
Depreciation charge ((25,500 - 2,550) ÷ 5)	4,590

(b)   The cost of a fixed asset is not just its purchase price but any other expenditure incurred necessarily in acquiring the asset and getting it into service. All of these costs will then be capitalised and spread over the estimated useful life of the asset by way of depreciation.

Interest however can be regarded either as a cost of acquiring the fixed asset or a cost of financing the business. If it is a necessary cost of acquiring the fixed asset then it should be capitalised and written off over the useful life of that asset, thereby matching the costs to the benefit from the fixed asset. However if it is a financing cost of the business then the interest should be written off over the life of the loan as it is incurred thereby matching with the finance method used.

In most cases it is unlikely that, under the concept of prudence, the interest cost would be viewed as a necessary cost of the asset. Instead the managing directors proposal would be rejected and the interest would be written off to the profit and loss account as it was incurred.

10   DYNOSAUR PLC

(a)   **Journal**

Date	Detail	Dr £	Cr £
30.9.19X3	Suspense	30,000	
	Ordinary share capital		25,000
	Share premium		5,000
	Issue of 50,000 50p shares @ 60p originally credited to suspense.		
30.9.19X3	Suspense	52,000	
	Fixed asset disposal		52,000
	Proceeds of sale of freehold buildings originally credited to suspense.		
30.9.19X3	Freehold land and buildings - depreciation	49,000	
	Fixed asset disposal	51,000	
	Freehold land and buildings - cost		100,000
	Transfer of cost and accumulated depreciation of building disposed of to fixed asset disposal.		
30.9.19X3	Fixed asset disposal	1,000	
	Depreciation (profit and loss)		1,000
	Profit on sale of freehold land and buildings netted off against depreciation.		
30.9.19X3	Bad debts (profit and loss)	8,000	
	Suspense		8,000
	Bad debts written off originally debited to suspense.		
30.9.19X3	Depreciation (profit and loss)	18,131	
	Freehold land and buildings - depreciation		4,531
	Plant and machinery - depreciation		13,600
	Depreciation for period (W1).		
30.9.19X3	Provision for bad debts	70	
	Bad debts (profit and loss)		70
	Reduction in bad debt provision to 5% of debtors (W2).		
30.9.19X3	Prepayments	3,637	
	Rent and rates		3,637
	Prepayment of rent and rates.		

Date	Detail	Dr £	Cr £
30.9.19X3	Electricity	1,967	
	Accruals		1,967
	Accrual for electricity.		
30.9.19X3	Sales	45	
	Trial balance difference		45
	Correction of amount of £363,772 posted to sales which should have been £363,727.		
30.9.19X3	Stock (balance sheet)	50,776	
	Stock (trading account)		50,776
	Inclusion of final stock in accounts (W3).		
30.9.19X3	Bank charges	3,637	
	Accruals		3,637
	Bank charges not provided for.		
30.9.19X3	Trial balance difference	841	
	Purchase ledger control account		841
	Purchase ledger payments column of cash book over-added.		

(b)

Trading and profit and loss account for year ended 30 September 19X3

	£	£
Sales		1,123,411
Less: Cost of sales:		
Opening stock	113,137	
Purchases	762,234	
	875,371	
Less: Closing stock	50,776	
		824,595
Gross profit		298,816
Less: Expenses:		
Depreciation	17,131	
Bad debts	7,930	
Rent and rates	30,630	
Electricity	27,353	
Bank charges	3,637	
Debenture interest	7,000	
Sundry expenses	21,417	
		115,098
Profit for period		183,718
Profit and loss account b/d		149,307
Profit and loss account c/d		333,025

Balance sheet as at 30 September 19X3

	Cost £	Depn £	£
Fixed assets:			
Freehold land and buildings	462,553	93,183	369,370
Plant and machinery	136,000	48,600	87,400
	598,553	141,783	456,770
Current assets:			
Stock		50,776	
Debtors	51,737		
Less: Provision	2,587		
		49,150	
Prepayments		3,637	
Bank		37,123	
		140,686	
Creditors: Amounts falling due within one year:			
Creditors	38,827		
Accruals (£1,967 + 3,637)	5,604		
		44,431	
			96,255
			553,025
Creditors: Amounts falling due after more than one year: 10% debentures			70,000
			483,025
Capital and reserves:			
Ordinary share capital			125,000
Share premium account			25,000
Profit and loss account			333,025
			483,025

WORKINGS

(W1)   **Land and buildings depreciation**

	£
Cost of buildings at beginning of period (£562,553 - 236,000)	326,553
Less: Cost of buildings disposed of in period	100,000
Cost of buildings at end of period	226,553

Depreciation thereon £226,553 × 2% = £4,531.

(W2)

Bad debt provision

	£		£
Bad debts	70	Balance b/d	2,657
Balance c/d (£51,737 × 5%)	2,587		
	2,657		2,657

(W3)   **Closing stock**

	£
As given	52,557
Less: Adjustment to lower of cost and net realisable value (£3,637 − 1,856)	1,781
	50,776

11   JETELECTRONICS PLC

(a)   **Journal**

No.	Detail	Dr £	Cr £
1	Fixed assets disposal	25,000	
	Plant - accumulated depreciation	51,000	
	Plant - cost		76,000
	Transfer of NBV of asset sold to fixed asset disposal.		
2	Debtors	16,000	
	Loss on disposal (profit and loss)	9,000	
	Fixed asset disposal		25,000
	Proceeds of sale and transfer of loss on disposal.		
3	Work-in-progress	26,910	
	Overhead expenses		26,910
	Transfer of overhead to work in progress.		
4	Purchase ledger control accounts	4,941	
	Sales ledger control accounts		4,941
	Contra - Minuscule Ltd		
5	Rent payable	4,500	
	Prepayments	1,500	
	Premises		6,000
	Revenue expenditure incorrectly capitalised.		
6	Accumulated depreciation	56,150	
	Depreciation (profit and loss)		56,150
	Correction of depreciation overcharge (see working).		
7	Prepayments	1,618	
	Accruals	1,618	
	Insurance		3,236
	Insurance prepayment wrongly taken as accrual.		

No.	Detail	Dr £	Cr £
8	Heating and lighting	10,084	
	Prepayments		5,042
	Accruals		5,042

Heating and lighting accrual wrongly taken as prepayment.

No.	Detail	Dr £	Cr £
9	Debtors	973	
	Prepayments	8,480	
	Overdraft interest	570	
	Bank charges	122	
	Bank		10,145

Omitted transactions.

(b)

Statement amending closing net assets employed figures as at 31 March 19X4

	− £	+ £
As originally extracted		4,999,650
Journal 2	25,000	16,000
Journal 3		26,910
Journal 5	6,000	1,500
Journal 6		56,150
Journal 7	10,084	3,236
Journal 8	10,084	
Journal 9	10,145	8,480
		973
	51,229	5,112,899
		51,229
Revised net assets at 31 March 19X4		5,061,670

(c)   **Net assets employed**

	£
At 1 April 19X3	4,268,490
At 31 March 19X4 (per (b) above)	5,061,670
	9,330,160
Average (£9,330,160 ÷ 2)	4,665,080
Assumed normal level	4,000,000
Excess	665,080
Amount due from the Ministry of Defence:	
Work performed	6,426,792
5% of £665,080 (excess)	33,254
	6,460,046
Received already	6,375,000
Balance due	85,046

Working - Correct depreciation

	£	£
Fixed assets at 1 April 19X3	2,582,500	
Disposals	76,000	
Fixed assets at 31 March 19X4	2,506,500	
Depreciation should be (10% straight line)		250,650
Originally charged		306,800
Reduction in charge required		56,150

---

12 SUSPENSE ACCOUNT AND PROVISION FOR DOUBTFUL DEBTS

(a)

Suspense account

	£		£
Discounts received (7,000 × 2)	14,000	Trial balance - difference	14,000
Current account of senior partner's wife	9,600	Discounts allowed (3,000 × 2)	6,000
		Creditors control account (237,386 − 233,786)	3,600
	23,600		23,600

(Tutorial note:

Error (iii), omission from the sales day book, will not have affected the suspense account as it does not affect the agreement of the trial balance totals. It is an error of omission ie, a transaction is completely omitted from the books of account.)

(b)

Provision for doubtful debts account

		£			£
Year 1	Debtors	2,345	Year 1	Bad debts (50,000 × 2%)	1,000
	Balance c/d (60,000 × 2%)	1,200		Bad debts (bal. fig.)	2,545
		3,545			3,545
Year 2	Debtors	37	Year 2	Balance b/d	1,200
	Bad debts (bal. fig.)	463			
	Balance c/d	700			
		1,200			1,200
			Year 3	Balance b/d	700

(Tutorial note:

In the provision for doubtful debts account, it should be noted that the **required provision** gives the closing balance, **NOT** the charge to the profit and loss account.

There are two different methods of recording bad debts written off. A debit may be made in the bad debts account or, alternatively, debited against the provision. The net amount shown as bad debt expenses will be the same using the two methods and also the balance sheet will look exactly the same whichever method is used.

The question requires bad debts to be charged against the provision and so this method must be followed.)

13   REASONS FOR CONTROL ACCOUNTS

(a)   A purchase ledger is required to give to the business information on the amounts owing to **each** supplier. Whether the ledger is part of the double entry system or not does not matter.

A purchase ledger control account acts as a check on the accuracy of the entries made in the purchase ledger as at any time the sum of the individual balances within the purchase ledger should equal the balance in the control account.

The effectiveness of the check is considerably improved if the preparation of the control account and the purchase ledger is performed by different people.

(b)   (i)   Increase £198.
(ii)   Decrease £100.
(iii)   No effect.
(iv)   Decrease £400.
(v)   Decrease £120.

(c)   In a computerised accounting system there is effectively only one preparer of accounting information - the accounting program. Assuming that information is keyed in correctly, the program will generate totals from the individual transactions keyed in and post the transactions and totals to the purchase ledger and control account respectively. There is thus no independent check and the control account serves little useful purpose.

Some form of control will still be required but this must take place outside the computer and in different ways from the preparation of a control account.

14   C LTD

(a)

Sales ledger control account

	£		£
Balance b/d	54,358.37	Balance b/d	1,194.26
Balance c/d (1,194.26 + 673.46)	1,867.72	SDB (W3)	500.00
		Sales returns under - cast (W4)	10.00
		Balance c/d (bal fig)	54,521.83
	56,226.09		56,226.09

Net Balance (54,521.83 − 1,867.72) = 52,654.11

		£
	Debtors per sales ledger listing (55,136.65 − 1,194.26)	53,942.39
(1)	Debt collection fees (increasing debtors)	108.81
(1)	Bad debts written off (decreasing debtors)	(474.16)
(2)	Credit balance taken as debit balance (2 × 673.46 in order to cancel debit and reinstate credit balance)	(1,346.92)
(4)	Contra entry error (2 × 378.82 - this should be a credit not a debit)	(757.64)
(5)	Transposition error (347.58 − 374.85)	(27.27)
(7)	Dishonoured cheque (601.75 + 607.15)	1,208.90
		52,654.11

(b)   As the name implies the purpose of control accounts is to provide some control or check on the entries in the ledgers. Both the totals of the sales ledger control account and the sales ledger should be equal. If they are not then investigation is required as there have obviously been errors made.

Control accounts also provide a summary of the many transactions that take place in a ledger and provide an instant balance for construction of financial statements.

WORKINGS

(W1)   Set up the sales ledger control account commencing with the closing balances given. Work through each of the facts discovered and adjust the sales ledger control account where relevant. Make a note on the examination paper of those facts which relate to the sales ledger individual customer balance listings.

(W2)   Now work through the remaining facts altering the list of individual balances in each case.

(W3)   Journal entry:

DR	Sales	£500	
CR	Sales ledger control		£500

(W4)   Journal entry:

DR	Returns inwards	£10	
CR	Sales ledger control		£10

15   IN SUSPENSE

(a)

Suspense account

	£		£
Sales ledger control	1,248	Difference per trial	
Cash book	66	balance	
Fixed asset disposal	740	(1,605,668 − 1,603,623)	2,045
		Telephone	9
	2,054		2,054

(b)

	£	£
Balance per sales ledger control account		327,762
Discount allowed	(1,248)	
Credit sale	857	
Contra (2 × 731)	(1,462)	
		(1,853)
Correct sales ledger control account balance		325,909
Adjustment to sales ledger account listing - SEC		(857)
Original sales ledger account listing total		325,052

(c)

	£	£
Net profit per draft accounts		412,967
Sales - SEC	857	
Telephone	(9)	
Purchases - day book error	(360)	
Loss on disposal of fixed asset	(60)	
		428
Corrected net profit		413,395

16   WHOLESALERS PLC

(a)

Sales ledger control account

	£		£
Opening balance	50,000	Sales return	5,000
Sales	107,000	Cash book receipts	111,000
		Discounts allowed	3,000
		Bad debts	2,000
		Contra	6,000
		Closing balance	30,000
	157,000		157,000
Balance b/f	30,000		

Provision for doubtful debts

	£		£
Closing balance	2,200	Opening balance	2,000
		Profit & loss account	200
	2,200		2,200
		Balance b/f	2,200

(Note: Provision is 4% of £30,000, plus £1,000 balance on C account.)

Summary memorandum ledger accounts
all figures in £000; credits in brackets

	A	B	C	D	E	F	G	Totals
Opening balance	10	20	8	9	6	(2)	(1)	50
Sales	30	35		18	9	8	7	107
Sales returns	(2)					(3)		(5)
Cash receipts	(35)	(30)	(5)	(20)	(12)	(5)	(4)	(111)
Discounts allowed	(2)					(1)		(3)
Bad debts			(2)					(2)
Contra					(2)		(4)	(6)
	1	25	1	7	1	(3)	(2)	30

(*Note:* The sales day book total in the 'unaudited information presented' was wrongly added.)

(b)   Two advantages are:

(1)   Control is improved because staff duties can be segregated and responsibilities can be split between staff.

(2)   The sales day book and purchases day book give a further arithmetical check on the information input into the accounting system.

Tutorial notes:

In order to ensure that you pick up a couple of easy marks for part (b) of the question it would be a good idea to answer that part of the question first, if you know the answer. Otherwise you may forget about part (b) or run out of time on the question before you have answered part (a) in full and have no time for part (b).

If you look at the model answer you will see that the summary memorandum accounts have been laid out side-by-side, if you can fit this number of figures across the page (perhaps by turning the page sideways) it will help you to save time, as the headings will only have to be written out once, and it will be easier to mark (getting the marker on your side can help your final mark).

This question tested your basic bookkeeping knowledge in a new way by asking you to perform some of the everyday bookkeeping required in a small business.

---

17   A NEW CLERK

(a)   (i)

Debtors ledger control account

	£		£
Per question	16,600	Adjustments (i)	909
		(iv)	800
		(v)	74
		C/fwd	14,817
	16,600		16,600

Debtors ledger debit balances:

Per question		15,547
	(ii)	216
	(iii)	(246)
	(v)	(74)
		15,443

Credit balances:

Per question	551

(ii)

Ledger balances 15,443 - 551 =	14,892
Control account	14,817
Difference	75

As at 1 January the difference was:

Ledger balances 10,483 - 497 =	9,986
Control account	10,000
Difference	(14)

The net amount of remaining errors appears to be 75 +14 = £89

(b)

Provision for doubtful debts

	£		£
DLCA	600	B/fwd 1/1/91	1,000
C/fwd 31/12/91 (i)	1,470		
		P & L account 31/12/91	1,070
			1,470
P & L account 31/12/92	520		1,470
C/fwd 31/12/92 (ii)	950		

Notes:

(i)   5% × £29,400
(ii)   5% × £19,000

(c)   The balance on the doubtful debts provision is not a liability. Although it is a credit balance, in common with liabilities, it is not an amount owed, as a liability is but a provision against an expected loss arising on the asset of debtors due to net realisable value being lower than gross debtors due.

18   ACCOUNTING CONCEPTS

(a)   (i)   **Historic cost**

This is the price paid for goods or services at the time of their purchase. For example, if a piece of machinery cost £4,000 five years ago then that is its historic cost.

(ii)   **Historic cost accounting**

This is a method of accounting which records assets and liabilities at their historic cost. No account is normally taken of any changes in value due to inflation. Changes in values may be recorded for specific reasons. Examples of these are when stock is reduced to its net realisable value or when the accounts values of buildings are increased due to a revaluation. Such changes are not made habitually.

(iii)   **Objectivity**

Objectivity is an attempt to deal with matters by reference to external standards and not in a manner coloured by personal beliefs or emotions. This means that results should not be influenced by the personality of the person who achieves those results.

(iv)   **Prudence**

Another word for prudence is caution. When applied to accounting it means that assets should not be overstated and profits should not be included until they are earned (usually when an item is sold). On the other hand a cautious view should be taken of possible losses and liabilities. For example if a liability is estimated to be between £700 and £800 then the figure of £800 is the one normally shown in the accounts.

(b)   Many people argue that historic cost accounting is objective because it records items at a readily determined figure of historic cost rather than some estimate of current value. However, there are a number of areas which have a subjective element. For example, in determining an appropriate depreciation rate to apply, an estimate should be made of the expected useful life of an asset. In stock valuation there are many areas of judgement such as valuation of work in progress and allocation of overheads.

Historic cost accounting normally gives asset values that are lower than current values - at least in times of rising prices. This is an argument for saying that historic cost accounting is prudent. However, this also means that items valued at yesterday's prices are matched against sales at today's price and this tends to give higher profits than a system involving inflation accounting.

---

19   ACCOUNTING TERMS

(a)   **Financial accounting** does not have a precise meaning but the central feature is the provision of financial information to individuals and enterprises outside the business. It tends to be concerned more with external reporting than internal reporting.

Some would also include the accounting preparation system within the term.

(b)   **Realisation** is a principle underlying the preparation of accounting information concerned with the time at which revenue and/or profits are recognised. The prudence concept in SSAP 2 states that revenue and profits are recognised by inclusion in the profit and loss account only when realised in the form of cash or of other assets, the ultimate cash realisation of which can be assessed with reasonable certainty. Realisation thus equates to a cash receipt or a reasonably certain cash receipt.

(c)   **The matching** concept is another name for the accruals concept. Revenue is accrued in the profit and loss account when it is earned. Costs are then matched with that revenue ie, charged in the profit and loss account of the same period.

A consequence of the matching concept is that costs which are not matched against current revenue but are likely to be matched against future revenue will be carried forward in the balance sheet as an asset (eg, stock).

(d)   **Materiality** is a concept used in financial accounting reporting to help determine:

(i)   whether an item should be adjusted by further information received after the draft accounts have been prepared;

(ii)   whether an item should be disclosed separately in the financial accounts.

There can be no hard and fast rule on the size of an item for it to be material. Factors to take into account include:

(i)   Relativity. £1,000 may be immaterial in a large company but material in a small business.

(ii)   Possible reaction of the user of the accounts. An item would be material if the user is likely to be influenced by the information if it were to be provided to him.

(e)   **Inflation** is a term defined by economists rather than accountants. It can be viewed as a general rise in the price of goods and services or as a fall in the purchasing power of money.

Traditionally accounts have been prepared on the basis that the unit in which data is measured - the £ - does not change in value over time. The effect of inflation, however, is that the value of the unit of measurement does change over time. Some attempts have been made to remedy this deficiency by showing accounting information in terms of 'constant purchasing power units' but the attempts have not met with success.

20   COST CONCEPTS

(a)   (i)   **Historical cost convention**

Under the historical cost convention, assets are stated in the balance sheet at their purchase price at the date of acquisition (less any amounts written off in respect of depreciation or diminution in value). Capital is simply the difference between assets and liabilities, and profit is calculated as revenues less original cost of resources used. If prices are rising, it is possible for a company to show a profit in its historical cost accounts despite having identical physical assets and owing identical liabilities at the beginning and end of its accounting period.

(ii)   **Going concern convention**

The going concern convention assumes that a business will continue in operational existence for the foreseeable future. This means, in particular, that the financial statements are drawn up on the assumption that there is no intention or necessity to liquidate or curtail significantly the scale of operation.

(b)   As stated above, the historical cost convention records assets at their original cost. However, to the extent that an asset is worth less to the business on a going concern basis, then the asset is stated at net realisable value.

For example, stock is normally stated at cost as it is expected to be sold at a higher price in the normal course of business. Slow moving stock effectively reflects a poor purchasing decision by the business and may need to be sold at less than cost. It is thus valued at NRV.

If the going concern basis did not apply in the previous paragraph, it is likely that more stock would have to be sold at less than cost on a 'forced sale' basis. Thus, the historical cost convention still requires the going concern concept to apply so that most items can be stated at original cost.

It could be argued, however, that the going concern convention is less important to the historical cost convention than the current cost convention, as the current cost convention tends to result in assets being revalued upwards to show their current value. The absence of the going concern convention may result in more reductions from current values to low values that would apply if it is assumed that the business would have to sell its assets quickly.

(c)   Certainly, some knowledge of the past is useful when predicting the future, as it is the past and current situations which develop into those of the future. Thus, a shareholder may well find a report on the past events extremely useful pertaining to his future returns (dividends) from the investment. On the other hand, a shareholder may find the management's estimate of future events to be directly useful to him. In this respect, income does not necessarily appear to be a significant factor in helping the shareholder to predict future liquidity positions. Rather, it is the cash-generating potential of the company which is likely to interest him.

21   AUDITED ACCOUNTS

The major points which should be included in the letter are:

(i)   The accounts only show the financial status of the client for last year.

(ii)   Both profit projections and cash flow projections are crucial to a business. The bank manager will tend to put greater emphasis on the cash flows of the business, even though published accounts tend to put greater emphasis on profits.

(iii)   The bank manager will require information about current value of assets, as he is concerned about asset backing for the loan.

(iv)   Accounts are largely prepared on a historic cost basis rather than a current cost basis and do not give an indication of the current state of the business in an economic sense.

(v)   The bank manager needs to know how likely and when the client will be able to pay the money back. Budgets and projections of the business will help him make the decision.

There are many factors that the past accounts do not disclose. The desire to keep to the money measurement concept and to be objective exclude a great deal of desirable information.

(Tutorial note: there are a number of points that could be raised here. However, credit is given for quality of answer and not merely for quantity of points mentioned.)

22   RESEARCH AND DEVELOPMENT

Answer plan
Define three types of research and development.
Application of matching; Conflict.
Application of prudence.
Application of going concern.

Research and development costs are split into three categories, each with their own characteristics.

Pure research is defined as experimental or theoretical work which is being undertaken in order to provide new knowledge but knowledge for its own sake rather than directed towards a particular practical aim. For example a pharmaceutical company may spend some time examining the effect of combining a number of chemical components.

Applied research is work undertaken in order to gain new knowledge but this time directed towards a specific practical aim. The same pharmaceutical company may be looking at the combination of a number of component chemicals with the aim of discovering a cure for the common cold.

Development is defined as the use of scientific or technical knowledge in order to produce new or substantially improved products or services or to install new processes or systems prior to the commencement of commercial production or applications. Therefore development is specifically the use of knowledge with the aim being a new or substantially improved commercial end product. An example here would be where the pharmaceutical company has discovered a cure for the common cold from its research and is now developing a drug for the market.

The matching concept is that wherever possible costs and their related revenues should be matched and dealt with in the same accounting period. Therefore under the matching concept if revenues from the research and development can be foreseen then the costs should be carried forward to match with these revenues when they are earned.

However this would appear to be in conflict with the concept of prudence. Following this concept revenues and profits should only be included in the profit and loss account when their realisation is assessed with reasonable certainty whereas provision should be made for all losses and expenses whether known for certain or merely estimated.

Therefore the accounting treatment adopted is that under the prudence concept pure and applied research is always written off in the profit and loss account in the period in which it is incurred. Development costs, in most instances, will also be written off when incurred but in certain circumstances can be carried forward and matched with the revenues from the new product, service or process.

Development costs can only be carried forward (ie, capitalised as an intangible fixed asset) if they satisfy a number of strict criteria which are essentially testing the certainty of the realisation of the revenues from the new product, service or process.

The going concern assumption is also included in the treatment of development costs as the future revenues from the new product or service could not be anticipated with certainty if the organisation was not a going concern.

The effect on the profit of the company of deferring development expenditure can be demonstrated with a simple example. A company incurs £1 million of development expenditure on a product which is soon to be sold on the market and is expected to have a sales life of 10 years. If this were to be capitalised as development expenditure and written off over 10 years then the charge to the profit and loss account would be £100,000 each year for 10 years. This compares to a charge of £1 million in the year in which it was incurred if the expenditure does not satisfy the criteria for deferral.

23   GOODWILL

Answer plan

Explain how goodwill is created.

Define inherent goodwill; Define purchased goodwill.

Accounting treatment of inherent goodwill; Reasons.

Accounting treatment of purchased goodwill; Reasons.

REPORT

To:	The Owner
From:	The Management Accountant
Date:	X-X-19XX
Subject:	Goodwill

As requested I have outlined below the relevant details regarding goodwill and the accounting treatment which is currently best accounting practice.

The goodwill of a business is generally created by good relations between a business and its customers. Such good relations may be caused by the attitude of the staff, the business's reputation for the reliability and quality of its products or services or by something as simple as the physical location of the business. Goodwill is defined as 'the difference between the value of a business as a whole and the aggregate of the fair values of its separable net assets'.

Whatever the cause of the goodwill it can be viewed as an additional asset of the business causing the business to be more highly valued with the goodwill than without it.

Inherent goodwill or 'internally generated' goodwill is the goodwill or reputation that has grown up with a business for any of the reasons mentioned above. Such goodwill has not been paid for and is extremely difficult to value objectively. The goodwill is also extremely volatile and can change rapidly and be lost for as many reasons as it can be created in the first place.

Purchased goodwill is inherent goodwill that has had a value assigned to it simply because it has been sold together with the business from one owner to another. If a business is purchased and the purchaser and vendor agree upon a price that is greater than the net asset value of the business then the premium being paid is for the goodwill of the business. This is termed purchased goodwill.

Inherent goodwill should never be included in the financial statements of a business. The owner may realise that it exists but it should not appear in the accounts as an asset.

The reason for not including inherent goodwill in the accounts as an asset is primarily because an objective value cannot be assigned to it and because it is such a volatile asset.

Purchased goodwill on the other hand has had a value assigned to it when the business changed hands and therefore it can be included in the balance sheet as an intangible fixed asset. However due to the volatility of this asset it would not be wise to keep it in the accounts indefinitely.

Therefore there are two alternative treatments for purchased goodwill in the financial statements. The goodwill could be written off immediately against the retained profits of the business. This is a very prudent approach recognising the instability of such an asset. However it ignores the matching concept in the sense that the goodwill will be earning profits for the business in the future.

The alternative treatment is to recognise that the asset goodwill will earn profits for a number of years into the future and include it in the balance sheet as an intangible fixed asset which is written off or amortised over the number of years of the goodwill's expected useful life. This is less prudent than immediate write off but recognises the value of the asset for what is estimated as its useful life and is therefore in accordance with the accruals concept.

24   FINANCIAL REPORTING

(a)   The fundamental objective of financial reporting is to furnish those having a right to such information with details of the company's activities during the period under review.

The objective of financial statements is to provide information about the financial position, performance and financial adaptability of an enterprise that is useful to a wide range of users for assessing the stewardship of management and for making economic decisions.

(b)   The information in the report is to be communicated to:

(i)   **Shareholders** - the owners of the company: existing and potential, including persons or groups interested in takeovers and mergers.

(ii)   **Providers of external finance**, long and short term, such as debenture holders and finance companies, both existing and potential.

(iii)   **Employees** past, present and potential.

(iv)   **Suppliers of goods and services, and customers**, past, present and prospective.

(v)   **Tax authorities**

(vi)   **Trade agencies, local authorities, environmental pressure groups, ratepayers** and any other members of the public who may require such information as is normally and legally contained in the report.

(vii)   **Analysts and advisers**, both of investors (stockbrokers, economists, statisticians and journalists) and of employees (trade unions).

(c)   The information contained in the report should be:

(i)   **Reliable** - so that conclusions drawn may be 'true and fair'.

(ii)   **Relevant** - so that information meets the needs and expectations of the users.

(iii)   **Understandable** - material matters should be disclosed without unnecessary complex detail.

(iv)   **Complete** - if an unbalanced or biased report is presented, readers will be unable to make sound judgements.

(v)   **Comparable** - the information contained in one period's report should be, as far as possible, calculated and presented on the same bases as in previous periods, so that comparisons are relevant.

(vi)   **Objective** - an unbiased view of the company's affairs, without regard to the interests of particular groups of interested parties, should be put forward.

(vii)   **Up-to-date** - companies are required to prepare their reports annually, and this is important from the point of view of investors and those advising them, for evaluation purposes.

(d)   The kind of information required by two of the groups is:

(i)   **Shareholders** - Shareholders are interested in the future performance of the business but require past figures as a guide to the future. Therefore, all financial information in the report is needed.

In addition, any general indication given in the report as to future prospects is relevant.

(ii)   **Tax authorities** - require past figures as a basis for computing tax liabilities.

25   REGULATORY INFLUENCES

Answer Plan

Companies Act; Accounting standards; Stock Exchange requirements; current position.

The three main regulatory influences on the preparation of the published accounts of quoted companies in the UK are the Companies Acts, accounting standards and the Stock Exchange regulations.

The Companies Acts, now consolidated in Companies Act 1989, lay down the basic framework for the keeping of books of accounts and the preparation of published accounts for quoted companies. As far as the preparation of the published accounts is concerned the Companies Acts set out the formats for the financial statements that should be followed, together with some details of information that should be disclosed in the financial statements. However much of the detail of which accounting techniques should be used and exactly what information should be disclosed is left to the accountancy bodies themselves to decide.

The accountancy bodies in the UK publish accounting standards to fill in the details of methods of accounting that are preferred and the precise information that should be disclosed in financial statements. These standards were, for many years, issued as Statements of Standard Accounting Practice (SSAPs) but under the new regulatory system are now published as Financial Reporting Standards (FRSs). A company's financial statements should comply with SSAPs and FRSs and if they do not the company risks investigation and possible disciplinary proceedings.

Finally quoted companies must comply with the Stock Exchange's own requirements in addition to those of the government and the accountancy profession. These requirements are usually disclosure requirements which are monitored by the Stock Exchange and companies must comply before their shares can be quoted or traded on the Stock Exchange.

In the past this regulatory system has not always been as effective as it might be. Certainly many companies have flouted the requirements of SSAP's such as SSAP 16 (which has since been withdrawn) and to some extent SSAP 22 without any form of penalties from the accountancy profession. There is currently a move towards greater internal regulation by the setting up of the Financial Reporting Review Panel which aims to monitor the accounts of quoted companies and instigate disciplinary proceedings against those that do not prepare their accounts in line with SSAPs and FRSs. There is also some debate as to whether accounting standards should be given legal backing in order to strengthen their position in the regulatory framework.

26 REVENUE

Answer Plan

(a) Reasonably certain; objective measurement.

(b) Stage F; stage G.

(c) Gross profit calculation.

(d) Prudence; doubtful debts.

(e) Production process.

(a) The general rule that accountants apply regarding the timing of revenue recognition is that revenue will only be recognised if it is prudent to do so. Therefore revenue will only be recognised when the value of the asset to be received in return is reasonably certain and when the value of that asset is capable of objective measurement.

When revenue is recognised it is included in the profit and loss account for that period.

(b) Applying the rules to the situation in the question it would appear that revenue should be recognised when it is reasonably certain and this will be when there is an agreement with the customer. In this case therefore the point of revenue recognition is likely to be stage F.

In practice the actual delivery of the goods, and the delivery note in particular, serve as evidence of the sale and therefore it could also be argued that revenue recognition could be delayed until stage G.

(c) The gross profit on goods is the selling price of the goods less the cost of the goods. In this instance the selling price of the product is £300 and the manufacturing cost of the goods is £170. Therefore the gross profit is £130.

There appears to be a further £10 of selling cost involved in the sale of the goods after the manufacturing stage. These costs will be charged to the profit and loss account in arriving at the net profit on the sale of the goods.

(d) One of the fundamental accounting concepts set out in SSAP2 is that of prudence. If prudence were to be taken to extremes then it could be argued that revenue should not be recognised until it was absolutely certain. This would be when the customer actually paid for the goods, ie stage H in this example.

At any time until the price of the goods is actually received in full there will always be some risk that the customer will not pay for the goods. Therefore it could be argued that by recognising revenue any earlier than at stage H there is a chance that revenue is being overstated. This would of course be contrary to the concept of prudence. However an alternative, prudent approach is to recognise the revenue at the point of sale, stage F, and then set up a provision for doubtful debts to cover the situation of some customers not eventually paying for their goods.

(e) If a product is of the type that requires manufacturing or production over a significant period of time it could be argued that the profit on the product is not just made at the time of the sale but that the profit has accrued over the period of production. In such a case it might be fairer, and in accordance with the matching concept from SSAP2, to recognise some of the revenue, and therefore profit, on the product at intervals throughout the production process.

In this example it could perhaps be argued that some revenue and profit should be recognised at stages B, C and D, throughout the production process, rather than it all being recognised at stage F. However this is contrary to the concept of prudence and SSAP2 states that where there is a conflict between matching and prudence then prudence should prevail.

27   FOLLOWING TERMS

(a)   (i)   **Asset***:* An asset is a resource owned or controlled by the business, acquired by means of a transaction which will give valuable benefits to the business in the future.

(ii)   **Fixed asset***:* Assets which the business intends to keep and utilise in the business for the long-term.

(iii)   **Current asset***:* An asset which the business expects to keep and utilise in the business for the short-term.

(iv)   **Depreciation:** The method by which the cost of a fixed asset is allocated to the accounting periods which benefit from its use. (That is over its useful economic life.)

(b)   (i)   **A screwdriver:** This is strictly within the definition of a fixed asset, however, on application of the concept of materiality such items would usually be written off as an expense to the profit and loss account.

(ii)   **A machine hired by the business:** As the asset has not been acquired and is not controlled by the business on a permanent basis the machine cannot be regarded as an asset. If the hire were on a permanent basis then there could be an argument that in fact the machine was controlled by the business and therefore the right to use the machine is an asset.

(iii)   **The good reputation of the business with its customers:** This is usually one component of the asset of goodwill. However as goodwill is usually created and not purchased, it is common for goodwill not to be valued as an asset in the accounts (following the concept of prudence).

(c)   The fixed assets have a value of £4.5 million, made up of £3 million of land, £1 million of buildings and £0.5 million of plant and equipment.

The land is stated at valuation, which means that it is stated at a value such as market value rather than original cost.

The buildings are stated at their original cost, which may have been incurred some time ago and which may be out of line with the current value of the building.

The plant and machinery figure is made up of the original cost of the plant after deduction of an amount of £1.5 million for depreciation to come to the net book value of £0.5 million.

The depreciation is an attempt to spread the cost of the plant, as an expense to the profit and loss account, over its useful economic life. Thus the £0.5 million is the remaining cost yet to be expensed to the profit and loss account in future years.

The total of £4.5 million therefore consists of three figures calculated on entirely different bases. It is therefore questionable whether this figure gives any meaningful information to the shareholders.

Tutorial notes:

This question asked about various aspects of accounting for fixed assets. As we have already mentioned, you can expect to find written questions in the exam asking you to explain certain accounting terms. The examiner has taken that kind of question one step further by asking you to categorise some items in accordance with these definitions and also to explain the figures in the accounts that these definitions produce. In this way he is testing whether you can do more than just deal with the arithmetic of accounting, and whether you actually understand what you are doing.

The examiner could set this kind of question relating to other aspects of accountancy.

28	EXPLAIN THE TERMS

(a)   (i)   **An expense** arises on the using up of a resource. In the context of accounts it normally means the total or partial using up of an asset or service.

        (ii)   **Matching** (sometimes referred to as accruals) is the process by which revenue is matched against expenditure incurred in making that revenue to arrive at the net profit of an enterprise.

        (iii)   **Prudence** is the convention applied by accountants in preparing accounts that tends to understate profit in times of uncertainty by only including revenue and profits in accounts when actually realised in the form of cash, etc., but including losses or expenses in accounts as soon as the loss, etc., is known about.

        (iv)   **Objectivity** in the context of accounts is the ability of the accountant to look at accounting problems without any bias as to the outcome of the figures, or their impact on one or other bodies interested in the accounts.

(b)

Address

Date

Dear Mr Smith

Invoice from Marketing Services Limited

Monthly fees

These fees relate to the period from 1 October 1992 to 31 December 1992 and as such they will be included as an expense in the accounts for the year ended 31 December 1992, in order to match the revenue of that three-month period with the full expenses of making that revenue. It is not important that you have not yet paid this invoice.

Photocopier

As the photocopier will benefit your business for a number of years the expenditure on this item will be shown in the balance sheet as a fixed asset.

We will then need to depreciate the asset. In order to decide how much of the cost of £10,000 should be depreciated each year we will need to decide two things:

(a)   the number of years you expect to use the asset
(b)   the resale value of the photocopier (if any) at the end of that time.

In deciding these factors we will have to use our judgement. For example, we may decide that the life of the copier is five years (in line with the life of the guarantee) and that it will be worth very little at that date (due to technological change) and so have a scrap value in five years of nil. If so, we would depreciate the copier cost evenly over the next five years. The charge for the year ended 31 December 1992 would be one quarter of one fifth of £10,000 as you only acquired the machine on 1 October 1992, with three months of your accounting year left to run.

Deposit paid for the advertisement

Applying the matching concept, as mentioned before, this is clearly an expense of the year ended 31 December 1993 and not the current year, because the benefit of the advertising will not be received until February 1993. In the accounts for the year ended 31 December 1992 this expense will be debited to an asset account on the balance sheet, instead of being an expense in the profit and loss account. This will recognise the fact that you will no doubt be entitled to receive a refund on these advertising monies should the adverts not proceed as arranged.

Newspaper advertising campaign

Following on from the arguments listed above, and applying the matching concept, as this expenditure is incurred in November 1992 it should be an expense in the profit and loss account for the year ended 31 December 1992. You could argue that as the effects on revenues of this campaign may extend beyond the year ended 31 December 1992, the cost should also be spread over this longer period of time. However, it would be hard to estimate the period of time over which the benefits would accrue and so it would be more prudent to account for the full cost of the advertising campaign in the 1992 accounts.

29   ACCOUNTING INFORMATION

(a)   The concept of objectivity, as related to accountants and accountancy, is that in solving accounting problems or preparing financial statements or accounting records there should be freedom from bias, subjectivity and uncertainty as far as possible. This is to ensure that accounting information would be presented in the same manner no matter who was preparing the information.

(b)   As shareholders may not be the managers of the company in which they hold shares they need to read accounts in order to evaluate the strength of their investment in terms of the profitability and liquidity of the company they have invested in. This information will help them to decide whether to maintain their existing investment, to invest further or to disinvest in whole or in part.

(c)   With the application of the concept of objectivity to accounts they are likely to be more free from bias and therefore more reliable. However, in order to arrive at objectivity accounts are prepared under the historical cost convention, which means that the information they disclose, based on historic costs of assets and liabilities, may not faithfully represent that which it purports to represent, such costs often being out of date. If shareholders wish to look to the future of their investment, then historic cost accounts. while reliable, may not in fact be relevant.

30   LEGAL CASES

Answer Plan
(a)   Define contingency; legal cases uncertain

(b)   Use paras 15 to 17 of SSAP

(c)   Only if provision in accounts

(d)   Items falling within paras 16 and 17; follow para 18

(e)   Extra disclosures; why different treatment of contingent gains v losses

(Tutorial note: the examiner wants to set questions that test your understanding of a topic rather than your ability to regurgitate the requirements of an accounting standard. It is essential in such questions to refer to the paragraphs of the standard in your answer. This also helps to avoid the unnecessary repetition of parts of the extract in your answer. For example, if the extracts had given the definition of a contingency, you will not gain any marks by repeating the definition in your answer.*)*

MEMORANDUM

To: Managing director

From: An accountant

Date: X-X-19XX

Subject: Accounting for legal cases

I set out below answers to your various queries.

(a)   **Relevance of SSAP 18**

Legal cases that have not been settled by the date the financial statements are approved by the directors are examples of contingent items.

A contingency is defined in SSAP 18 as a condition that exists at the balance sheet date where the outcome will be confirmed only on the occurrence or non-occurrence of one or more uncertain future events.

Each of the legal cases has an uncertain outcome.

(b)   **Accounting treatment**

Paragraphs 15 to 17 of SSAP 18 set out the accounting treatment. Different treatments apply depending on whether the contingency may result in a gain or a loss and how probable the contingency is.

Case	Type of contingency	Treatment
P	'Less than probable' gain	Not accrued and not disclosed in notes
Q	'Probable' gain	Not accrued but disclosed in notes
R	'Less than probable' loss	Not accrued but disclosed in notes
S	'Probable' loss	Accrued and therefore not disclosed in notes

For item R it may be possible to argue that the loss is 'remote' and thus under paragraph 16 of SSAP 18, no disclosures in the notes are required.

(c)   **Journal entries**

The only journal entry required is for case S.

Dr		Profit and loss account	40,000	
	Cr	Provision for damages		40,000

(d)   **Contents of notes to the accounts**

Notes to the accounts are required in the cases of Q and R. As S is accrued in the accounts no disclosure is required in the notes (per paragraph 16).

The notes need to give the details required by paragraph 17. For both cases references would be made to the existence of the court cases and the firm's view of the strength of its cases. The amount of the contingent loss (£30,000) and contingent gain (£20,000) would be disclosed.

(e)   **Consideration of whether SSAP 18 provides a satisfactory representation**

SSAP 18 is suggesting that users of financial statements require information about possible or probable future events. Due to the inherent uncertainties relating to contingent items, in most cases the information is best provided by additional disclosures in the notes to the accounts rather than accruing for the amounts in the balance sheet.

However it could be argued that the treatment of gains and losses is not a fair representation as the treatment is not symmetrical. Losses are more readily accrued than gains, and losses are more readily disclosed than gains. The reason for the lack of symmetry is due to the prudence concept. This concept requires for example losses to be recognised in the accounts as soon as they are foreseen whereas gains should not be recognised until they are realised (which means a cash receipt is highly probable).

SIGNATURE

31   EXPLANATIONS

Answer Plan

(b)   Current cost basis; matching costs to sales; CPP basis; changing sales and costs; loss of objectivity.

(Tutorial note: part (a) should gain you high marks. All the terms are commonly tested. In part (b) it is important to write something. The questions asked in the discussion parts of the exam are often difficult to answer but the examiner will mark your answer fairly generously. Make as many reasonable points as you can.)

(a)   **Matching**

Matching is the process of comparing the revenues of an entity with the costs incurred in earning those revenues. Profits arise where there is an excess of revenues over costs, and losses occur where there is a shortfall.

Prudence

Prudence is the concept by which profits and revenues are not recognised in financial statements until they have been realised. By way of contrast, immediate provision is made for all anticipated losses and costs, even if they are unrealised. As a result of this, profits for a period will tend to be understated rather than overstated. Similarly, reported assets will tend to be understated and reported liabilities overstated. The valuation of stock at the lower of cost and net realisable value is an example of the prudence concept.

Inflation

Inflation is the rise in the general level of prices. Alternatively, it can be viewed as the general fall in the value of money because in times of inflation the amount of goods which can be purchased with a fixed amount of money will decrease.

Historical cost accounts take no account of the fall in the value of money and assume that the value of the pound is constant.

Price changes

Price changes are alterations in the market price of specific goods and services. In the context of a business these prices may be costs or sales proceeds. Prices are determined uniquely for a particular item in a particular business at a particular point in time.

Going concern

This is the assumption that a business or enterprise will continue in existence for the foreseeable future. It therefore enables the financial statements to be drawn up on the basis that there is no intention to liquidate the business or to significantly reduce the scale of its activities. For this reason the value of fixed assets to the business can be based on the assumption that they will continue to be used over their estimated useful life. If the going concern assumption were not valid, the assets would have to be included in the balance sheet at their market value and any resulting reduction in value would be recognised immediately.

Objectivity

Financial statements should be as objective as possible. In most cases this is not a problem because the figures used can be independently checked - for example, the recording of a sale can be checked to an invoice. However, accounting is not a precise science - there are situations where estimates must be made and these can create two different results from the same set of circumstances. Such estimates should therefore be as free from personal bias as possible. This is often achieved by making the estimate on a consistent basis eg, a general doubtful debt provision may be taken as 1% of debtors every year.

(b)   Changing prices can be taken into account in the matching process by updating expense figures from an historic basis to reflect the price level on the date when the sale is made. This will result in the matching of expenses at today's level with revenues at today's level rather than matching expenses at yesterday's level with revenues at today's level. This is considered by many to be a better indication of performance but will result in lower profits in times of rising prices. This more prudent approach helps to ensure that more funds are retained in the business because profits are lower and so dividends tend to be lower. This will help to maintain the long-term operating capacity of the business.

This is the approach taken in current cost accounting.

The current purchasing power model matches sales and costs of sales by converting items denominated in a currency to units of current purchasing power. Thus sales and costs are matched on the same price basis. The claimed advantage of the method is that it removes the distorting effect caused by inflation when costs and revenue originate at different dates.

On the other hand, it may be argued that the process of updating data to today's price levels can lead to loss of objectivity. There are several ways to update the price, each giving a different result.

Provided the weaknesses of historical cost accounting are appreciated and a business is financially well managed, the potential erosion of operating capacity should not be a problem. With good financial planning there should be sufficient working capital available even when a business is growing in times of inflation.

32   AMATEUR FOOTBALL CLUB

(a)   *(Tutorial note:* the question asked for those journals which affect the 19X3 accounts. Items 1 and 4 are applicable to 19X4. It is wise to state in the answer, however, why no journals have been given for these transactions. In some marking schemes it is necessary to state a reason for omission of an item.)

Journal		Dr £	Cr £
(1)	Does not affect 19X3 accounts		
(2)	Equipment	36.70	
	Creditors (Sports Equipment Ltd)		36.70
	Equipment acquired on 20 December 19X3		
(3)	Prepayments	15.00	
	Bank		15.00
	19X4 match fee paid in 19X3		
(4)	Does not affect 19X3 accounts		
(5)	Fixtures and fittings	268.30	
	Repairs and renewals	60.55	
	Creditors (Plumbing Services)		328.85
	Work carried out in November 19X3		
(6)	Wages	11.21	
	Creditors		11.21
	Part-time groundsman's wages earned to 31 December 19X3		

Journal		Dr £	Cr £
(7)	Depreciation	61.00	
	Equipment depreciation (20% × £36.70)		7.34
	Fixtures and fittings depreciation (20% × £268.30)		53.66
	Charge for depreciation on capital expenditure on (2) and (5) above.		

(b)

Balance sheet item

	£	£
Assets:		
Equipment	36.70	
Depreciation	(7.34)	
		29.36
Fixtures	268.30	
Depreciation	(53.66)	
		214.64
Prepayments		15.00
Bank		(15.00)
Liabilities:		
Creditors	36.70	
	328.85	
	11.21	
		376.76
Accumulated fund		
Change in expenses		
Repairs	60.55	
Wages	11.21	
Depreciation	61.00	
Decrease		132.76

33   SPRINGTIME GARDENERS' CLUB

(a)

Accumulated fund as at 1 January 19X6

	£	£	£
Fixed assets - building plot			2,000
Current assets:			
Stock - seeds		250	
Debtors - lawn mower sales		400	
Balance at bank		876	
		1,526	
Current liabilities:			
Creditors:			
Lawn mowers	800		
Seeds	110		
Subscriptions in advance	240		
		(1,150)	
Net current assets			376
			2,376

(b)

Income and expenditure account for year ended 31 December 19X6

	£	£
Income - subscriptions (240 + 7,190 − 390)		7,040
Expenditure:		
Loss on seed sales	136	
National Gardening Show	3,690	
Rent	500	
Gardening magazines	390	
Secretarial expenses	940	
		(5,656)
Surplus of income over expenditure		
transferred to accumulated fund		1,384

(c)

Balance sheet as at 31 December 19X6

	£	£	£
Fixed assets:			
Land at cost		2,000	
Architect's fees		1,000	
			3,000
Current assets:			
Stock		560	
Debtors		1,370	
		1,930	
Current liabilities:			
Creditors (170 + 340)	510		
Subscriptions in advance	390		
Bank overdraft	270		
		(1,170)	
Net current assets			760
			3,760
Accumulated fund:			
Balance at 1 January 19X6			2,376
Surplus of income over expenditure for year			1,384
Balance at 31 December 19X6			3,760

(Tutorial note: a separate profit or loss must be calculated for each activity undertaken by the non-profit making entity eg, seed sales, lawn mower sales, bar sales, etc.)

WORKINGS

(W1)   **National Gardening Show**

	£	£
Income from ticket sales		400
Expenditure:		
Tickets and brochures	3,600	
Coaches	490	
		(4,090)
Loss		(3,690)

(W2)   **Seed sales**

	£	£
Seed sales		1,684
Opening stock	250	
Purchases (1,900 − 110 + 340)	2,130	
Closing stock	(560)	
		1,820
Loss		(136)

(W3)   **Lawn mower sales**

	£
Sales (3,800 − 400 + 1,370)	4,770
Purchases (5,400 − 800 + 170)	(4,770)
Profit	Nil

34   HB TENNIS CLUB

(a)

HB Tennis Club income and expenditure account for the six months ended 30 September 19X0

	£	£
Income		
Subscriptions (W3)		7,050
Net income from tournaments (465 − 132)		333
Bank interest		43
Profit from sale of club ties (W4)		103
Life membership (W5)		210
		7,739
Expenditure		
Groundsman's wages (4,520 + 40)	4,560	
Rent and rates (636 − 68)	568	
Heating and lighting (674 + 53)	727	
Postage and stationery (41 + 12)	53	
Court maintenance	1,000	
Depreciation of equipment (W6)	403	
		7,311
Excess of income over expenditure		428

(b)

HB Tennis Club Balance Sheet as at 30 September 19X0

	Cost £	Dep'n £	NBV £
Fixed assets			
Equipment	4,080	403	3,677
Current assets			
Stock of ties ($\frac{40}{100} \times 450$)		180	
Subscriptions in arrears ($5 \times 300 \times \frac{6}{12}$)		750	
Rates paid in advance		68	
Balance at bank		6,148	
		7,146	
Current liabilities			
Subscriptions in advance ($12,600 \times \frac{6}{12}$)	6,300		
Accrued expenses (40 + 12 + 53)	105		
	6,405		
		741	
		4,418	

	£
Financed by	
Excess of income over expenditure	428
Life membership fund (W5)	3,990
	4,418

WORKINGS

(W1)   The income and expenditure account is simply a list of income followed by a list of all expenditure for the period. Therefore set up a simple proforma and then work through the question line by line entering the figures where relevant and ticking them off on the question paper when used.

(W2)   Items such as the subscriptions and various expenses should be dealt with on the accruals basis and matched to the six month period of the income and expenditure account.

A further feature of income and expenditure accounts is that income and expenditure on a particular item or event should be netted off. Therefore the net figure is shown for income from tournaments and profit from the sale of club ties.

(W3)   The subscriptions received of £12,600 are for a full year and we are also told that 5 subscriptions were paid after 30 September.

	£
Subscriptions paid for 6 month period ($\frac{6}{12} \times 12,600$)	6,300
Subscriptions in arrears ($5 \times \frac{6}{12} \times 300$)	750
Subscription income	7,050

Alternatively this may be presented:

Subscriptions account

	£		£
Income and expenditure	7,050	Bank	12,600
Bal c/d subscriptions in		Bal c/d subscriptions in	
advance ($\frac{6}{12} \times 12,600$)	6,300	arrears ($5 \times 300 \times \frac{6}{12}$)	750
	13,350		13,350

Note also that the remaining £6,300 that has been paid for subscriptions but which relates to the six months from 1 October 19X0 to 31 March 19X1 will be shown as a creditor, subscriptions in advance, in the balance sheet.

(W4)

	£	£
Sale of ties		373
Cost of sales		
Purchases	450	
Closing stock ($\frac{40}{100} \times 450$)	(180)	
		270
Profit on sale of ties		103

(W5) The life membership fees paid of £4,200 are to be taken to the income and expenditure account over 10 years or 120 months. Therefore the amount to be taken to income and expenditure in this 6 month period is $6/120 \times £4,200 = £210$.

This will leave £4,200 – £210 = £3,990 in the Life membership fund on 30 September 19X0.

(W6)

	£
Cost of equipment	4,080
Less: Estimated scrap value	50
	4,030

This is to be depreciated over 5 years or 60 months.

Depreciation charge $\frac{6}{60} \times 4,030 = £403$.

(W7) Having completed the income and expenditure account you should now list all of the remaining figures from the question in the balance sheet. Remember all of the accruals and prepayments including subscriptions in advance and in arrears.

35 HAPPY TICKERS

(a) **Profit on cafe operations**

	£	£
Sales		4,660
Less: Cost of sales		
Opening stock	800	
Purchases (1,900 + 80)	1,980	
	2,780	
Less: Closing stock	850	
		1,930
		2,730
Wages of cafe manager		2,000
Profit		730

Profit on sale of new sports equipment

	£	£
Sales		900
Less: Cost of sales		
Opening stock	1,000	
Purchases (1,000 × 50%)	500	
	1,500	
Closing stock (bal. fig.)	900	
		600
Gross profit (900 × $^{50}/_{150}$)		300

(Tutorial note: there is no profit to be recorded on the sale of used sports equipment as this is sold at book valuation.*)*

(b) **Subscription income**

	£
Subscription for 1990 (120 + 1,100 + 80)	1,300
Life subscriptions allocated for the year	
(11 × 200 × $^1/_{10}$)	220
	1,520

(c)   **Income and expenditure account for the year ended 31 December 1990**

	£	£
Income:		
Subscription		1,520
Cafe surplus		730
Sports equipment surplus		300
		2,550
Expenditure:		
Rent	1,200	
Insurance $(900 \times {}^{12}\!/_{18})$	600	
1989 subscriptions written off $(60 - 40)$	20	
Share of roller repairs $(450 \times 50\%)$	225	
Depreciation of roller $(£2,000 \times 10\% \times 50\%)$	100	
Sports equipment used $(500 - 14)$	486	
		2,631
Excess of expenditure over income		81

Balance sheet as at 31 December 1990

	£
Half-share in motorised roller $(600 - 100)$	500
New sports equipment unsold (part a)	900
Used sports equipment at valuation	700
Rent $(200 + 1,200 - 1,200)$	200
Insurance $(900 - 600 - 150)$	150
Carefree Conveyancers - motor roller repairs	225
Subscriptions 1990 in arrears	80
Cafe stocks	850
Cash and bank $(1,210 + 6,994 - 7,450)$	754
	4,359
Subscriptions in advance	80
Life subscriptions $(1,400 + 200 - 220)$	1,380
Cafe suppliers	80
	1,540
Accumulated fund $(2,900 - 81)$	2,819
	4,359

(d)   The life subscriptions are debited to the cash account on receipt but instead of being credited to the income and expenditure account immediately are instead credited to a life subscriptions account. This credit balance is then transferred to the income and expenditure account over a 10 year period.

The remaining credit balance on the life subscriptions account appears in the balance sheet and seems to be a liability although it is in fact known as a deferred income account. Eventually all of this balance will be transferred to the income and expenditure account but until this takes place then the funds are effectively owed back to the life subscription members.

36   THINGUMMY LTD

(Tutorial note: a balance needs to be struck in a question such as this between opening accounts for every adjustment and working at speed. In general if only one adjustment is required this can be shown on the face of the solution (ie, the trial balance).)

Trial balance as at 31 December 19X9

	£'000 Dr	£'000 Cr
Share capital (200 + 50)		250
Share premium		25
Revaluation reserve		40
Profit and loss account		80
Purchases	300	
Discount received		10
Creditors (W2)		65
Sales		500
Debtors (W1)	120	
Bad debt provision (10% × 120)		12
Discount allowed	15	
Bad debts expenses (20 + (12 − 4))	28	
Operating expenses (4 + 95 − 10)	89	
Land and buildings	150	
Plant and machinery - cost (140 + 60 − 18 (W4))	182	
- depreciation (50 − 9 (W4))		41
Stock	100	
Bank (W3)	45	
Profit on disposal		6
	1,029	1,029

WORKINGS

(W1)

Sales control

	£'000		£'000
Balance b/d	100	Receipts	440
Sales	500	Bad debts	20
		Contra	5
		Discounts	15
		Balance c/d	120
	600		600

(W2)

Purchases control

	£'000		£'000
Payments	310	Balance b/d	90
Contra	5	Purchases	300
Discounts	10		
Balance c/d	65		
	390		390

(W3)

Bank

	£'000		£'000
Receipts	440	Balance b/d	20
Shares	75	Payments	310
Plant	15	Operating expenses	95
		Fixed assets	60
		Balance c/d	45
	530		530

(W4)

Disposal of plant

	£'000		£'000
Profit (given)	6	Proceeds (given)	15
Cost	18	Depreciation	9
	24		24

(Tutorial note:

Cost and depreciation in the disposal account are not given except that depreciation is half of cost. Therefore as proceeds (a credit) exceed profit (a debit) by £9,000, cost must be at least £9,000 plus a further amount to allow depreciation to be half of cost ie, another £9,000.

It is doubtful if many candidates worked this out in the examination.)

37   DELTIC

(a)

Trading and profit and loss account for year ended 30 September 19X4

	£	£	
Sales		142,850	(100%)
Opening stock	Nil		
Purchases	115,538		
Closing stock	(8,400)		
Cost of sales		107,138	(75%)
Gross profit		35,712	(25%)
Expenses:			
Cleaning	520		
Sundries	780		
Depreciation:			
Van	1,500		
Leasehold premises	3,000		
Telephone	1,021		
Wages	19,182		
Rent and rates	1,424		
Repairs	4,022		
		31,449	
Net profit		4,263	

(b)

Balance sheet as at 30 September 19X4

	Cost £	Depn £	£
Fixed assets:			
Leasehold premises	150,000	3,000	147,000
Van	6,000	1,500	4,500
	156,000	4,500	151,500
Current assets:			
Stock		8,400	
Debtors		10,350	
Prepayment		258	
Cash at bank		61,313	
Cash in hand		250	
		80,571	
Current liabilities:			
Trade creditors	29,957		
Accruals	125		
		30,082	
			50,489
			201,989
Capital account:			
Capital introduced			200,000
Add: Net profit			4,263
Less: Drawings			(2,274)
			201,989

WORKINGS

Cash

	£		£
Balance b/d	Nil	Wages (£75 × 52)	3,900
Total sales (bal. fig.)	132,500	Cleaning (£10 × 52)	520
		Sundries (£15 × 52)	780
		Drawings (£25 × 52)	1,300
		Bank	125,750
		Balance c/d	250
			132,500
	132,500		

Drawings

	£		£
Cash	1,300	Capital account	2,274
Bank	323		
Total purchases	651		
	2,274		2,274

Wages

	£		£
Cash	3,900	Profit and loss	19,182
Bank	15,282		
	19,182		19,182

Telephone

	£		£
Bank	896	Profit and loss	1,021
Balance c/d	125		
	1,021		1,021

Rent and rates

	£		£
Bank	1,682	Profit and loss	1,424
		Balance c/d	258
	1,682		1,682

Total purchases (creditors)

	£		£
Bank	86,232	Trading account	115,538
Balance c/d	29,957	Drawings (bal.fig.)	651
	116,189		116,189

Repairs

	£		£
Bank	3,637	Profit and loss	4,022
Bank	385		
	4,022		4,022

Total sales

	£		£
Trading account (bal.fig.)	142,850	Cash	132,500
		Balance	10,350
	142,850		142,850

38   I WRIGHT

(a)

Profit and loss account for year ended 31 May 19X2

	£	£
Royalties received		22,750
Fees for articles		8,000
Serialisation fees		5,400
Publicity fees (£2,734 − 456)		2,278
Lecture fees		250
		38,678
Less: Expenses:		
Secretarial	6,866	
Travelling expenses (£3,427 − 370)	3,057	
Telephone charges (W1)	748	
Stationery (£659 -123)	536	
Postages	414	
Photocopying	640	
Artist's fees	715	
Heating and lighting (W2)	244	
Rates (W3)	150	
Insurance (W4)	118	
Subscriptions:		
Periodicals	226	
Professional societies	70	
Miscellaneous (£691 − 86)	605	
Depreciation:		
Equipment (25% × £2,200)	550	
Furniture (20% × 600)	120	
		15,059
Net profit for year		23,619

Balance sheet as at 31 May 19X2

	Cost £	Depn £	Net £
Fixed assets:			
Office equipment	2,200	1,050	1,150
Office furniture	600	210	390
	2,800	1,260	1,540
Current assets:			
Stock of stationery		123	
Prepayments		36	
Bank balance		2,265	
Cash in hand		28	
		2,452	
Current liabilities:			
Advance royalties	900		
Trade creditors (£180 + 15 + 40)	235		
Accruals	60		
		1,195	
Net current assets			1,257
			2,797
Financed by:			
Opening capital			2,150
Add: Net profit for year			23,619
			25,769
Less: Drawings (W5)			22,972
			2,797

WORKINGS

(W1)

Telephone

	£		£
Per list	762	Drawings (£762 × ⅓)	254
Balance c/d (£270 × ⅔) +		Profit and loss	748
(£270 × ⅔ × ⅓)	240		
	1,002		1,002

(W2)

Heating and lighting

	£		£
Per list	916	Drawings (£916 × ¾)	687
Balance c/d (£60 × ¼)	15	Profit and loss	244
	931		931

(W3)

Rates

	£		£
Per list	440	Drawings (£440 × ¾)	330
Balance c/d (£480 × ¼ × ⅔)	40	Profit and loss	150
	480		480

(W4)

Insurance

	£		£
Per list	308	Drawings (£308 × ½)	154
		Profit and loss	118
		Balance c/d (£72 × ½)	36
	308		308

(W5)

Drawings

	£		£
Bank	21,547	Capital account	22,972
Telephone	254		
Heating and lighting	687		
Rates	330		
Insurance	154		
	22,972		22,972

(b)   The answer should contain the following points:

(i)   The indicator suggested by Wright is totally inappropriate to the circumstances of his profession because his profit is not principally generated from the use of business assets. This is in direct contrast to the circumstances of a trading or manufacturing business.

(ii)   The only feasible overall indicator in Wright's circumstances is to express net profit as a percentage of fee income.

(iii)   Control can be exercised over individual expenses in the conventional manner by expressing them as a percentage of total expense or fee income.

39   BENDS

(a)

Trading account for new cars

	£'000	£'000	£'000
Sales (27 × £10,000 × 120%)			324
Purchases (37 × £10,000)		370	
Less:			
Car lost in fire	10		
Cars taken as fixed assets	20		
		30	
		340	
Less: Closing stock (7 × £10,000)		70	
			270
Gross Profit			54

(b)

Trading account for second-hand cars

	£'000	£'000
Sales (W1)		93
Purchases	93	
Less: closing stock (6 + 6 + 7 + 8)	27	
		66
Gross Profit		27

(c)

Profit and loss account for the year ended 31 December

	£'000	£'000
Gross Profit (54 + 27)		81
Expenses:		
Loan interest (£50,000 × 10%)	5	
Wages	36	
Rent (£3,000 × 4)	12	
Depreciation of furniture (£5,000 × 20%)	1	
Depreciation of equipment (£5,000 × 20%)	1	
Depreciation of cars (£20,000 × 20%)	4	
Insurance, electricity and stationery	7	
Bank charges	1	
Loss of car in fire	10	
Bad debt written off	5	
		82
Net loss for the year		1

(d)

Balance sheet as at 31 December

	£'000	£'000	£'000
Fixed assets:			
Cars	20	4	16
Furniture and equipment	10	2	8
	30	6	24
Current assets:			
Stock (70 + 27)		97	
Debtors (£10,000 × 120%)		12	
Prepayments - rent (15 − 12)		3	
Cash at bank (550 − 508)		42	
		154	
Creditors: amounts falling due within one year			
Creditors for new cars (370 − 320)	50		
Loan interest due	5		
		55	
Net current assets			99
			123
Creditors: amounts falling due after more than one year			
Loan			50
			73
Represented by:			
Capital			100
Net loss for the year			1
			99
Drawings			26
			73

*(**Tutorial note:** the loan could also be shown in the bottom part or capital part of the balance sheet giving a balance sheet total of £123,000.)*

WORKING

(W1)

	£'000
Receipts from customers	400
Receipts from sales of new cars (26 × £10,000 × 120%)	312
Receipts from sale of second-hand cars	88
Add: Worthless cheque	5
	93

40   RACKETS UNLIMITED

(a)

Member:	Income year to 30.6.90	Income year to 30.6.91	Balance c/f at 30.6.91 Dr	Cr
A	10			
B	10	10		
C	10	10		
D	10	10		17
E	10	9		8
F	10	10		27
G	10	10		80
H	10	10		100
I	10	10		9
J		10	10	
K		10		17
L	10			10
M	10	9		
N		10	10	

(b)   Many different comments could be made, here is a selection of the possible answers:

(1)   Spreading subscriptions over 10 years seems the logical conclusion from the information given, however this practice is in fact an arbitrary method of allocating the subscriptions.

(2)   If a member pays a subscription in advance and receives a deduction for this it could be viewed as a discount with the gross subscription being treated as £10 per year.

(3)   It is possible that L's payment in June 1991 was related to the subscription due in the previous year.

Tutorial notes:

Again make sure that you attempt part (b) of the question and that you don't miss out on these two relatively easy marks.

This question concentrates on the preparation of a subscriptions account for a club. In other questions the examiner will incorporate an analysis of the subscriptions account (on a smaller scale than in this question) with the preparation of full-scale club accounts.

41   ALBERT ZWEISTEIN

Albert Zweistein

Profit and loss account for the eighteen months ended 30 June 1993

	£	£
Sales (W2)		175,700
Less: cost of goods sold		
Opening stock	nil	
Purchases (W1)	106,150	
Less: returns	(200)	
Less: cost of exchange	(100)	
	105,850	
Add factory wages	30,000	
	135,850	
Closing stock	(18,000)	
		(117,850)
Gross profit		57,850
Expenses		
Rent	15,000	
Sundry	18,300	
Cost of guarantee returns	200	
Office wages	13,000	
Depreciation	40,100	
Bank charges	500	
Bad debts	200	
Gain on clock exchange (W4)	(50)	
		(87,250)
Net operating loss		(29,400)
Loan interest		(18,000)
		47,400
Formation costs		(2,000)
Net loss		49,400

Albert Zweistein

Balance sheet as at 30 June 1993

	£	£	£
Fixed assets			
Machines and vehicles - cost (W5)		142,000	
Depreciation (W6)		(40,100)	
			101,900
Current assets			
Stock		18,000	
Debtors		1,500	
Cash at bank (W3)		60,500	
Cash in hand		3,500	
		83,500	
Current liabilities			
Creditors	6,000		
Interest	6,000		
Rent	5,000		
		(17,000)	
Net current assets			66,500
			168,400
Loan from Russell			(120,000)
Net assets			48,400
Represented by:			
Capital			120,000
Loss			(49,400)
Drawings			(22,200)
			48,400

Workings

1

Creditors ledger control account

	£		£
Payments	25,000	Purchases	106,150
	5,000		
	26,000		
	6,000		
	30,000		
	7,000		
Standing order	1,000		
Exchange	150		
C/fwd	6,000		
	106,150		106,150

2

Debtors ledger control account

	£		£
Sales (net of returns)	175,700	Receipts	10,000
			30,000
			12,000
			50,000
			9,000
			60,000
		Standing order	3,000
		Bad debts	200
		C/fwd	1,500
	175,700		175,700

3

Bank

	£
As per question	59,000
Standing order	3,000
	62,000
Less: bank charges	(500)
Standing order	(1,000)
	60,500

4

Clock exchange account

	£		£
Purchases	100	Creditors ledger	150
Profit on exchange	50		
	150		150

5

Machine at cost

	£		£
1 Jan	125,000	C/fwd	134,000
1 July	9,000		
	134,000		134,000
B/fwd	134,000		
1 Jan	8,000	C/fwd	142,000
	142,000		142,000
B/fwd	142,000		

6

Provision for depreciation account				
	£			£
		30 June		12,500
		31 Dec		13,400
C/fwd	40,100	30 June		14,200
	40,100			40,100
		B/fwd		40,100

---

42   HEAD, HANDS AND FEET

(a)

Trading and profit and loss and appropriation accounts for the year ended 31 December 19X3

	£	£
Sales:		
For three months to 31 March 19X3		24,000
For nine months to 31 December 19X3		96,000
		120,000
Less: Cost of goods sold:		
Opening stock	11,000	
Purchases	100,000	
	111,000	
Less: Closing stock	14,500	
		96,500
Gross profit		23,500

	Three months to 31 Mar 19X3		Nine months to 31 Dec 19X3
	£	£	£
Gross profit allocated on sales basis 24 : 96		4,700	18,800
Less: Fixed overheads:			
Sales salaries	6,240		
Rent and rates	1,400		
Depreciation (£9,000 × 20%)	1,800		
General expenses	2,580		
	12,020		
Allocated on time basis 1 : 3		(3,005)	(9,015)
Less: Bad debt			(110)
		1,695	9,675

	Total £	Head £	Hands £	Feet £
Three months to 31 March 19X3:				
Interest for three months	375	250	125	
Profit shares 3 : 2	1,320	792	528	
	1,695	1,042	653	
Nine months to 31 December 19X3:				
Salaries for nine months	2,625	1,125	750	750
Profit shares 3 : 2 : 1	7,050	3,525	2,350	1,175
	9,675	4,650	3,100	1,925
Total	11,370	5,692	3,753	1,925
Less: Drawings	9,400	4,500	3,200	1,700
	1,970	1,192	553	225

(b)

Partners' capital accounts

	Head £	Hands £	Feet £		Head £	Hands £	Feet £
Goodwill contra			2,000	Balance b/d	20,000	10,000	
Balance c/d	21,200	10,800	4,000	Cash			6,000
				Goodwill contra (3 : 2 of 2,000)	1,200	800	
	21,200	10,800	6,000		21,200	10,800	6,000

(Tutorial note:

As the question has given a figure of Feet's share of goodwill this has been used to make adjustments in the capital accounts.)

An alternative approach is to calculate total goodwill from the figure given for Feet's share ie, if £2,000 represents a one sixth share (which is his profit share), total value for goodwill is 2,000 × 6 = £12,000. The capital accounts would be shown as:

Partners' capital accounts

	Head £	Hands £	Feet £		Head £	Hands £	Feet £
Goodwill written down (3 : 2 : 1 of 12,000)	6,000	4,000	2,000	Balance b/d	20,000	10,000	
Balance c/d	21,200	10,800	4,000	Cash			6,000
				Goodwill written up (3 : 2 of 12,000)	7,200	4,800	
	27,200	14,800	6,000		27,200	14,800	6,000

(c)

Balance sheet as at 31 December 19X3

	£	£	£
Fixed assets:			
Fixtures and fittings			15,000
Less: Depreciation			7,800
			7,200
Current assets:			
Stock		14,500	
Debtors (£19,000 – 110)		18,890	
Prepayment		100	
Cash at bank		4,920	
		38,410	
Current liabilities:			
Creditors	7,400		
Accrual	240		
		7,640	
			30,770
			37,970

	Capital £	Current £	£
Capital employed:			
Partners' accounts:			
Head	21,200	1,192	22,392
Hands	10,800	553	11,353
Feet	4,000	225	4,225
	36,000	1,970	37,970

---

43   ALPHA AND BETA

(a)   (i)

Capital accounts

	Alpha £'000	Beta £'000	Gamma £'000		Alpha £'000	Beta £'000	Gamma £'000
Goodwill				Balance b/d	30	25	
written down	4	4	4	Loan			20
Balance c/d	44	39	16	Goodwill written			
				up	6	6	
				Revaluation			
				(84 – 60)	12	12	
	48	43	20		48	43	20
				Balance b/d	44	39	16

(ii)

Current accounts

	Alpha £'000	Beta £'000		Alpha £'000	Beta £'000
Drawings	4	5	Balance b/d	3	4
Balance c/d	11	7	Profit share	12	8
	15	12		15	12
			Balance b/d	11	7

(Tutorial note: Gamma is not a partner till the **end** of the year and therefore does not participate in profits for the year.)

(iii)

Trading, profit and loss, and appropriation account for year to 31 December 19X9

	£'000	£'000
Sales (200 − 6)		194
Opening stock	30	
Purchases	103	
Less: Closing stock (24 + 2)	(26)	
Cost of sales		107
Gross profit		87
Less: Expenses:		
Operating expenses	64	
Interest (10% × 30)	3	
		67
		20

(iv)

Balance sheet of Alpha, Beta and Gamma as at 31 December 19X9

	Cost £'000	Dep'n £'000	£'000
Fixed assets			
Land and buildings	84		84
Plant and machinery	70	40	30
			114
Current assets			
Stock		26	
Debtors (40 − 6)		34	
		60	
Current liabilities			
Creditors	33		
Interest accrued	3		
Bank overdraft	11		
		47	
			13
			127
Loan - Beta			10
			117

	Alpha £'000	*Beta* £'000	*Gamma* £'000	£'000
Capital accounts	44	39	16	99
Current accounts	11	7	-	18
	55	46	16	117

(Tutorial note:

Goods on sale or return are not legally sold until the return date has elapsed or the customer has formally accepted the goods. If goods are actually returned then obviously no sale has been made.

As the goods were not formally accepted until after the year end then no sale has been made in 19X9. The original entry by the business was to credit sales £6,000 (we are told this). Where then did the debit go? To debtors, so these must be reduced as well.

As the items are not sold they remain the stock of the business and therefore must be added to the stock 'on hand'.)

(b)

To: Gamma

From: Accountant

Date: X - X - 19XX

Subject: Capital account balance

Your capital account balance is lower than Alpha's and Beta's for two reasons:

(i)   Alpha and Beta had larger amounts in their capital accounts brought forward from earlier years than you have contributed upon admission.

(ii)   The disparity is further increased by the adjustments made relating to goodwill. The goodwill valuation of £12,000 records an asset built up by Alpha and Beta before you became a partner. Therefore their capital accounts were increased by equal shares in this sum.

As goodwill is not to be shown in the balance sheet however, the asset was written off each of your capital accounts. It has been written off in your account as well as you are now a third owner of all the partnership assets including goodwill.

I should stress you have not lost any money here. The £16,000 standing to the credit of your capital account represents your share in the net tangible assets of the business. In addition you have one third share in an asset not recorded on the balance sheet.

44   RIVER, STREAM AND POOL

(a)

River, Stream and Pool
Profit and loss appropriation account
for the year ended 30 September 19X7

	£	£
Net profit (see working)		47,300
Partner's salary - Pool		(11,000)
Interest on capital (see part (b))		
River	950	
Stream	1,230	
Pool	470	
		(2,650)
		33,650
Balance in PSR		
River	16,825	
Stream	10,095	
Pool	6,730	
		(33,650)

WORKINGS

	£
Net profit for the year per draft accounts	46,300
Reduction in valuation of opening stock	2,000
	48,300
Interest on River's loan account 10% × £10,000	1,000
	47,300

(Tutorial note: it is necessary to work out the adjustments to the partner's capital accounts in part (b) before the interest can be computed for part (a).)

(b)

Partners' capital accounts year ended 30 September 19X7

	R £	S £	P £		R £	S £	P £
Adjustment				Balance b/d	30,000	20,000	15,000
Stock valuation	1,000	1,000		Goodwill	14,000	14,000	
Goodwill	14,000	8,400	5,600	(see working)			
(see working)							
Transfer to loan							
account	10,000						
Balances c/d	19,000	24,600	9,400				
	44,000	34,000	15,000		44,000	34,000	15,000
				Balances b/d	19,000	24,600	9,400

(Tutorial note: stock at 1 October 19X7 represents an asset of the business into which Pool is being admitted as a partner. A change in an asset value from its book value creates a revaluation surplus or deficit which must be reflected in the existing partners' capital accounts.)

Partners' current accounts year ended 30 September 19X7

	R £	S £	P £		R £	S £	P £
Drawings	21,000	13,000	11,000	Balance b/d	1,000	700	-
Balance c/d			7,200	Loan interest	1,000		
				Salary			11,000
				Interest on			
				capital	950	1,230	470
				Balance of			
				profit	16,825	10,095	6,730
				Balance c/d	1,225	975	-
	21,000	13,000	18,200		21,000	13,000	18,200
Balances b/d	1,225	975		Balance b/d			7,200

Goodwill

	£		£
Goodwill written up in old PSR		Goodwill written down in new PSR	
River ½	14,000	River 5	14,000
Stream ½	14,000	Stream 3	8,400
		Pool 2	5,600
	28,000		28,000

---

45   TIMMY AND LUCY

(a)

Partners' capital accounts

	Timmy £	Lucy £	Charlie £		Timmy £	Lucy £	Charlie £
Revaluation 1/1/93	8,400	8,400	4,200	B/fwd	30,000	40,000	
				Capital			
				introduced			20,000
Revaluation 31/12/93	1,100	1,100	550	Revaluation			
C/fwd	31,000	41,000	15,250	1/1/93	10,500	10,500	
	40,500	50,500	20,000		40,500	50,500	20,000

Working

Revaluations	£
1/1/93:	
Land (20,000 - 12,000)	8,000
Buildings (30,000 - [25,000 - 2,000])	7,000
Goodwill (16,000 - 10,000)	6,000
Gain	21,000
31/12/93:	
Buildings - cost	25,000
- depreciation	(2,250)
Net book value	22,750
New value	(20,000)
Loss	2,750

(b)

Appropriation account

	Timmy £	Lucy £	Charlie £	Total £
Interest on capital	3,210	4,210	1,580	9,000
Profit share	12,400	12,400	6,200	31,000
	15,610	16,610	7,780	40,000

(c)

Partners' current accounts

	Timmy £	Lucy £	Charlie £		Timmy £	Lucy £	Charlie £
B/fwd 1/1/93		4,000		B/fwd 1/1/93	3,000		
Drawings	4,000	4,000	4,000				
C/fwd 31/12/93	14,610	8,610	3,780	Profits	15,610	16,610	7,780
	18,610	16,610	7,780		18,610	16,610	7,780

(d) **Summary balance sheets as at 31 December 1993**

Capital accounts	£	£
Timmy	31,000	
Lucy	41,000	
Charlie	15,250	
		87,250
Current accounts		
Timmy	14,610	
Lucy	8,610	
Charlie	3,780	
		27,000
		114,250

Goodwill	10,000
Land	12,000
Buildings	20,000
Machinery (30,000 - 19,000)	11,000

	53,000
Net current assets (balancing figure)	61,250
	114,250

(e) **Net current asset reconciliation**

Net current assets at 1/1/93	10,000
Add: profit	40,000
Add: expenses charged not affecting net current assets	
Depreciation	3,250
Add: capital introduced	20,000
Less: partners' drawings	(12,000)
Net current assets 31/12/93	61,250

46   A, B AND C PARTNERSHIP

(a) **Journal entries**

	Dr £	Cr £
(i) Provision for depreciation of motor vehicles	4,000	
Provision for depreciation of motor vehicles		5,000
Depreciation	1,000	

Being the adjustment required to reverse the original depreciation charge and replace it with the charge using the new depreciation rate of 25% (see working below).

	Dr	Cr
(ii) Provision for depreciation of fixtures and fittings	1,000	
Cost of fixtures and fittings		3,000
Current account (A)	2,500	
Profit on disposal of fixed assets		500

Being the entries required to account for the disposal of a fixed asset to Partner A.

	Dr	Cr
(iii) Loan interest	2,400	
Current account (A) (see TN1)		1,800
Creditors		600

Being the entries required to account for the interest at 12% on the loans from A and D.

	Dr	Cr
(iv) Bank charges	500	
Bank overdraft		500
Bank overdraft	1,000	
Debtors		1,000
Debtors	2,000	
Bank overdraft		2,000

Being the posting of items from the December bank reconciliation which have not yet been accounted for.

WORKINGS

NBV of motor vehicles after a depreciation charge of 20% = £(40,000 - 24,000) =   £16,000

∴ NBV of motor vehicles before depreciation charge of 20% = £16,000 × $\frac{100}{80}$ =   £20,000

∴ Depreciation charge at 25% (reducing balance) = £20,000 × 25% =   £5,000

[Original depreciation charge was £(20,000 - 16,000) = £4,000]

(Tutorial notes:

(i)   Loans from partners to a partnership in excess of their agreed capital contribution will be treated as normal commercial loans. Therefore, interest will be included as an expense in the profit and loss account rather than appearing in the appropriation account.

(ii)   No adjustment required for the £3,000 unpresented cheque.*)*

(b)

Partners' capital accounts

	A £	B £	C £		A £	B £	C £
Goodwill written down in new PSR	20,000	20,000	10,000	Balances b/d	50,000	30,000	-
				Goodwill written up in old PSR	5,000	5,000	-
Property revaluation surplus written down in new PSR	12,000	12,000	6,000	Property revaluation surplus written up in old PSR	15,000	15,000	-
Balances c/d	38,000	18,000	4,000	Capital introduced	-	-	20,000
	70,000	50,000	20,000		70,000	50,000	20,000

WORKINGS

Goodwill

	£		£
Balance b/d	40,000	Written down in new PSR:	
Written up in old PSR:		A	20,000
A	5,000	B	20,000
B	5,000	C	10,000
	50,000		50,000

Partners' current accounts

	A £	B £		A £	B £
Drawings	7,000	6,000	Balances b/d	12,000	3,000
Disposal of fixed asset	2,500	-	Interest on capital	5,000	3,000
			Salary	5,000	-
Balances c/d	51,100	36,800	Balance of profit	36,800	36,800
			Loan interest	1,800	-
	60,600	42,800		60,600	42,800

(c)   **Profit and loss and appropriation account for the year ended 31 December 19X1**

	£	£
Sales		250,000
Cost of sales		120,000
Gross profit		130,000
Operating expenses	40,000	
Additional depreciation	1,000	
Bank charges	500	
Profit on disposal of fixed assets	(500)	
Loan interest	2,400	
		(43,400)
		86,600
Net profit allocated: A	46,800	
B	39,800	
		(86,600)

Balance sheet as at 31 December 19X1

	Cost £	Accumulated depreciation £	Net book value £
Fixed assets:			
Property	90,000	-	90,000
Motor vehicles	40,000	25,000	15,000
Furniture and fittings	37,000	13,000	24,000
	167,000	38,000	129,000
Current assets:			
Stocks		20,000	
Debtors		41,000	
Balance at bank		20,000	
		81,000	
Current liabilities:			
Creditors	30,600		
Bank overdraft	11,500		
		(42,100)	
			38,900
Loans from A and D (£15,000 + £5,000)			(20,000)
			147,900

Represented by:

	Capital accounts £	Current accounts £	Total £
A	38,000	51,100	89,100
B	18,000	36,800	54,800
C	4,000	-	4,000
	60,000	87,900	147,900

47   MYDDLETON ACCESSORIES

(a)   (i)   Entries for each of these shareholders would have been made in the Register of Members when the shares were originally acquired. On disposal of the shares these entries will be amended by indicating the date on which Dupp and Kint ceased to be members.

There is no bookkeeping entry to record the disposal.

(ii)   Entry would be made in the Register of Members detailing Mrs Gamble's name, address, number of shares and nominal value thereof. The date of her purchase would also be recorded.

There is no bookkeeping entry as Mrs Gamble did not buy the shares from the company.

(iii)   Once again an entry would be made in the Register of Members. As regards Universal Investment Trust plc, its name and registered office would be entered, together with the number and nominal value of the shares involved and the date.

Myddleton Accessories plc must additionally enter the details in a Register of Shareholders with 3% (or more) interests. Universal Investment Trust plc is obliged to tell Myddleton within two days that its holding exceeds 3% of the nominal value of issued shares.

(iv)   Further entries would be made against Richer's name in the Register of Members.

As Richer holds over 3% of the nominal value of the new issued ordinary share capital, he is obliged to notify the company of this fact. Myddleton Accessories plc will then include Richer on its Register of Shareholders with 3% (or more) interests.

In the case of (iii) and (iv) entries will be made in the nominal ledger to record the issue.

(b)   Both registers mentioned must be available for public inspection for a minimum of two hours per day during business hours, normally at Myddleton Accessories plc's registered office.

48   ANNUAL REPORT

(a)   Goodwill purchased (an intangible asset).

(b)   The excess is share premium.

(c)   It does not have a precise meaning but normally means ordinary shares. It denotes those shares which are capable of fully participating in the profits.

(d)   The new shareholders will not receive the impending dividend payable to the existing shareholders.

(e) (i) The rate of interest payable computed on the nominal value of the stock, ie, £500,000 × 8%.

(ii) The debentures may be redeemed within those years - the precise dates of redemption depend on the terms of the issue.

(f) (i) The dividend payable provided that there are sufficient profits available. The 6% is applied to the nominal value of £20 million.

(ii) The shares are redeemable by the company. The issue terms may contain provisions as to redemption but there may be no dates set.

(g) The company is reorganising the financial structure of the business. Presumably market rates of interest have declined since the original issue.

(h) This depends on the definition of gearing that is used. Some would treat preference shares in the same way as loan stock ie, as debt. Preference shares are similar to stock as a fixed rate of return is payable. Thus the gearing has increased. Others treat preference shares as shareholders - thus decreasing the gearing. Legally preference shares are shareholders and also the dividend is variable as, if sufficient profits are not made, there will be no payment.

(j) Debenture interest is an expense deductible in arriving at profit. Dividends are a return of profit once the profit has been determined.

(k) Debenture holders are creditors of the company. Shareholders own the company.

49 FIDDLES PLC

(a)

Note no.	Details	Dr £	Cr £
(i)	Creditors control (5,000 × 2)	10,000	
	Debtors control		10,000
	Contra between debtors and creditors not recorded on correct side		
	Operating profit (13,345 – 12,345)	1,000	
	Debtors control		1,000
	Sale overstated due to incorrect total in day book		
	Operating profit	4,000	
	Suspense		4,000
	Omission of sales returns from initial trial balance		
(ii)	Bank	2,000	
	Debtors control		2,000
	Omission of standing order from debtor		
	Operating profit	1,000	
	Bank		1,000
	Bank charges		

Note no.	Details	Dr £	Cr £
(iii)	Operating profit	1,000	
	Debtor control (bad debts)		1,000
	Write off of debtor		
	Provision for doubtful debts (W1)	1,140	
	Operating profit		1,140
	Adjustment to provision for doubtful debts (1% of debtors)		
(iv)	Stock	2,000	
	Operating profit		2,000
	Understatement of closing stock		
	Profit and loss b/f	1,000	
	Operating profit		1,000
	Overstatement of opening stock		
(v)	Suspense (W2)	3,000	
	Operating profit		3,000

(Tutorial note: the overstatement of opening stock merely changes the amount of profit recorded last year and this year. The effect is therefore a transfer within the profit and loss account.)

(b)

Profit and loss account

	£
Operating profit (W3)	80,140
Less: Debenture interest $(180,000 \times 16\% \times \frac{3}{12})$	7,200
Net profit	72,940
Dividend $(100,000 \times 10\%)$	10,000
Retained profit	62,940
Profit and loss account b/f $(200,000 - 1,000)$	199,000
Profit and loss account c/f	261,940

Balance sheet

	£	£	£
Fixed assets			
Land			100,000
Buildings			120,000
Plant and machinery - cost		170,000	
- depreciation		120,000	
			50,000
			270,000
Current assets			
Stock (190,000 + 2,000)		192,000	
Debtors (W1)	186,000		
Less: Provision for doubtful debts (W1)	1,860		
		184,140	
Bank (W4)		13,000	
		389,140	
Current liabilities			
Creditors (110,000 – 10,000)	100,000		
Debenture interest	7,200		
Dividends proposed	10,000		
		117,200	
Net current assets			271,940
			541,940
16% debentures			180,000
Net assets			361,940
Capital and reserves			
Share capital			100,000
Profit and loss account			261,940
			361,940

WORKINGS

(W1)

Debtors account

	£		£
Per trial balance	200,000	Creditors *(note (i))*	10,000
		Operating profit *(note (i))*	1,000
		Bank *(note (ii))*	2,000
		Operating profit *(note (iii))*	1,000
		Balance c/d	186,000
	200,000		200,000
Balance b/d	186,000		

Provision for doubtful debts account

	£		£
Bad debts (bal.fig.)	1,140	Per trial balance	3,000
Balance c/d (186,000 × 1%)	1,860		
	——		——
	3,000		3,000
	——		——
		Balance b/d	1,860

(W2)

Suspense account

	£		£
Trial balance - difference	1,000	Operating profit *(note (i))*	4,000
Operating profit (bal.fig.)	3,000		
	——		——
	4,000		4,000
	——		——

*(**Tutorial note:** we are not told in the question whether the £1,000 is a debit or credit balance. The other balances therefore need to be totalled.*

Credit balances exceed debit balances by £1,000; therefore the suspense account balance is £1,000 debit.)

(W3)

Operating profit

	£		£
Debtors	1,000	Per trial balance	80,000
Suspense account	4,000	Provision for doubtful debts	1,140
Bank	1,000	Stock	2,000
Debtors	1,000	Profit and loss b/d	1,000
Balance c/d	80,140	Suspense	3,000
	——		——
	87,140		87,140
	——		——
		Balance b/d	80,140

(W4)

Bank account

	£		£
Per trial balance	12,000	Operating profit	1,000
Debtors	2,000	Balance c/d	13,000
	——		——
	14,000		14,000
	——		——
Balance b/d	13,000		

50   PARTIZAN PLC

(a)   **Journal**

			Dr £	Cr £
(1)	Profit and loss account		120,000	
	Revaluation reserve			120,000
	Surplus on revaluation of land and buildings			
	credited to correct account			
(2)	Suspense account		300,000	
	Share capital			100,000
	Share premium			200,000
	Issue of 400,000 ordinary shares at a			
	premium of 50p per share			
(3)	P&L - Taxation charge		130,000	
	Corporation tax creditor			130,000
	Provision for the year			
(4)	P&L - appropriations		58,000	
	Preference dividends payable			10,000
	Ordinary dividends payable			48,000
	Proposed dividends for the year			
(5)	Provision for doubtful debts		60,000	
	Bad debts - P&L account			60,000
	Reduction in the provision			
(6)	Debenture stock		200,000	
	Share premium		20,000	
	Profit and loss account			220,000
	Transfer of payment to redeem debentures			
	out of the profit and loss account to correct			
	accounts including premium on redemption			
(7)	Audit fee		30,000	
	Accruals			30,000
	Accrued audit fee for the year			

(b)   **Partizan plc**

Balance sheet at 31 December 19X7 (extract)

	£
Capital and reserves	
Ordinary shares of 25p each	600,000
10% preferences shares of £1 each	100,000
Share premium account (150 + 200 − 20)	330,000
Revaluation reserve	120,000
Profit and loss account (see working)	1,192,000
	2,342,000

WORKING

Profit and loss account	£'000
Profit for year in draft accounts	380
Less: Revaluation reserve removed	120
Less: Corporation tax	130
Less: Dividends	58
	72
Add: Reduction in PDD	60
Add: Debenture redemption payment	220
	352
Less: Audit fee	30
	322
Add: Balance brought forward	870
	1,192

51   QUEUE PLC

Profit and loss account for year to 31 December 19X8

	£	£
Sales		100,000
Opening stock	12,000	
Purchases	70,000	
	82,000	
Closing stock	10,000	
Closing stock		72,000
Gross profit		28,000
Expenses (11,000 + 200)	11,200	
Depreciation less profit on disposal (W5)	875	
Interest:		
Bank	250	
Debentures (W2)	1,125	
		13,450
Net profit before tax		14,550
Corporation tax		5,000
Profit after tax		9,550
Dividends:		
Paid	1,500	
Proposed (30,000 × 6p)	1,800	
		3,300
		6,250
Profits brought forward		5,500
Profits carried forward		11,750

Balance sheet as at 31 December 19X8

	£	£	£
Fixed assets:			
Freehold properties at cost			40,000
Motor vehicles at cost (10,000 + 4,000 − 4,500)		9,500	
Less: Depreciation (W3)		3,125	
			6,375
			46,375
Current assets:			
Stock		10,000	
Debtors (25,000 − 500)		24,500	
Bank (W1)		11,800	
		46,300	
Current liabilities:			
Creditors	15,000		
Accruals:			
Debenture interest (W2)	375		
Motor vehicle (4,000 − 2,750)	1,250		
Dividend	1,800		
Corporation tax	5,000		
		23,425	
Net current assets			22,875
			69,250
Debentures			(15,000)
			54,250
Share capital (£1 ordinary shares) (30,000 + 10,000)			40,000
Share premium (10,000 × 25p)			2,500
Profit and loss account			11,750
			54,250

WORKINGS

(W1)

Cash book

	£		£
Debtors	500	Balance b/d	1,000
Share issue	12,500	Standing order - Expense account	200
		Balance c/d	11,800
	13,000		13,000

(W2)   **Debenture interest**

	£
Charge should be:	
10% × 15,000 × $\frac{9}{12}$	1,125
Paid	750
Accrual	375

(W3)

Motor vehicles - depreciation

	£		£
Disposal (4,500 × 75%)	3,375	Balance b/d	4,000
Balance c/d	3,125	Charge for year (10,000 × 25%)	2,500
	6,500		6,500

(W4)

Disposal account

	£		£
Cost	4,500	Accumulated depreciation	3,375
Profit on disposal	1,625	Part exchange value	2,750
	6,125		6,125

(W5)   **Depreciation to profit and loss**

	£
Charge	2,500
Less: Profit on sale	1,625
	875

---

52   TOBY LTD

Profit and loss account for year to 31 December 19X8 (format 1)

	£	£
Turnover (100 − 1) − (4 − 1)		96,000
Cost of sales (W1)		(65,300)
Gross profit		30,700
Distribution costs	6,800	
Administrative expenses	7,300	
Interest payable (10% × 30,000)	3,000	
		(17,100)
Profit on ordinary activities before taxation		13,600
Tax on profit on ordinary activities		(3,000)
Profit on ordinary activities after taxation and amount set aside to reserves		10,600

(Tutorial note:

Format 1 should be chosen for the profit and loss account as there is insufficient information presented in the question to show format 2; in particular stocks are not split between raw materials, WIP and finished goods, and staff costs are not given.)

Balance sheet as at 31 December 19X8

	Cost £	Depr. £	£
Fixed assets			
Tangible assets			
Land and buildings	40,000	-	40,000
Plant and machinery	40,000	16,000	24,000
			64,000
Current assets			
Stocks		18,000	
Debtors (18,000 – 900 (W3))		17,100	
Prepayment (W4)		500	
		35,600	
Creditors: Amounts falling due within one year			
Bank overdraft (W4)	9,000		
Creditors and accruals	7,000		
Interest payable	3,000		
Taxation	3,000		
		22,000	
Net current assets			13,600
Total assets less current liabilities			77,600
Creditors: Amounts falling due after more than one year			
Debentures			30,000
			47,600
Capital and reserves			
Share capital - £1 ordinary shares			15,000
Share premium account			3,000
Profit and loss account (19,000 + 10,600)			29,600
			47,600

WORKINGS

(W1)   **Analysis of costs**

	Cost of sales £	Dist. £	Admin. £
Opening stock	15,000		
Purchases	61,000		
Returns	(4,000)		
Closing stock	(18,000)		
Operating expenses	9,000		
Admin			7,000
Selling		6,000	
Provision netted off against selling expenses		800	
Bad debts (W3)			100
Rates £500 (W3)	450		50
Rates in operating expenses	(150)		150
Depreciation (W5)	4,000		
Profit on sale of plant (W5)	(2,000)		
	65,300	6,800	7,300

(Tutorial note: as the cost classification headings are not defined in the legislation there is some choice as to how various costs are allocated. Bad debts for example could be shown under any heading.

What is important is the production of a working paper showing where you have allocated items.)

(W2)

Suspense account

	£		£
Share capital	5,000	Balance b/d	10,000
Share premium (5,000 × 0.6)	3,000		
Disposal proceeds	2,000		
	10,000		10,000

(W3)

Provision for doubtful debts

	£		£
		Reversal of error - selling expenses	800
Balance c/d 5% × (20,000 – 2,000)	900	Profit and loss	100
	900		900

(Tutorial note: care is needed with the sales returns incorrectly entered. As the company has control accounts, totals are entered from the various books of prime entry to the sales account and sales ledger control account etc. Sales are overstated by £1,000 and thus debtors are overstated by £1,000 (ie, debit to the control account was overstated). In addition sales returns are understated by £1,000 and thus debtors are again overstated by £1,000.)

(W4)   **Standing order for rates**

		Expense account £	Bank overdraft £
(a)			8,000
	Enter into books	1,000	1,000
			9,000
(b)	Prepayment	(500)	
		500	

(W5)   **Disposal - plant**

	Per trial balance	
	Plant cost £	Depreciation £
	50,000	22,000
Eliminated on disposal	(10,000)	(10,000)
	40,000	12,000
Depreciation charge for year 10% × 40,000		4,000
		16,000
Profit on sale = cash proceeds =		2,000

---

53   PERCIVAL PLC

Sales ledger control

	£'000		£'000
Balance	200	Discounts allowed	20
Credit sales	1,500	Contra	15
		Bad debts	25
		Bank	1,450
		Closing balance	190*
	1,700		1,700

Purchase ledger control

	£'000		£'000
Dicounts received	30	Balance	220
Contra	15	Purchases	900
Closing balance	280		
Bank	795*		
	1,120		1,120

* Derived balancing figure

Bank

	£'000		£'000
Balance	20	Plant purchases	120
Cash sales	100	Debenture interest	30
Plant proceeds	30	Interim dividend	20
Scrapped stock	10	Bank charges	8
Sales control	1,450	Purchase control	795
		Wages and salaries	250
		Operating expenses	240
		Closing balance	147*
	1,610		1,610

Plant - cost

	£'000		£'000
Balance	450	Disposals	90
Additions	120	Closing balance	480*
	570		570

Plant - depreciation

	£'000		£'000
Disposals	80	Balance	180
Closing balance	148*	Profit and loss	48
	228		228

Operating expenses

	£'000		£'000
Balance	10	Balance	11
Bank	240	Profit and loss	237*
Balance	12	Balance	14
	262		262

Plant - disposal

	£'000		£'000
Cost	90	Depreciation	80*
Profit and loss	20	Proceeds	30
	110		110

* Derived balancing figure

Trading, profit and loss account, year to 31 December 1991

	£'000	£'000	£'000
Sales (1,500 + 100)			1,600
Opening stock		225	
Purchases	900		
Damaged by fire	40		
	860		
		1,085	
Closing stock		170	
			915
Gross profit			685
Loss on fire (40 - 10)		30	
Discounts (20 - 30)		(10)	
Depreciation – property		4	
– plant		48	
– profit on disposal		(20)	
Bad debt		25	
Reduction in bad debts provision		(1)	
Wages		250	
Operating expenses		237	
Bank charges		8	
Debenture interest		30	
			601
Net profit			84
Dividends (20 + 20)			40
Net profit retained for year			44

Summary balance sheet, 31 December 1991

	Cost £'000	Depr. £'000	Net £'000		£'000	£'000
Land			350	Share capital	400	
Property	200	28	172	Share premium	100	
Plant	480	148	332	Revaluation reserve	100	
				Retained profit	244	
			854			844
Stocks		170		Debentures		200
Debtors (190 - 19)		171				
Prepayments		14		Creditors	280	
Bank		147		Accruals (12 + 20)	32	
		502				312
		1,356				1,356

Tutorial notes

This is a straightforward accounts preparation question without the complications of incomplete records or suspense accounts.

Although the workings above are shown as separate to the financial statements, it would be possible to save time and put the workings on the face of the financial statements in brackets, next to the figure being calculated, and only do separate workings where the complexity of the item makes it necessary.

The Balance Sheet you produce need not be in the horizontal form shown, but could be in vertical format if you wish.

54   LINCOLN PLC

Lincoln plc

Profit and loss account for the year ended 31 December 1992

	£'000	£'000	£'000
Sales			5,000
Less: returns			(100)
			4,900
Less: cost of goods sold			
Opening stock		300	
Purchases	2,400		
Less returns	(150)		
Less stock taken for private use	(10)		
		2,240	
		2,540	
Closing stock		(400)	
			(2,140)
Gross profit			2,760
Operating expenses			
Figure given	1,300		
Property depreciation	16		
Machinery depreciation	108		
Cash discounts (20 - 10)	10		
			(1,434)
Net operating profit			1,326
Payment for injury	50		
Debenture interest paid and proposed	90		
Less gain on redemption	(20)		
			(120)
Net profit			1,206
Dividends paid	100		
proposed	110		
			(210)
Retained profit for the year			996
Retained profit B/fwd			200
Retained profit C/fwd			1,196

Lincoln plc

Balance sheet as at 31 December 1992

Fixed assets	Cost/valuation £'000	Depreciation £'000	Net £'000
Land	1,500	nil	1,500
Property	800	216	584
Machinery	1,600	608	992
			3,076
Current assets			
Stock		400	
Debtors		1,000	
Due from director		10	
		1,410	
Current liabilities			
Creditors	400		
Dividends	110		
Debenture interest	30		
Bank overdraft	30		
		(570)	
Net current assets			840
Long term liabilities			
Debentures (15%)			(400)
Net assets			3,516
Represented by:			
Share capital			1,100
Share premium			620
Revaluation reserve			600
Profit and loss account reserves			1,196
			3,516

Workings

1

Suspense account			
	£'000		£'000
B/f	210	Redemption of debentures	380
Share issue	220	Payment - injury	50
	430		430

2   Depreciation

Machinery

	Cost £'000	Depreciation £'000
Balance per question	1,600	500
Depreciated to scrap value	(160)	(150)
	1,440	350

Remaining net book value	1,090	
Scrap value - not to be depreciated	(10)	
	1,080	

---

55   NANTRED TRADING CO LTD

(a)   **Profitability**

*(**Tutorial note:** the question has asked for three areas of the business to be highlighted. Profitability is the key area. Without profits a business cannot survive. Be prepared, therefore, to derive a profit figure for the two years.)*

Profit and loss accounts

	19X5 £	19X6 £
Profit (bal.fig)	21,500	37,500
Taxation	(11,400)	(13,100)
Dividends	(17,000)	(17,000)
Retained for year	(6,900)	7,400
Reserves b/d	26,100	19,200
Reserves c/d	19,200	26,600

$$\frac{\text{Net profit before tax}}{\text{Sales}} \qquad \frac{21,500}{202,900} \times 100 \qquad \frac{37,500}{490,700} \times 100$$

$$= 10.6\% \qquad\qquad = 7.6\%$$

Return on capital employed:

$$\frac{\text{Net profit before taxation}}{\text{Net assets employed}} \qquad \frac{21,500}{119,200} \times 100 \qquad \frac{37,500}{326,600} \times 100$$

$$= 18.0\% \qquad\qquad = 11.5\%$$

Liquidity:

Current ratio:

$$\frac{\text{Current assets}}{\text{Current liabilities}} \qquad \frac{66,500}{52,300} \qquad \frac{152,500}{85,900}$$

$$= 1.3 \qquad\qquad = 1.8$$

Quick ratio:

| Current assets - Stock / Current liabilities | 35,300 / 52,300 = 0.7 | 57,200 / 85,900 = 0.7 |

Financial stability:

Gearing:

| Long-term debt / Net assets employed | Nil | $\frac{100,000}{326,600} \times 100$ = 30.6% |

| Liabilities / Shareholders' funds | 52,300 / 119,200 = 0.4 | 185,900 / 226,600 = 0.8 |

(b)   **Comment**

(Tutorial note: comments need not be long. It is better that they are short and to the point. It is a good idea to state whether each ratio is showing a better or worse position compared to last year.)

Profitability

Profitability in relation to sales and capital employed has fallen. However, the fall has occurred in a period of sales increasing two and a half times and capital increasing due to the issue of loan stock.

It will take time to invest the additional capital efficiently.

The decline in the profitability compared to sales may also be a short-term problem. For example overheads are not being kept under control in the period of rapid expansion. Alternatively the sales volume may have been achieved by cutting gross profit margins.

Liquidity

The current ratio has increased to give a comfortable level of cover for short-term creditors. Most of the increase, however, is derived from higher stocks. The quick ratio is constant.

Whether these two ratios are good or bad depends on what is normal/efficient in the type of business that Nantred is in.

Financial stability

There has been a major injection of long-term finance during the year, producing a gearing ratio of 30%. The business is thus in a riskier position than last year but the expansion of the business may be necessary to protect the existing business (by becoming larger it may be better able to protect itself).

The liabilities to shareholders' funds show a similar position as the gearing (and for the same reasons).

56   GRAVELEA HAULAGE CO PLC

(a)   Redeemable means that the shares or debentures can be bought back by the company from the holders and cancelled. Debentures, being loans to the company, are almost invariably redeemable. Any type of share may be redeemable but the most common is preference shares.

(b)   Redeemable shares and debentures provide medium-term finance regularly as in this instance to provide funds for an expansion programme. When the project has provided sufficient funds to be self-financing, the need for the securities no longer exists and thus they may be redeemed. Additionally, the facility to redeem gives the company:

(i)   the opportunity to introduce gearing; and

(ii)   flexibility in its capital structure.

In most instances the company has no choice other than to redeem, because of the terms under which the shares or debentures were issued. Shareholders, and especially debenture holders, are likely to require their investment returned under the terms of issue.

(c)   The dates signified are the earliest and latest dates at which the debentures may be redeemed. Depending on the terms of issue, the debentures will be redeemed within that period either at the company's option or the option of the debenture holders, more normally the former. The absence of a precise date gives the company the option of taking advantage of favourable financial conditions or avoiding unfavourable conditions.

Once again, depending on the terms of issue, the debentures may be redeemed by equal annual amounts, piecemeal or in one lot.

(d)   The dividend will be calculated on the nominal value and could alternatively be expressed in pence per share.

(e)

	Scheme A (i) £	Scheme B (ii) £	Scheme C (iii) £
Profit before interest and taxation	704,000	704,000	704,000
Less: Interest	4,000	4,000	4,000
Debenture interest (7% × £500,000)	35,000	-	-
Profit after interest, before taxation	665,000	700,000	700,000
Less: Corporation tax (40%)	266,000	280,000	280,000
Profit after taxation	399,000	420,000	420,000
Less: Preference dividends (10% × 500,000)	-	50,000	-
Earnings	399,000	370,000	420,000
Number of ordinary shares in issue	3,000,000	3,000,000	3,400,000
Earnings per share	13.3p	12.3p	12.4p

(f)

	Scheme A £	Scheme B £	Scheme C £
Fixed interest loans	500,000	-	-
Fixed dividend share capital	-	500,000	-
Total	500,000	500,000	Nil
Ordinary share capital	3,000,000	3,000,000	3,400,000
Gearing	14.3%	14.3%	Nil

(Tutorial note: shareholders' funds should be used in the calculation of gearing but there is insufficient information regarding the reserves of the company.)

57   ANTIPODEAN ENTERPRISES

(a)

Cash flow statement for the year ended 31 December 19X3

	£	£
Net cash inflow from operating activities		56,490
Returns on investments and servicing of finance		
Interest paid (3,000 – 400)		(2,600)
Capital expenditure		
Payments to acquire tangible fixed assets		
(36,400 + 19,860)	(56,260)	
Receipts from sales of tangible fixed assets		
(5,630 + 1,270)	6,900	
		(49,360)
Acquisitions and disposals		
Purchase of long-term investments		(8,000)
Drawings paid		(15,130)
Management of liquid resources		
Purchase of short-term investments		(1,200)
Financing		
Part repayment of business development loan	(3,000)	
Owners' capital withdrawals	(6,500)	
Net cash outflow from financing		(9,500)
Decrease in cash (28,200 + 1,100)		(29,300)

Note to the cash flow statement

Reconciliation of operating profit to net cash inflow from operating activities

	£
Operating profit (25,200 + 3,000)	28,200
Depreciation charges	7,000
Loss on sale of tangible fixed assets (740 – 430)	310
Decrease in stocks	7,830
Decrease in debtors	2,450
Increase in creditors ((32,050 – 400) – 20,950)	10,700
Net cash inflow from operating activities	56,490

WORKINGS

(W1)

Equipment account - NBV

	£		£
Balance b/d	17,600	NBV disposal	5,200
Additions (bal.fig.)	36,400	Depreciation provided for year	3,000
		Balance c/d	45,800
	54,000		54,000

(W2)

Equipment disposal account

	£		£
NBV disposals	5,200	Sale proceeds (bal.fig.)	5,630
Profit on disposal	430		
	5,630		5,630

Cars account - NBV

	£		£
Balance b/d	4,080	NBV disposals	2,010
Additions (bal. fig.)	19,860	Depreciation for year	3,000
		Balance c/d	18,930
	23,940		23,940

Cars disposal account

	£		£
NBV disposals	2,010	Loss on sale	740
		Sale proceeds (bal.fig.)	1,270
	2,010		2,010

(b) Antipodean Enterprises has increased in profit from £15,300 to £25,200 which, on the face of it, must be an encouraging sign.

However, in the year ended 31 December 19X3 there has been a substantial increase in the overdraft, being largely explained by purchases of equipment and cars, although the proprietor has, rather surprisingly, seen fit to increase his long-term investments, which also helps to explain the increase.

In fact the increase would have been even more substantial had it not been for the large reduction in stock levels and, to a lesser degree, the fall in the debtors, and a very large increase in creditors. Divestment in working capital has been around £20,000.

Overall criticisms of business management could be:

(i) There has been excessive withdrawal of profits at a time of expansion when funds are needed by the business.

(ii) The owner has long and short term investments, along with a substantial overdraft. The cash position would ease considerably if he could dispose of the investments, or increase long term loans to finance the fixed asset expenditure.

58 CASH FLOW PLC

(a)

Summarised estimated balance sheet as at 31 December 19X4

	£'000	£'000	£'000
Fixed assets			
Cost (200,000 + 190,000)		390	
Depreciation (40,000 + 30,000)		70	
		—	
			320
Current assets			
Stock (45,000 + 9,000)	54		
Debtors (37,000 - 23,000)	14		
	—		
		68	
Current liabilities			
Creditors (30,000 + 25,000)	55		
Bank overdraft (24,000 - 18,000)	6		
	—		
		61	
Net current assets			7
			—
			327
10% debentures (0.75 × 100,000)		75	
15% debentures		100	
		—	
			175
			—
Net assets			152
			—
Capital and reserves			
£1 ordinary shares [50,000 + (30,000 × 1)]			80
Share premium (40,000 - 30,000)			10
Profit and loss account (Working)			62
			—
			152
			—

WORKING

	£'000	£'000
Balance b/d		70
Profit for 19X4		20
		—
		90
Less: Dividends paid (33,000 - 10,000)	23	
Premium on redemption $(30,000 - \frac{100,000}{4})$	5	
	—	
		28
		—
Profit and loss balance		62
		—

*(**Tutorial note:** the changes in the elements of working capital can only be distinguished as increases or decreases if the relationship of profits to cash flow is understood. An increase in debtors represents a utilisation of cash resources. It would thus be a deduction from profit in arriving at net cash inflow. In the question the change in debtors is an addition to profit, thus it must represent a reduction in debtors.)*

(b)

Report

To:

From: Accountant

Date: X - X 19XX

Subject: Strengths and weaknesses of Cash Flow plc

(i)   The expenditure on fixed assets is high, and is only partly financed by new shares and debentures. The gearing position has worsened.

(ii)   Both creditors and stocks have gone up. The bank balance has gone down. In other words, the liquidity position is moving unfavourably, even though there is a decrease in debtors.

(iii)   Profits are low considering the size of the company. Retained profits for the year are expected to be negative even without paying a final dividend.

(iv)   The 10% debentures have to be redeemed in each of the years 19X5, 19X6 and 19X7, at a cost of £30,000 each year. On the basis of the existing financial status of the company, it is doubtful that the business would have sufficient liquid resources to meet its current liabilities.

(v)   The expansion of fixed assets is significant and the fixed assets are apparently either new or nearly new. This is possibly sufficient to form the basis for a more profitable future.

Taking into account of all the limited data given, the prospect of Cash Flow plc is highly uncertain.

(Tutorial notes:

(i)   Part (b) can best be answered on the basis of the data already provided in the cash flow statement rather than the data calculated in part (a).

(ii)   Questions to be considered are:

    (1)   The likelihood of the firm being able to afford to redeem £75,000 debentures, presumably at a cost of £90,000, over the next three years.

    (2)   Whether the fixed asset expansion would significantly increase profits in future years.

Simply reporting the variances between the two balance sheets without providing any interpretation of their significance is not sufficient to answer the question.

(iii)   Do **NOT** attempt to work out the ratios. The calculation of ratios is not required, as stated in the question.)

59   AIDA PLC

(a)   **Statement of net cash flow from trading operations**

	£
Operating profit (see working)	17,000
Depreciation	9,000
Increase in debtors	(16,000)
Decrease in stock	2,000
Decrease in creditors	(7,000)
Net cash inflow from operating activities	5,000

WORKING

	£
Operating profit before interest (bal fig)	17,000
Interest charged	
$(10\% \times 20,000) + (15\% \times 40,000)$	(8,000)
Dividend	(9,000)
Retained for year	Nil

(Tutorial note: there is no set format for the statement required in part (a). The approach adopted in the answer is to present a note that would normally be prepared reconciling operating profit to net cashflow.

In order to arrive at operating profit a further statement/working is required as the question does·not give a profit and loss account for the year.)

(b)   **Cash flow statement for the year ended 31 December 19X1**

	£	£
Net cash inflow from operating activities		5,000
Returns on investments and servicing of finance		
Interest paid	(8,000)	
		(3,000)
Capital expenditure		
Purchase of fixed assets		
Property (20 - 3 revaluation)	(17,000)	
Plant	(16,000)	
		(33,000)
Equity dividends paid		(5,000)
		(41,000)
Financing		
Issue of shares	10,000	
Issue of debentures	40,000	
Redemption of debentures	(20,000)	
		30,000
Decrease in cash		(11,000)

60   FRED PLC

(a)   Firstly we have to consider why an accountancy student might be worried by these accounts at first sight. The current assets of the business appear to be much lower than the current liabilities. This would appear to indicate liquidity problems. However, it is also possible to draw the conclusion that this state of affairs is due to the efficiency of the organisation. Sales are paid for quickly, so there are few debtors; stock turnover period is short with stock being sold quickly, and not held in current assets; creditors do not mind waiting for payment, so creditors in current liabilities seem high.

It is unusual to see a company with such low debtors and such a high cash balance (£2,000,000).

The positive aspects of the company's balance sheet appear to outweigh the negative ones:

- The group still has very low gearing (despite a 5,400% year-on-year increase since 1991).

- Its financing appears to come from its ability to pay its creditors after it has received the sales income from its debtors.

There appears to be no shortage of cash within the company.

Turning to the profit and loss account, the profitability of the company also appears sound. Profit in relation to sales is not too high, but as a return on the capital invested in the company profitability is high; the EPS on the 10p ordinary shares stands at 16p per share.

As the question refers to the return an ordinary shareholder can expect from this company, it is useful to calculate what that return might be: 31/142 = 21.8%.

This seems a good return but should be compared with the returns available on a similar investment elsewhere.

Given the peculiarities of this type of cash-based company, the accountancy student's initial impression seems unfounded and it would not seem appropriate to sell shares in this company.

(b)   (i)   The loan redemption fund is a sum of money being put aside by the company to pay for the redemption of the company's loan in the future.

    (ii)   The common definition of an asset can be taken to be a resource possessed or controlled by a business and expected to give benefit to that business, and which has been acquired by the business through some market transaction.

        The question of use is not mentioned. Therefore future anticipated use would be sufficient and the item not yet in use could be an asset.

        As to the question of charging depreciation to the profit and loss account, as depreciation aims to match the revenue derived from an asset with the cost of that asset, if the asset is not yet in use the matching or depreciation will not have commenced. There is therefore no charge to the profit and loss account in respect of these assets not yet in use.

    (iii)   Interest is being capitalised, that is, transferred from the interest expense account to an asset (probably the fixed asset) account. This will result in a higher profit now as the interest charged to the profit and loss account is reduced, but profit will be reduced in later years when the increased value of the fixed asset is depreciated. The expense of the interest is therefore deferred and not removed.

        This accounting treatment comes about as a result of treating the cost of a loan to purchase a fixed asset as part of the cost of acquiring that asset. This is not a universally accepted accounting policy, because on the grounds of prudence it would be preferable to recognise the expense of the interest immediately.

61   LIMITED COMPANIES

(a)   (i)   Shares

        A share is a part of a company, and ownership of that share denotes ownership of a proportion of the company. The share entitles the owner to dividends as and when declared and to a share of the reserves of a company after all other liabilities have been met.

(ii)   Reserves

A reserve is the equivalent of a special creditor owed by the company to the shareholders of the company over and above the share capital the shareholders have invested.

(iii)   Debentures

A debenture is a formal loan to a business, witnessed by a formal written agreement of terms of interest and repayment.

(iv)   Shareholders' equity

This is the total claim the shareholders have on a company, totalling share capital and reserves.

(v)   Capital employed

This is the shareholders' equity plus the long-term loans raised, which together make the total monies invested in the operation of the business for the long term.

(b)   Return on capital employed (ROCE) is the ratio between the amount of capital employed in the business for the long term and the return generated on that capital by the business.

The 'return' is the return or profit made for the shareholders plus any interest normally deducted from that profit for payment to long-term shareholders.

ROCE is of use to many people, including bankers, investors, and managers, because it measures how efficiently the funds invested are being used to generate income.

9 NEW SYLLABUS EXAMINATIONS

Note: **With effect from June 1997, there will no MCQs in the examination. The sample items previously issued by the ACCA are included here for the sake of completeness.**

Section A - Multiple Choice Questions (Sample items)

The multiple choice questions set in the examinations until December 1996 are not available for publication. The following are sample items issued by the Association.

1   On checking the list of balances on the creditors' ledger accounts, it is found that the total is £2,250 more than the balance on the creditors control account.

Which of the following errors could, by itself, account for this difference?

A   The total of contra entries against debtor accounts is overstated by £1,125.
B   Purchases day book has been overcast by £2,250.
C   A credit note to the value of £1,125 has been omitted from a creditors ledger account.
D   A creditors ledger account with a debit balance of £1,125 has been treated as a credit balance.

Answer

D   A creditors ledger account with a debit balance of £1,125 has been treated as a credit balance.

Option A could partially explain the difference, but is insufficient, in itself, at £1,125. Option B increases the size of the difference and is, therefore, incorrect. Option C will narrow the difference but, again, cannot account for it in itself. Option D provides a full explanation by reducing the list of balances by £2,250 through correcting the treatment of a debit balance of £1, 125.

2   Waverly Products acquired a new mainframe computer system for £50,000 on 1 November 1993. The computer's estimated useful life is five years, at the end of which it is expected to have a scrap value of £4,550. If the company's financial year ends on 31 March, and straight line depreciation is applied on a time-apportioned basis, what is the depreciation charge on the computer in the profit and loss account for the year to 31 March 1994?

A   £3,788
B   £4,167
C   £9,090
D   £10,000

Answer

A   £3,788

Annual depreciation (straight line)

$$= \frac{£50,000 - £4,500}{5}$$

$$= £9,090$$

Time apportioned charge (rounded)
= 5/12 × £9,090
= £3,788 (rounded)

3   On 30 November, Hayman Services Limited receives a $3,500 (US Dollar) cheque from a customer in Florida, enters this cheque as £3,500 in its accounting records and lodges the cheque in its usual bank account (£ sterling). On 2 December, the bank discovers this error and adjusts the company's bank account with the sterling equivalent of £1,950.

In order to correct the company's records, which of the following is the sole adjusting journal entry?

A	Debit: Bank - Current Account	£1,950
	Credit: Debtors	£1,950
B	Debit: Bank- Current Account	£1,950
	Credit: Debtors	£1,550
	Credit: Losses on Exchange	£400
C	Debit: Debtors	£1,550
	Credit: Bank - Current Account	£1,550
D	Debit: Debtors	£1,550
	Debit: Losses on Exchange	£400
	Credit: Bank - Current Account	£1,950

Answer

C	Debit: Debtors	£1,550
	Credit: Bank - Current Account	£1,550

The original entry (including the error) will have debited the bank account and credited debtors with £3,500 i.e. overstating bank and therefore, the correcting journal entry requires the difference of £1,550 to be credited to bank and debited to debtors.

Section B - ALL THREE questions are compulsory and MUST be attempted

62	**(Question 1 of examination)**

1   The trial balance of Zed Ltd at 1 January 1993 contains the following items.

	£'000
Bank overdraft	7
Building - cost	80
- depreciation	5
Creditors - trade	28
- operating expenses	2
16% Debentures	50
Debtors	24
Land, at valuation	125
Machinery - cost	90
- depreciation	43
Ordinary shares, £1 each	100
10% Preference shares, £1 each	40
Profit and loss account	34
Revaluation reserve	45
Stocks	35

Summarised transactions and events for the year to 31 December 1993 are as follows.

(i)

	£'000
Sales	920
Purchases	500
Bad debts written off	5
Contras between debtors and creditors accounts	8
Operating expenses paid	360

(ii)   30,000 £1 ordinary shares were issued at £2.00 per share on 1 January 1993; this transaction was not reflected in the trial balance above.

(iii)   Debenture interest and the preference dividend for the year were all paid on 31 December. An ordinary dividend of 20p per share was paid on 31 December.

(iv)   The land is revalued at 31 December 1993 at £130,000. The machinery is to be depreciated at 10% on cost and the buildings are to be depreciated on the straight line basis over eighty years.

(v)   At 31 December 1993:

	£'000
- additional operating expenses owing are	10
- closing stock is	40
- closing debtors are	35
- closing trade creditors are	25

Required:

Prepare the balance sheet at 31 December 1993 and the profit and loss account for the year ended 31 December 1993. These statements do not need to comply with Companies Act disclosure requirements, but should be presented in a format which is generally accepted and which presents the information helpful to the reader. Submit all workings. Ignore taxation.

                                                         (18 marks)

63   (Question 2 of examination)

2   In Appendix A you are given Paragraphs 1, 2, 3, 4, 5, and 39 of SSAP 9, 'Stocks and Long-term Contracts' which may help you answer parts (a) and (c) of this question.

(a)   A firm buys and sells two models, P and Q. The following unit costs are available (all figures are in £s and all the costs are borne by the firm):

	P	Q
Purchase cost	100	200
Delivery costs from supplier	20	30
Delivery costs to customers	22	40
Coloured sales packaging costs	15	18
Selling price	150	300

Required:

Calculate the figure to be included in closing stock for a unit of each model, according to SSAP 9.

(3 marks)

(b)   A firm has the following transactions with its product R.

Year 1

Opening stock: nil
Buys 10 units at £300 per unit
Buys 12 units at £250 per unit
Sells 8 units at £400 per unit
Buys 6 units at £200 per unit
Sells 12 units at £400 per unit

Year 2

Buys 10 units at £200 per unit
Sells 5 units at £400 per unit
Buys 12 units at £150 per unit
Sells 25 units at £400 per unit.

Required:

Calculate on an item by item basis for both year 1 and year 2:

(i)   The closing stock
(ii)   The sales
(iii)   The cost of sales
(iv)   The gross profit

using, separately, the LIFO and the FIFO methods of stock valuation. Present all workings clearly.

(10 marks)

(c)   Paragraph 39 of SSAP 9 suggests that the LIFO stock figure at the end of year 1 in (b) above would be a 'misstatement of balance sheet amounts' and would potentially cause a 'distortion of current and future results'.

Required:

Comment on these suggestions, using the situation and calculations from part (b) above as an illustration. Your answer should indicate the extent to which you agree with the comment in Paragraph 39 as regards the use of the LIFO method of stock valuation.

(7 marks)
(Total: 20 marks)

64	**(Question 3 of examination)**

---

3   (a)   Define each of the following terms as used in financial accounting:

          (i)   asset
          (ii)   revenue
          (iii)   expense
          (iv)   matching.   **(8 marks)**

    (b)   Explain the purposes, and the weaknesses, of a balance sheet.

                                                                       (8 marks)

    (c)   It has become common in recent years, particularly in the UK, for companies not to provide any depreciation on their freehold buildings, which simply remain in the balance sheet at the same cost figure each year.

Required:

Describe arguments for and against the validity of this treatment, and explain whether you regard this policy as acceptable.

                                                                      (6 marks)
                                                      (Total: 22 marks)

Appendix A

Extracts from SSAP 9

1   The determination of profit for an accounting year requires the matching of costs with related revenues. The cost of unsold or unconsumed stocks will have been incurred in the expectation of future revenue, and when this will not arise until a later year it is appropriate to carry forward this cost to be matched with the revenue when it arises; the applicable concept is the matching of cost and revenue in the year in which the revenue arises rather than in the year in which the cost is incurred. If there is no reasonable expectation of sufficient future revenue to cover cost incurred (e.g., as a result of deterioration, obsolescence or a change in demand) the irrecoverable cost should be charged to revenue in the year under review. Thus, stocks normally need to be stated at cost, or, if lower, at net realisable value.

2   The comparison of cost and net realisable value needs to be made in respect of each item of stock separately. Where this is impracticable, groups or categories of stock items which are similar will need to be taken together. To compare the total realisable value of stocks with the total cost could result in an unacceptable setting off of foreseeable losses against unrealised profits.

3   In order to match costs and revenue, 'costs' of stocks should comprise that expenditure which has been incurred in the normal course of business in bringing the product or service to its present location and condition. Such costs will include all related production overheads, even though these may accrue on a time basis.

4   The methods used in allocating costs to stocks need to be selected with a view to providing the fairest possible approximation to the expenditure actually incurred in bringing the product to its present location and condition. For example, in the case of retail stores holding a large number of rapidly changing individual items, stock on the shelves has often been stated at current selling prices less the normal gross profit margin. In these particular circumstances this may be acceptable as being the only practical method of arriving at a figure which approximates to cost.

5   Net realisable value is the estimated proceeds from the sale of items of stock less all further costs to completion and less all costs to be incurred in marketing, selling and distributing directly related to the items in question.

39   In particular, the use of the LIFO method can result in the reporting of current assets at amounts that bear little relationship to recent costs. This may result in not only a significant misstatement of balance sheet amounts but also a potential distortion of current and future results. This places a special responsibility on the directors to be assured that the circumstances of the company require the adoption of such a valuation method in order for the accounts to give a true and fair view.

EXAMINER'S COMMENTS

Paper 1, the foundation accounting exam, has not changed much, compared with its predecessor (Paper 1.1). The only major alteration is the extension of the syllabus to include some SSAPs. Broadly speaking, both this examination and candidates' performance continued the pattern of recent years. Candidates' ability in discussion and discursive questions was significantly lower than in numerical work, and they should work hard to improve this aspect of their performance. Candidates must recognise that accounting is all about communication.

Question 1 required the preparation of final accounts from an opening trial balance and a summary of the events of the year. It was a straightforward question except that the closing bank balance had to be calculated indirectly via the use of control accounts to derive sales receipts and purchases payments. Some candidates missed this aspect completely.

Question 2 tested various aspects of stock valuation and SSAP 9. The 'lower of cost and market value' rule, surprisingly, was often not well understood, but FIFO and LIFO calculations were usually sound. The final discussion part concerning the SSAP arguments against the use of LIFO was generally unsatisfactory. Clarity of thought and expression are essential in such situations, and neither was regularly forthcoming.

Question 3 tested in part (a) the definitions of some central terms, in part (b) the purposes and weaknesses of a balance sheet, and in part (c) discussion of non-depreciation on freehold buildings. The question required purely written answers, and results were often poor. In part (a), 'expense' was particularly poorly explained and often not properly distinguished from the earlier attempt to define 'asset'. Parts (b) and (c) were more open-ended, requiring clear, logical argument and a rational conclusion and opinion. The ability to chart a passage through a situation where conflicting arguments exist requires significant development by the majority of candidates.

ANSWERS TO JUNE 1994 EXAMINATION

62 (Answer 1 of examination)

1 Working (all figures £'000)

Debtors ledger control

	£		£
Opening balance	24	Closing balance	35
Sales	920	Bad debts	5
		Contra	8
		Cash	896
	944		944

Creditors ledger control

	£		£
Closing balance	25	Opening balance	28
Contra	8	Purchases	500
Cash	495		
	528		528

Bank control

	£		£
Debtors ledger control	896	Opening balance	7
Share issue	60	Creditors ledger control	495
		Operating expenses paid	360
		Debenture interest	8
		Preference dividends	4
		Ordinary dividends	26
		Closing balance	56
	956		956

Trading and profit and loss account, year to 31 December 1993
(all figures £'000)

Sales		920
Opening stock	35	
Purchases	500	
	—	
	535	
Closing stock	40	
	—	
Cost of sales		495
		—
Gross profit		425
Operating expenses	368	
Depreciation - machinery	9	
- building	1	
Bad debts	5	
	—	
		383
		—
Operating profit		42
Debenture interest		8
		—
Net profit		34
Preference dividend		4
		—
Ordinary shareholders' earnings		30
Ordinary dividends		26
		—
Retained profit for the year		4
		—

Balance sheet at 31 December 1993
(all figures £000)

Fixed assets	Cost	Depreciation	
Land at valuation			130
Building	80	6	74
Machinery	90	52	38
			242
Current assets			
Stock		40	
Debtors		35	
Bank		56	
		131	
Current liabilities			
Creditors		35	
Net current assets			96
			338
Ordinary shares of £1 each			130
Preference shares of £1 each			40
Share premium			30
Revaluation reserve			50
Profit and loss			38
Shareholders equity			288
Debentures			50
Capital employed			338

---

63 (Answer 2 of examination)

2 (a) Model P

Cost	100 + 20 + 15	= 135[1]
Net realisable value	150 - 22	= 128[2]
Lower of cost and net realisable value		£128

Model Q

Cost	200 + 30 + 18	= 248[1]
Net realisable value	300 - 40	= 260[2]
Lower of cost and net realisable value		£248

[1] purchase cost + delivery costs from supplier + packaging costs
[2] selling price - delivery costs to customers

(b)   LIFO

Year 1	Purchases	Cost of sales	Stock	Sales
buy 10 at 300	3,000		3,000	
buy 12 at 250	3,000		6,000	
sell 8 at 400		2,000[1]	4,000	3,200
buy 6 at 200	1,200		5,200	
sell 12 at 400		2,800[2]	2,400	4,800
	7,200	4,800	2,400	8,000

Year 2	Purchases	Cost of sales	Stock	Sales
Opening stock			2,400	
buy 10 at 200	2,000		4,400	
sell 5 at 400		1,000[3]	3,400	2,000
buy 12 at 150	1,800		5,200	
sell 25 at 400		5,200[4]	0	10,000
	3,800	6,200	0	12,000

[1] 8 at 250
[2] 6 at 200 + 4 at 250 + 2 at 300
[3] 5 at 200
[4] 12 at 150 + 5 at 200 + 8 at 300

FIFO

Year 1	Purchases	Cost of sales	Stock	Sales
buy 10 at 300	3,000		3,000	
buy 12 at 250	3,000		6,000	
sell 8 at 400		2,400[5]	3,600	3,200
buy 6 at 200	1,200		4,800	
sell 12 at 400		3,100[6]	1,700	4,800
	7,200	5,500	1,700	8,000

Year 2	Purchases	Cost of sales	Stock	Sales
Opening stock			1,700	
buy 10 at 200	2,000		3,700	
sell 5 at 400		1,100[7]	2,600	2,000
buy 12 at 150	1,800		4,400	
sell 25 at 400		4,400[8]	0	10,000
	3,800	5,500	0	12,000

5 8 at 300
6 2 at 300 + 10 at 250
7 2 at 250 + 3 at 200
8 3 at 200 + 10 at 200 + 12 at 150

Trading accounts		LIFO		FIFO	
	£	£	£	£	£
Year 1					
Sales		8,000			8,000
Opening stock	0			0	
Purchases	7,200			7,200	
	7,200			7,200	
Closing stock	2,400			1,700	
Cost of sales		4,800			5,500
Gross profit		3,200			2,500
Year 2					
Sales		12,000			12,000
Opening stock	2,400			1,700	
Purchases	3,800			3,800	
	6,200			5,500	
Closing stock	0			0	
Cost of sales		6,200			5,500
Gross profit		5,800			6,500

(c)   There are a variety of points, arguments and attitudes possible here. Marks will be given for any coherent and logically-supported suggestions.

We are asked to consider the effects of the LIFO method on the stock figure at the end of year 1, and on both the gross profit figures. Since the closing stock at the end of year 2 is nil, the situation is presented with unusual clarity. Note however that purchase costs are falling, not rising which is more common.

Relevant points to mention might include the following.

- at the end of year 1 the closing stock is higher under LIFO than under FIFO, the cost of sales is lower, and therefore the gross profit is higher, than under FIFO. With these particular figures it could be argued that LIFO lacks prudence, but this would mean that in the normal situation where costs are rising rather than falling, FIFO would lack prudence as compared with LIFO.

- because the closing stock in year 1 is obviously the opening stock of year 2, the effect reverses in year 2. The choice of method affects the annual gross profit, and will affect the trend of annual gross profits, but does not affect the long-run amount of the gross profit. This is demonstrated by the figures, as total gross profit for the two years is £9,000 under both methods.

- the cost of sales figure under LIFO is more up-to-date than under the alternative historical cost methods. This means that expense and revenue figures are more internally consistent in terms of dates, and therefore it can be argued that the matching principle is better followed by LIFO than by FIFO. SSAP 9 seems to take the opposite view.

- the balance sheet figure will often be based on very out-of-date costs under LIFO

- LIFO can be regarded as having some similarity to replacement cost accounting as regards profit calculation (though not as regards the balance sheet stock figure).

64   (Answer 3 of examination)

3   (a)   (i)   An asset is a resource which is under the control of a business, is expected to be of future benefit to the business, and which was obtained via a past transaction between the business and another party.

            (ii)   A revenue is a benefit received or receivable where the asset receivable is capable of objective measurement and its receipt is reasonably certain. In practice a revenue is usually recognised when goods are delivered to and accepted by the customer.

            (iii)   An expense is a resource used or consumed in the operations of the business, or one which has no reasonable possibility of future beneficial use.

            (iv)   Matching is the process of allocating against revenues any expenses relating to the generation of those revenues, the net result being profit.

   (b)   (The following is a fuller answer than would be expected from the average pass candidate).

A balance sheet is in bookkeeping terms just a list of balances. In accounting terms it is often described as a statement of financial position at a point in time, or as a snapshot of the financial position. It shows the assets (resources) of the business, and the liabilities (claims) against the business, at a point in time. The ownership claims are regarded as a liability of the business in this sense.

The asset and external liability figures are arrived at by applying appropriate accounting conventions, such as matching, prudence, etc. and a valuation system. The generally accepted valuation systems are either historical cost (based on the original cost of the item), or modified historical cost (where some of the fixed assets are revalued periodically). The closing ownership claim, i.e. the closing capital, is then the balancing figure between the assets and the external liabilities.

It is clear from the above discussion that a balance sheet is essentially a statement of unexpired costs, i.e. a statement of resources acquired but not yet used. its major weakness perhaps is that it does not seem to have any clear positive definition or positive purpose. It is not a summary of the values of the individual assets. It is certainly not a statement of the value of the business as a whole. To confuse the average reader of a balance sheet even more, the figures included for the assets are not even consistently evaluated between themselves. For example if debtors are at expected realisable value and stocks are at cost, what can we say about the meaning of the total of stock and debtors? Very little!

   (c)   Arguments for the validity of not providing depreciation might include:

-    the asset has not fallen in value over the year. This argument, often heard, is not logically acceptable. Depreciation is an application of the matching convention, as explained in (a) above, not an attempt at a current valuation, so the change in value in the year is irrelevant to the issue.

-    the estimated net realisable value of the building to the firm is not less than the original cost, making the net cost to be allocated over the useful life equal to nil.

-    unnecessary or excessive depreciation would lead to the creation of secret reserves, which is illegal.

-    maintenance expenditure is charged to profit calculation to avoid dilapidation, to charge depreciation as well would in effect be double-counting.

Arguments against the validity of not providing depreciation might include:

-    buildings do wear out and do have a finite useful life, and all such fixed assets should be consistently depreciated in logic and in law
-    consistency with other assets consumed in the production or operational process requires it.

The acceptability of the policy on balance is of course an individual matter. Maybe the real problem is the fact that practice in this area is so variable and inconsistent.

DECEMBER 1994 QUESTIONS

Note: **With effect from June 1997, there will no MCQs in the examination.**

The Multiple Choice Questions set under the old examination format until December 1996 were not released by the examiner. Some sample items were issued in 1994 and are reproduced with the June 1994 examination questions on page 161.

Section B - ALL THREE questions are compulsory and MUST be attempted

65   (Question 1 of examination)

1   A, B and C have been in partnership for many years, sharing profits equally. Their trial balance at 1 January 1994 is as follows:

			£'000	£'000
A	Capital			30
	Current			2
B	Capital			28
	Current			4
C	Capital			32
	Current		4	
Land and buildings	- Cost		70	
Plant and machinery	- Cost		100	
	- Depreciation			66
Stock			40	
Trade debtors			30	
Bank			3	
Creditors	- Trade			40
	- Operating expenses			5
Loan from D, at 10% per annum				40
			247	247

With effect from 1 January 1994, the partnership agreement is changed. Profits are to be shared A: B: C: 3: 2: 1.

At 1 January 1994, the partnership goodwill is agreed at £60,000 but a ledger account for goodwill is not to be maintained in the accounting records. The land and buildings are agreed to be worth £100,000 and this figure is to be recorded in the accounting records.

At the end of each year each partner is to be allowed interest of 10% on the opening net balance on capital and current accounts (i.e. on the given balances before any adjustments).

The following information relating to 1994 should be taken into account as necessary.

(i)   The cash book summary for 1994 is as follows:

	£'000			£'000
Opening balance	3	To trade suppliers		110
Received from customers	172	For operating expenses		30
From sale of old plant	10	For new plant		50
		Drawings	A	10
			B	11
Balance c/d	38		C	12
	223			223

(ii)   At 31 December 1994 £10,000 is prepaid for rent, and £2,000 is to be accrued for electricity. Rent and electricity are both included in operating expenses.

(iii)   All plant and machinery is depreciated at 10% p.a. straight-line basis, assuming no scrap value, and with a full year's depreciation in the year of purchase and none in the year of sale. The old plant sold in 1994 had been bought in June 1986 at a cost of £60,000.

(iv)   At 31 December 1994 trade creditors were £35,000. Trade debtors, after deducting £4,000 of bad debts, were £40,000. Gross profit is consistently 50% of cost of sales.

Required:

Prepare trading, profit and loss and appropriation accounts for 1994 for the partnership, and a summary balance sheet at 31 December 1994. Submit all workings which must be clear and legible. Ignore taxation.

(25 marks)

66   (Question 2 of examination)

2   SSAP 2, Disclosure of Accounting Policies, issued in 1971, distinguishes between fundamental concepts, accounting bases and accounting policies. Part of Paragraph 14 of the SSAP, which defines the four suggested 'fundamental concepts', is attached as Appendix A.

Required:

(a)   explain and distinguish between

(i)   fundamental concepts
(ii)   accounting bases
(iii)   accounting policies

as the terms are used in SSAP 2.   **(6 marks)**

(b)   Explain and give an example of the effect on a set of published financial statements of a company if the going concern convention is held *not* to apply.

(6 marks)

(c)   A number of documents and reports in recent years have attempted to produce something loosely described in the syllabus for this paper as a 'conceptual framework'.

Required:

Explain in general terms what such proposals are trying to achieve. Why is SSAP 2 apparently no longer considered adequate?

(7 marks)
(19 marks)

67   (Question 3 of examination)

3   For each of the following pairs of concepts, carefully explain the distinction between the first member of each pair and the second:

(a)   Reserves; cash in hand.
(b)   Ownership interest; capital employed.
(c)   Liability; expense.
(d)   Contingent liability; provision.

(16 marks)

Appendix A

Extract from paragraph 14 of SSAP 2

(a)   the 'going concern' concept: the enterprise will continue in operational existence for the foreseeable future. This means in particular that the profit and loss account and balance sheet assume no intention or necessity to liquidate or curtail significantly the scale of operation;

(b)   the 'accruals' concept: revenue and costs are accrued (that is, recognised as they are earned or incurred, not as money is received or paid), matched with one another so far as their relationship can be established or justifiably assumed, and dealt with in the profit and loss account of the period to which they relate; provided that where the accruals concept is inconsistent with the 'prudence' concept (paragraph (d) below), the latter prevails. The accruals concept implies that the profit and loss account reflects changes in the amount of net assets that arise out of the transactions of the relevant period (other than distributions or subscriptions of capital and unrealised surpluses arising on revaluation of fixed assets). Revenue and profits dealt with in the profit and loss account are matched with associated costs and expenses by including in the same account the costs incurred in earning them (so far as these are material and identifiable);

(c)   the 'consistency' concept: there is consistency of accounting treatment of like items within each accounting period and from one period to the next;

(d)   the concept of 'prudence': revenue and profits are not anticipated, but are recognised by inclusion in the profit and loss account only when realised in the form either of cash or other assets the ultimate cash realisation of which can be assessed with reasonable certainty; provision is made for all known liabilities (expenses and losses) whether the amount of these is known with certainty or is a best estimate in the light of the information available.

EXAMINER'S COMMENTS

General comment

This paper was similar in pattern to the June 1994 paper.

Question 1: required the preparation of partnership final accounts, involving a change in the partnership agreement and necessitating the calculation of a number of figures before the final accounts could be prepared.

Most candidates made a good attempt at this question. A common error was to put the loan interest in the profit and loss account, quite correctly, and then ignore it altogether in the balance sheet.

Question 2: related SSAP 2, Disclosure of accounting policies, to the recent 'conceptual framework' developments.

Part (a) was a piece of bookwork from the SSAP, often poorly answered. If an appendix is included in the paper, candidates cannot expect marks for quoting the appendix back to the examiner.

Part (b) asked for the effect on published accounts if the going concern convention is held not to apply. Many answers demonstrated that concepts had been learnt by rote but not necessarily understood.

Part (c) required reference in general terms to the purpose of the various 'conceptual framework' projects going on around the world. Many answers were poor. Some insight into the nature of the framework is an essential part of the foundation stage.

Question 3: required verbal distinctions between pairs of accounting terms.

Reserves were particularly poorly understood. Candidates should note that describing different types of reserves is not a substitute for an explanation of what reserves are.

ANSWERS TO DECEMBER 1994 EXAMINATION

65   (Answer 1 of examination)

1   *Note*: (⊗ indicates balancing item.)

Debtors control account

	£		£
Opening balance	30,000	Bank	172,000
Sales ⊗	186,000	Bad debt	4,000
		Closing debtors	40,000
	216,000		216,000

Creditors control account

	£		£
Bank	110,000	Opening creditors	40,000
Closing creditors	35,000	Purchases ⊗	105,000
	145,000		145,000

Plant disposal account

	£		£
Cost transferred	60,000	Depreciation transferred (8 years)	48,000
		Proceeds	10,000
		Loss on disposal ⊗	2,000
	60,000		60,000

Operating expenses account

	£		£
Bank	30,000	b/f	5,000
c/d	2,000	c/d	10,000
		Charge for year ⊗	17,000
	32,000		32,000

Plant and machinery - cost

	£		£
b/f	100,000	To disposal	60,000
Purchased	50,000	c/d ⊗	90,000
	150,000		150,000

Plant and machinery - depreciation

	£		£
To disposal	48,000	b/f	66,000
⊗ c/d	27,000	Charge for year	9,000
	75,000		75,000

Trading account - Year to 31 December 1994

Sales		186,000
Opening stock	40,000	
Purchases	105,000	
	145,000	
⊗ Closing stock	21,000	
	124,000	
Gross profit (1/3 of 186,000)	62,000	
		186,000

Profit and loss account - Year to 31 December 1994

Gross profit		62,000
Operating expenses	17,000	
Depreciation	9,000	
Loss on disposal	2,000	
Bad debt	4,000	
Interest on loan from D	4,000	
	36,000	
Net profit	26,000	

Appropriation account - Year to 31 December 1994

Net profit				26,000
Interest on net capital	A	3,200		
	B	3,200		
	C	2,800		
			9,200	
Profit	A	8,400		
	B	5,600		
	C	2,800		
			16,800	
				26,000

	A	B	C		A	B	C
	£	£	£		£	£	£
Capital accounts				Opening	30,000	28,000	32,000
Goodwill	30,000	20,000	10,000	Goodwill	20,000	20,000	20,000
				Land	10,000	10,000	10,000
⊗ Closing	30,000	38,000	52,000				
	60,000	58,000	62,000		60,000	58,000	62,000
Current accounts							
Opening	-	-	4,000	Opening	2,000	4,000	-
Drawings	10,000	11,000	12,000	Interest	3,200	3,200	2,800
⊗ Closing	3,600	1,800	(10,400)	Profits	8,400	5,600	2,800
	13,600	12,800	5,600		13,600	12,800	5,600

Summary balance sheet 31 December 1994

Fixed assets

Land and buildings			100,000
Plant and machinery	90,000	27,000	63,000
			163,000

Current assets

Stock		21,000	
Debtors		40,000	
Prepayment		10,000	
		71,000	

Less: Current liabilities

Creditors - Trade	35,000		
- Electricity	2,000		
Loan interest D	4,000		
Bank overdraft	38,000		
		79,000	
			(8,000)
			155,000

Capital employed	A	30,000	3,600	33,600
	B	38,000	1,800	39,800
	C	52,000	(10,400)	41,600
				115,000
Loan from D				40,000
				155,000

66	**(Answer 2 of examination)**

2   (a)   Formal definitions are as follows.

Fundamental accounting concepts are the broad basic assumptions which underlie the periodic financial accounts of business enterprises.

Accounting bases are the methods developed for applying fundamental accounting concepts to financial transactions and items, for the purpose of financial accounts, and in particular (a) for determining the accounting periods in which revenue and costs should be recognised in the profit and loss account and (b) for determining the amounts at which material items should be stated in the balance sheet.

Accounting policies are the specific accounting bases selected and consistently followed by a business enterprise as being, in the opinion of the management, appropriate to its circumstances and best suited to present fairly its results and financial position.

It is clear that the three types form a hierarchy. The concepts are basic parameters, the bases are possible ways of applying those parameters to particular problems, and the policies are the actual methods chosen, from the available bases, by a specific company.

(b)   The effect is likely to be extremely dramatic. As the SSAP says, the going concern convention implies no intention or necessity to liquidate or curtail significantly the scale of operations. This assumption is crucial to the application of the matching convention. It is the matching convention which allows (and requires) the deferral of expenses to future periods, i.e. until they are actually used in the operating process to generate recognised revenue. Most of the asset figures in a balance sheet are in fact future expenses in this way and the balance sheet figures therefore assume future usage under the normal operating procedures of the business. To take the extreme case, if a company is depreciating its buildings over, say, 50 years, then this assumes a useful life *to the business* of 50 years. If such an assumption ceases to be valid then the whole basis of accounting practice ceases to be applicable and breakup figures would need to be used instead. These would presumably be breakup figures assuming a forced sale (i.e. again, not through normal business activities and time scales) and would be different from, probably lower than, market values as regularly used for such purposes as 'lower of cost and market value' calculations.

(c)   It is generally recognised, and it is certainly easy to demonstrate, that the usual list of traditional accounting conventions are mutually conflicting and somewhat illogical when considered as a set. The framework idea could perhaps be characterised as an attempt to provide a coherent and internally consistent set of ideas, which could then be applied to any particular accounting problem. If the ideas are coherent and consistent, and they are applied 'rationally', then the set of solutions to all the various accounting problems which would emerge from such application should itself be consistent. The extent to which this objective is possibly achievable given the subjective nature of the accounting discipline is debatable.

SSAP 2 obviously sets itself much lower targets. Its main concern, as its title suggests, was that companies should disclose what they were doing. It did not really set out to change what companies were doing, nor to progress accounting thought. In that sense if the target is some form of complete coherent structure for accounting problem-solving, then SSAP 2 is clearly inadequate, as to achieve such a result was never its intention.

67	(Answer 3 of examination)

3   (a)   Reserves are the ownership interest in the business other than the share capital itself which for limited companies must always be shown separately as such. Reserves represent claims by the owners on business resources. The bigger the reserves then, other things equal, the bigger the resources in the business attributable to the owners. Cash in hand, on the other hand, means the amount of actual money - coin or note - which is owned by a business at the relevant date. Cash in hand is an asset, indeed the most liquid asset of all. Reserves are one of the claims on the assets.

(b)   Ownership interest is the total of share capital and reserves. It is the total ownership claim on a business. It indicates the total resources held in a business at a point of time which 'belong' to the owners, both put in by the owners and gained by successful business activity, according to the measurement bases used in the accounts.

Capital employed is the total of ownership interest plus long-term liabilities. It represents the 'permanent' sources of finance being used by the business.

(c)   A liability is an existing obligation of a business, arising from past events, the settlement of which is expected to involve a sacrifice of money or money's worth. Liabilities are claims on the business assets other than claims from the owners.

An expense arises through the use or consumption of an asset or resource. When a resource has been used for its beneficial purpose then the recorded figure for the resource becomes an expense and the resource is no longer regarded as an asset. If the expense is recognised before the resource is acquired then a liability will also arise.

(d)   A contingent liability is a possible or potential liability which may or may not actually occur. It relates to a past event but there may very well be no crystallisation of a liability, and therefore there may be no money sacrifice. An example would be a court case where no actual liability exists unless or until the judgement goes against the business.

A provision is an estimated liability. The existence of the liability is known (unlike with a contingent liability), but the amount of the liability is not.

JUNE 1995 QUESTIONS

Note: **With effect from June 1997, there will no MCQs in the examination.**

The Multiple Choice Questions set under the old examination format until December 1996 were not released by the examiner. Some sample items were issued in 1994 and are reproduced with the June 1994 examination questions on page 161.

Section B – ALL FOUR questions are compulsory and MUST be attempted

68 (Question 1 of examination)

1   Paragraphs 10 to 13 of SSAP 12, Accounting for depreciation, are included in this paper as Appendix A.

Your client has drawn your attention to part of the balance sheet you have prepared for her, which reads as follows.

	£'000	£'000
Fixed assets		
Land and buildings, at cost		150
Plant and machinery at cost	100	
Less: Depreciation	(60)	
		40
		190

Required

Answer her questions, which are as follows.

(a)   What are the purposes of providing for depreciation?   **(4 marks)**

(b)   In what circumstances is the reducing balance method more appropriate than the straight-line method? Give reasons for your answer.   **(4 marks)**

(c)   In a balance sheet prepared in accordance with SSAP 12, what does the net book value (carrying value) represent?   **(4 marks)**

(d)   In a set of financial statements prepared in accordance with SSAP 12, is it correct to say that the net book value (carrying value) figure in a balance sheet cannot be greater than the market (net realisable) value of the partially used asset as at the balance sheet date? Explain your reasons for your answer.   **(4 marks)**

(Total 16 marks)

69 (Question 2 of examination)

2 The balance sheet of CF plc for the year ended 31 December 1994, together with comparative figures for the previous year, is shown below.

	1994 £'000	1994 £'000	1993 £'000	1993 £'000
Fixed assets		270		180
Less: Depreciation		(90)		(56)
		180		124
Current assets				
Stock	50		42	
Debtors	40		33	
Cash	–		11	
		90		86
Current liabilities				
Trade and operating creditors	(33)		(24)	
Taxation	(19)		(17)	
Dividend	(28)		(26)	
Bank overdraft	(10)		–	
		(90)		(67)
Net current assets		–		19
Net assets		180		143
Represented by:				
Ordinary share capital £1 shares		25		20
Share premium		10		8
Profit and loss account		65		55
Shareholders' funds		100		83
15% Debentures, repayable 1998		80		60
Capital employed		180		143

You are informed that:

–   there were no sales of fixed assets during 1994;
–   the company does not pay interim dividends;
–   new debentures and shares issued in 1994 were issued on 1 January.

Required

(a)   Show your calculation of the operating profit of CF plc for the year ended 31 December 1994.

(4 marks)

(b)   Prepare a cash flow statement for the year, in accordance with the revised FRS 1 *Cash flow statements*, including the note required by that standard reconciling the operating profit to net cash inflow from operating activities.   **(10 marks)**

(c)   State the headings of the other notes which you would be required to include in practice under FRS 1 (revised).   **(2 marks)**

(d)   Comment on the implications of the information given in the question plus the statements you have prepared, regarding the financial position of the company.   **(6 marks)**

(e)   FRS 1 (revised) supports the use of the indirect method of arriving at the net cash inflow from operating activities, which is the method you have used to prepare 'Note 1' required in part (b) of this question.

What is the direct method of arriving at the net cash inflow from operations?

State, with reasons, whether you agree with the FRS 1 (revised) acceptance of the indirect method.

(3 marks)
(Total 25 marks)

---

70   (Question 3 of examination)

3   A company maintains a debtors control account in the nominal ledger, and includes the balance on this account in its trial balance. It also maintains a memorandum individual debtors ledger.

The following errors relating to debtors have been discovered.

(a)   A credit note for £90 had been entered as if it were an invoice.

(b)   Sales of £400 had been entered on the wrong side of a customer's account in the individual debtors ledger.

(c)   A prompt payment discount of £70 had been completely omitted from the records.

(d)   An invoice of £123 had been entered in the sales day book as £321.

(e)   No entry had been made to record an agreement to contra an amount owed to P of £600 against an amount owed by P of £700.

(f)   Bad debts of £160 had been omitted from the individual debtors accounts, though otherwise correctly treated.

Required

Prepare journal entries to correct each of the errors described in (a) to (f) above. Accounts should be fully named, but narrative descriptions are not required.

(12 marks)

---

71   (Question 4 of examination)

4   Examine the arguments for and against the proposition that all limited liability companies, of whatever size, should be legally required to have an independent audit.

(7 marks)

APPENDIX A

Paragraphs 10 to 13 of SSAP 12 *Accounting for depreciation*

Depreciation is the measure of the wearing out, consumption or other reduction in the useful economic life of a fixed asset whether arising from use, effluxion of time or obsolescence through technological or market changes.

The *useful economic life* of an asset is the period over which the present owner will derive economic benefits from its use.

Residual value is the realisable value of the asset at the end of its useful economic life, based on prices prevailing at the date of acquisition or revaluation, where this has taken place. Realisation costs should be deducted in arriving at the residual value.

Recoverable amount is the greater of the net realisable value of an asset and, where appropriate, the amount recoverable from its further use.

EXAMINER'S COMMENTS

Overall results were disappointing for this session. Many candidates appeared to be under-prepared for the question on cash flow statements under FRS 1, despite the lengthy period which has elapsed since it entered the Foundation Stage syllabus. Candidates should bear in mind, that whilst questions are not intended to be complicated, they are designed to test understanding, as well as knowledge of key issues.

Question 1: sought an understanding of the purposes and effects of depreciation, with particular reference to the resulting balance sheet figures.

Candidates did not perform well on this question and should remember that SSAP 12 does not require a fixed asset to be shown at the lower of depreciated cost and net realisable value. The answer published in the Question and Answer booklets will provide further guidance.

Question 2: concerned cash flow statements under FRS 1.

Many candidates produced poor answers and a surprising number of candidates did not attempt this question at all. Those candidates who understood the principles of cash flow performed very well.

Question 3: concerned journal entries to correct errors.

Many candidates produced journal entries that corrected the trial balance accounts, rather than producing entries to correct each of the errors as was required. Again, the answers published in the Q&A booklets will provide further guidance.

Question 4: required a brief discussion of the role of the independent audit for limited liability companies.

Many candidates had a grasp of the major issues in this area, although some gave an explanation of limited liability. A good number of candidates stated their views clearly with supporting arguments. It is to be hoped that this development continues in the future.

ANSWERS TO JUNE 1995 EXAMINATION

68 (Answer 1 of examination)

1 (a) The purpose of depreciation is to apply the matching principle to long-lived productive assets. The benefits (ie, the net revenues that arise from the use of the assets) are spread over a number of years and the essential purpose of depreciation is to spread the costs incurred in obtaining the long-lived productive asset over the useful life so that they can be matched against the benefits. According to SSAP 12, depreciation should be allocated so as to charge against income a fair proportion of cost or valuation of the asset to each accounting period expected to benefit from its use.

Depreciation is thus concerned with a 'proper' profit calculation. It is not primarily concerned with balance sheet figures, nor with replacing the asset, though it may be regarded as supporting the principle of capital maintenance, though which version of the principle depends on the valuation basis used for the 'gross' asset figure.

(b) The theoretical answer to this question is that the reducing balance method is better when it gives a series of expense figures which charge a fairer proportion of the cost or valuation of the asset to each accounting period expected to benefit from its use. This does not get us very far. The logical support for a declining annual charge, would be a declining annual benefit ie, the asset becomes significantly less useful as it gets older. If 'usefulness' is considered 'net' ie, after taking account of repair and maintenance costs, the argument for a declining charge method perhaps becomes stronger, as the repair and maintenance costs affecting the 'net usefulness' will be at their lowest in the early years. Therefore the net usefulness will be at its highest, and therefore the depreciation charge should perhaps be at its highest too.

(c) As suggested above, depreciation is essentially concerned with the calculation of profit, not with the provision of rational or helpful figures in the balance sheet. The profit and loss charge may be defined perhaps as the amount of the net cost (or other basic value) of the asset which is fairly allocated under the matching principle to be charged against the results of beneficially operating the asset during the accounting period. This logically leads to a laborious definition of the balance sheet net figure as something like that amount of the cost (usually but not necessarily the historic cost) of the asset which has not yet been allocated as an expense under the fair application of the matching principle. The balance sheet figure does not purport to be a current value on the market or a value in use to the business.

(d) No, it is not correct. What is correct is that the balance sheet figure so prepared cannot be greater than the recoverable amount, defined (as given in the question), as the greater of the net realisable value of the asset and, where appropriate, the amount recoverable from its further use. Therefore the balance sheet figure may need to be reduced to the *higher* of market (net realisable) value and the amount recoverable from its further use. In most ongoing situations market value would be the lower of these two alternatives.

69 (Answer 2 of examination)

2 (a) **Calculation of operating profit**

	£'000
Increase in profit and loss account balance	10
Add: Interest on debentures	12
Taxation	19
Dividends	28
	69

(b)   Note 1: Reconciliation of operating profit to net cash inflow from operating activities.

	£'000
Operating profit	69
Depreciation	34
Increase in stocks	(8)
Increase in debtors	(7)
Increase in creditors	9
	97

Cash flow statement for the year ended 31 December 1994

	£'000	£'000
Net cash inflow from operating activities		97
Returns on investments and servicing of finance		
Interest paid		(12)
Tax paid		(17)
Capital expenditure		
Acquisition of fixed assets		(90)
		(22)
Equity dividends paid		(26)
		(48)
Financing		
Issue of ordinary share capital	7	
Issue of debentures	20	
		27
Decrease in cash		(21)

(c)   The other notes are:

Note 2: Reconciliation of the movement of cash with the movement in net debt.

Note 3: Material non-cash transactions undertaken during the year.

(d)   The company is evidently seeking to expand. There has been major acquisition of fixed assets during the year, costing £90,000. It is clear from the cash flow statement that much of this investment has been internally financed from successful operating activities during the year. However, the new long-term financing of £27,000 was not enough to fill the gap, and the result was a decrease in cash of £21,000. Note also that the debentures are all repayable in 1998.

On the face of it the picture seems to have deteriorated considerably from a cash and liquidity viewpoint, but we do not have enough information to know whether any real concern is necessary – information over several years is really needed. If the investment in fixed assets is more-or-less complete, and given that a full year of use of the new assets should lead to greater operating profits and greater net cash flows from operating activity, then the decrease in cash will automatically be reversed. But care is needed, and at minimum the situation should be watched carefully.

(e)   Briefly, the direct method of arriving at the net cash inflow from operations uses the actual cash flows. In particular cash receipts from customers in the year and cash payments to suppliers, employees and for services acquired will be netted out directly against each other. FRS 1 recommends the indirect method as the ASB does not believe that the benefits to the users of the direct method outweigh the additional preparation costs involved. This argument seems rather surprising. The costs should be minimal (which companies do not know what their cash is spent on?) and the benefits of using true cash flows in a statement called a cash flow statement would seem hard to deny.

70   (Answer 3 of examination)

3

		Dr £'000	Cr £'000
(a)	Sales	180	
	Debtors control		180
	Memorandum individual debtor		180
(b)	Memorandum individual debtor	800	
(c)	Discounts allowed	70	
	Debtors control		70
	Memorandum individual debtor		70
(d)	Sales	198	
	Debtors control		198
	Memorandum individual debtor		198
(e)	Purchases (creditors) control	600	
	Debtors control		600
	Memorandum individual creditor	600	
	Memorandum individual debtor		600
(f)	Memorandum individual debtors		160

71   (Answer 4 of examination)

4   The argument for an independent audit might perhaps be related to the old idea of stewardship. The directors of the business have control of the money provided by the shareholders and creditors, who have neither the possibility nor the intention to keep an everyday watch on the actions of the directors and the company. It is argued that the directors, as managers of the company, should be held accountable to the providers of finance, and that the veracity of their report should be confirmed by a theoretically independent party acting on behalf of those outsiders taking the most risk – ie, the shareholders.

In the case of small owner-managed companies it can be argued that this rationale breaks down. There is no need for the actions of the directors to be verified on behalf of the shareholders if the directors *are* the shareholders. On the other hand this still leaves the position of the creditors to be considered, although personal guarantees from the directors, and the laws of fraud, should considerably safeguard their position. In practice, of course, cost-benefit considerations cannot be ignored, and a truly independent audit of a small company costs, in relative terms, a great deal of money. As a final practical point, how truly independent are typical 'small' audits anyway? How can a genuine safeguarding of, say, a creditor, be carried out when all decisions, information and explanations come from the same managing individual? However, it can still be argued that the privilege of limited liability justifies the existence of external audit.

DECEMBER 1995 QUESTIONS

Note: **With effect from June 1997, there will no MCQs in the examination.**

The Multiple Choice Questions set under the old examination format until December 1996 were not released by the examiner. Some sample items were issued in 1994 and are reproduced with the June 1994 examination questions on page 161.

Section B - ALL THREE questions are compulsory and MUST be attempted

72   (Question 1 of examination)

1   (a)   A and B are in partnership sharing profits equally. The summarised balance sheet of AB and Co at the close of business on 30 June 1995 is as follows.

	£'000		£'000
Land	30	Capital A	50
Buildings	100	Capital B	70
Other assets	70	Creditors	80
	200		200

The partners have agreed between themselves as follows.

(i)   With effect from 1 July 1995 profits are to be shared in the ratio A three fifths, B two fifths.

(ii)   As at 30 June 1995 the land is valued at £55,000. The new valuation is not to be recorded in the asset account.

(iii)   As at 30 June 1995 the buildings are valued at £65,000. This new valuation is to be recorded in the asset account.

(iv)   As at 30 June 1995 the business, i.e. the net assets, is valued at £170,000 (the 'other assets' and 'creditors' figures are valued as shown in the above balance sheet). The assets side of the balance sheet at commencement of business on 1 July 1995 is not to be altered from the figures at close of business on 30 June 1995 except for the figure for buildings which is to be reduced to the newly agreed value.

Required:

Prepare a summarised balance sheet at the commencement of business on 1 July 1995, taking account of the above agreement between the partners. Show workings clearly.

(8 marks)

(b)   Partner A, on receipt of the balance sheet you have prepared in Part (a), is not pleased. He is particularly concerned because the balance on his capital account, as compared with B's, has changed in both absolute and relative terms.

Required:

Draft a memorandum to A clarifying the whole situation. Your memorandum is required to contain five sections. The first four, referenced (i), (ii), (iii) and (iv), should explain the implication of the corresponding point in the four-part agreement between the partners given in the question. The final section, referenced (v), should summarise the reasons for the change in the balance on A's capital account and should include a comparison with the change in the balance on B's capital account.

(12 marks)

(c)   It is often said that the function of a balance sheet is to show the financial position of a business at a point in time.

Required:

To what extent do you believe that the balance sheets for AB and Co., one given in the question and one prepared in your answer to part (a), satisfy that function? Explain your answer briefly.

(5 marks)

(Total: 25 marks)

---

73   (Question 2 of examination)

2   (a)   Curd Ltd buys milk in bulk, and sells bottled milk. For many years they have manufactured their own glass bottles, but during the year ended 31 December 1994 the bottle-making plant was closed and the workers from the plant were made redundant. A trial balance for the company as at 31 December 1994 has been prepared, containing the following figures.

	£'000
Ordinary shares of 50p nominal value	100
10% Preference shares of 50p nominal value	50
16% Debenture loan stock	100
Prepayments for operating expenses as at 1 January	25
Accruals for operating expenses at 1 January	30
Operating expenses paid	112
Sales	600
Sales returns	14
Cost of sales	290
Stock at 31.12.94	90
Trade debtors	150
Provision for doubtful debts as at 1.1.94	7
Bad debts expense	16
Fixed assets at cost	350
Depreciation as at 1 January	180
Profit and loss account balance (credit)	70
Trade creditors	80
Redundancy and closure costs	90
Bank deposits and cash floats	80

You are informed that:

- depreciation should be provided at 10% per annum on cost,
- the bad debts provision is required to be 2% of debtors,
- corporate taxation for 1994 should be taken as £10,000,
- accruals and prepayments for operating expenses as at 31 December 1994 are £33,000 and £29,000 respectively.

All calculations should be made to the nearest £000.

Required:

Produce a profit and loss account for 1994, highlighting the following items:

(i)   gross profit
(ii)   net operating profit
(iii)   net profit
(iv)   profit for the year available for ordinary shareholders.

Submit all workings and calculations.   **(13 marks)**

(b)   A friend tells you that she thinks FRS 3, Reporting Financial Performance, is relevant to the preparation of a profit and loss account for Curd Ltd for publication purposes.

Required:

In what way is FRS 3 relevant, and what further information, beyond that already given in the question, would you need to know about the results of Curd Ltd for the year 1994 in order to apply FRS 3?

(8 marks)
(Total: 21 marks)

74   (Question 3 of examination)

3   (a)   Explain the purposes, and the relative importance, of

(i)   a profit and loss account, and
(ii)   a cash flow statement.

(8 marks)

(b)   To what extent do you think auditors of limited company accounts serve a useful function? Explain your answer.

(6 marks)
(Total: 14 marks)

EXAMINER'S COMMENTS

General comments

The general level of performance for this examination was poorer than in previous diets and was generally disappointing.

Question 1: tested the basic principles of changes in partnership profit ratios.

Candidates struggled with this question, often showing a lack of understanding of balance sheet structures, partner claims, and of the implications of unrecorded asset values.

Question 2: required (a) the preparation of a profit and loss account with appropriate headings, and (b) a discussion of FRS 3, *Reporting Financial Performance,* and its possible relevance to the situation.

Part (a) was generally well answered by candidates. However many of the answers to part (b) were disappointing. Many candidates appeared to know very little about FRS 3 and many confused it with FRS 1. FRS 3 has been in the paper 1 syllabus from the December 1994 sitting and it is important that students ensure that they are fully conversant with this area.

Question 3: was a discussion question on the roles of the profit and loss account, the cash flow statement, and auditors. Candidates need to be prepared to discuss these areas in quite some detail. For example, the profit and loss account is designed to show the profit or loss. However candidates should also be able to give consideration to the purpose of presenting profit or the cash flow.

ANSWERS TO DECEMBER 1995 EXAMINATION

72   (Answer 1 of examination)

1   (a)   Working

All figures are given in £000s.

The separable assets are worth 55 + 65 + 70 - 80 = 110 at 30 June.

The business is worth 170 at 30 June.

Goodwill is therefore 60 at 30 June.

Land					Buildings				
30 June	30	Capital a/c	25		30 June	100	Capital a/c	35	
Capital a/c	25	1 July	30				1 July	65	
	55		55			100		100	

Capital A					Capital B				
Land	15	30 June	50		Land	10	30 June	70	
Buildings	17.5	Land	12.5		Buildings	17.5	Land	12.5	
Goodwill	36	Goodwill	30		Goodwill	24	Goodwill	30	
1 July	24				1 July	61			
	92.5		92.5			112.5		112.5	

Goodwill			
Capital a/c	60	Capital a/c	60

Summary balance sheet at 1 July 1995

Land	30	Capital A	24
Buildings	65	Capital B	61
Other assets	70	Creditors	80
	165		165

(b)   Draft memorandum to A.

Prepared by:

Date:

(i)   This point means that A has a greater entitlement to future profits, including future gains on fixed assets and goodwill in excess of balance sheet figures.

(ii)   Land has increased in value by £25,000, before 30 June. This gain belongs to A and B in the profit-sharing ratio ruling up to 30 June, i.e. half each, and should be credited to A and B in their old profit-sharing ratio and debited to A and B in their new profit-sharing ratio. This is because if in the future the land is sold, the gain would then be allocated to the partners in the ratio then ruling, i.e. the new ratio. The eventual overall effect, therefore, is that changes in value occurring *before* 30 June 1995 are attributed to the partners in the profit-sharing ratio ruling before 30 June 1995, and changes in value occurring after 30 June 1995 are attributed to the partners in the ratio ruling after 30 June 1995.

(iii)   Buildings have reduced in value by £35,000, before 30 June. This loss belongs to the partners in the profit-sharing ratio ruling up to 30 June, i.e. half each, and should be debited to the partners in their old profit-sharing ratio. The fall in the value of the buildings is retained in the revised balance sheet, as agreed, the loss already having been deducted from the partners capital accounts in the old profit-sharing ratio.

(iv)   The recorded assets are agreed to be worth £110,000 (55 + 65 + 70 - 80), but the business itself is agreed to be worth £170,000. The excess of £60,000 is the goodwill of the business and can be attributed to expected future profits arising from past developments, or to the synergy arising between the individual assets. The whole is greater than the sum of the parts. The £60,000 should be credited to A and B in their old profit-sharing ratio and debited in their new profit-sharing ratio.

(v)   The reductions in A's capital account are caused as follows: (all figures (000s)

17.5	being A's share of the fall in value of the building (B also losing 17.5).
2.5	being the net effect of the adjustment in the land figure affecting A (B gaining the 2.5).
6.0	being the net effect of the adjustment in the goodwill figure affecting A (B gaining the 6.0)
26.0	

B has a net reduction of only 9.0.

However, there are significant unrecorded assets of 85 (land 25 and goodwill 60), all of which belong to A and B in the ratio of 3:2. Therefore A's share of the unrecorded assets is 60% of 85 = 51 whereas B's share is only 40% = 34. A's reduction being greater than B's by 17.0 (26.0 minus 9.0) is thus equalled by A's *unrecorded* increase being greater than B's by 17.0 (51.0 minus 34.0).

(c)   A balance sheet shows the financial position or state of affairs in so far as it comprises a list of the assets and liabilities of an entity at a specific point in time. Such balance sheets are largely, but not consistently, prepared under the historical cost convention and are therefore more of a record of money spent on items not yet consumed (assets) and where it was obtained from (liabilities or claims). Only in the limited sense of 'money put in', therefore can a balance sheet be regarded as showing the financial position of the business at the relevant date. The treatment of the building in the July 1 balance sheet means that even this limited statement is not strictly true.

Note. Other sensibly argued views will be marked on their logical merits.

73   (Answer 2 of examination)

2   (a)   Curd Ltd profit and loss account for year to 31 December 1994
                                        All figures in £000

Sales (600 - 14)		586
Cost of sales		(290)
Gross profit		296
Operating expenses (W)	(111)	
Bad debts (16 - 4) (W)	(12)	
Depreciation (10% of 350)	(35)	
		(158)
Net operating profit		138
Redundancy and closure costs	(90)	
Debenture interest (16% of 100)	(16)	
		(106)
Net profit		32
Tax		(10)
Profit after tax		22
Preference dividend (10% of 50)		(5)
Available for ordinary shareholders		17

Operating expenses account

b/f	25	b/f	30
Paid	112	Profit and loss a/c	111
c/d	33	c/d	29
	170		170

Calculation of bad debt provision.
Debtors are 150. 2% of 150 = 3
To correct provision account, debit it with 4 and credit profit and loss account with 4.

(b)   The essential purpose of FRS 3 is to require a layered format to be used for the profit and loss account to highlight a number of important components of financial performance. These components are:

(i)   results of continuing operations;

(ii)   results of discontinued operations;

(iii)   profits or losses on the sale or termination of an operation, costs of a fundamental reorganisation or restructuring and profits or losses on the disposal of fixed assets (these three are shown separately for continuing and for discontinued operations):

(iv)   extraordinary items

The item which may make FRS 3 relevant to Curd Ltd is the 'redundancy and closure costs' of £90,000. This figure is obviously material. If the bottle manufacturing is held to be a 'discontinued operation' then the revenues and expenses associated with it in the year ended 31 December 1994 must be segregated from the other revenues and expenses, so that they can be shown separately. Since the bottles were not sold separately there would seem to be no revenues involved, which perhaps suggests that the bottle-making was not a separate operation now discontinued. This needs to be investigated and resolved.

Whichever way this is resolved, some of the £90,000 will undoubtedly relate to losses on the disposal of fixed assets used to manufacture the bottles and some is redundancy relating to the termination of an operation, and probably also other incidental costs associated with the cessation of production. The £90,000 will therefore need to be split so as to allow the presentation of the separate components required by FRS 3, as already described.

74   (Answer 3 of examination)

3   (a)   Perhaps the two most important things a shareholder needs to be able to appraise are first, future profits and dividends by extension from past and current results, and secondly the capacity and abilities of management which of course will significantly affect profits and dividends in the longer run. In the last analysis a business exists to make profits, i.e. an excess of revenues over expenses defined and evaluated in accordance with the accruals or matching convention. Profits are surely the ultimate criterion of success for a business and for its management. All this suggests that the profit and loss account might be argued as of superior importance.

However, an adequate cash position is essential in the short term both to ensure the very survival of the business (i.e. to avoid insolvency) and to ensure the capacity to pay out dividends to the level consistent with profits and retention needs. An adequate cash position is also essential in the longer term to allow asset replacement and expansion. Distributable profits and cash are necessary to pay dividends to shareholders and so a statement of changes in financial position, to help present the cash position and cash trends is also a very important provider of information.

The rational conclusion therefore might be that both types of statement are essential components in a reporting package.

(b)   The function of the auditor might be summarised as being to provide a check, or to ensure that the system itself provides a check, on the actions and financial work of individuals within enterprises, and on the financial statements prepared on behalf of the business as a whole. Auditors can create or improve the system of 'automatic' check (internal control) and can (from either an internal or an external stance) increase the reliability of figures, results and accounts produced.

Auditors also, in the context of limited companies, have to form an opinion on whether the accounts give a true and fair view. All this increases (but does not guarantee) the reliability and usefulness of the accounts. It therefore reduces the risks inherent in acting on the contents of those accounts and statements. A business whose accounts are regarded as reliable is likely to be able to raise finance more easily and more cheaply *ceteris paribus*, than a business not in that position.

JUNE 1996 QUESTIONS

Note: **With effect from June 1997, there will no MCQs in the examination.**

The Multiple Choice Questions set under the old examination format until December 1996 were not released by the examiner. Some sample items were issued in 1994 and are reproduced with the June 1994 examination questions on page 161.

Section B - ALL THREE questions are compulsory and MUST be attempted

75   (Question 1 of examination)

1   You have agreed to take over the role of bookkeeper for the AB sports and social club.

The summarised balance sheet on 31.12.94 as prepared by the previous bookkeeper contained the following items. All figures are in £s.

Assets		
Heating oil for clubhouse		1,000
Bar and cafe stocks		7,000
New sportswear, for sale, at cost		3,000
Used sportswear, for hire, at valuation		750
Equipment for grounds person		
Cost	5,000	
Depr	3,500	1,500
Subscriptions due		200
Bank		
Current account		1,000
Deposit account		10,000
Claims		
Accumulated fund		23,150
Creditors		
Bar and cafe stocks		1,000
Sportswear		300

The bank account summary for the year to 31.12.95 contained the following items.

Receipts	
Subscriptions	11,000
Bankings	
Bar and cafe	20,000
Sale of sportswear	5,000
Hire of sportswear	3,000
Interest on deposit account	800
Payments	
Rent and repairs of clubhouse	6,000
Heating oil	4,000
Sportswear	4,500
Grounds person	10,000
Bar and cafe purchases	9,000
Transfer to deposit account	6,000

You discover that the subscriptions due figure as at 31.12.94 was arrived at as follows.

Subscriptions unpaid for 1993	10
Subscriptions unpaid for 1994	230
Subscriptions paid for 1995	40

Corresponding figures at 31.12.95 are:

Subscriptions unpaid for 1993	10
Subscriptions unpaid for 1994	20
Subscriptions unpaid for 1995	90
Subscriptions paid for 1996	200

Subscriptions due for more than 12 months should be written off with effect from 1.1.95.

Asset balances at 31.12.95 include:

Heating oil for club house	700
Bar and cafe stocks	5,000
New sportswear, for sale, at cost	4,000
Used sportswear, for hire, at valuation	1,000

Closing creditors at 31.12.95 are:

For bar and cafe stocks	800
For sportswear	450
For heating oil for clubhouse	200

$\frac{2}{3}$rds of the sportswear purchases made in 1995 had been added to stock of new sportswear in the figures given in the list of assets above, and $\frac{1}{3}$ had been added directly to the stock of used sportswear for hire.

Half of the resulting 'new sportswear for sale at cost' at 31.12.95 is actually over two years old. You decide, with effect from 31.12.95, to transfer these older items into the stock of used sportswear, at a valuation of 25% of their original cost.

No cash balances are held at 31.12.94 or 31.12.95. The equipment for the grounds person is to be depreciated at 10% per annum, on cost.

Required

Prepare the income and expenditure account and balance sheet for the AB sports club for 1995, in a form suitable for circulation to members. The information given should be as complete and informative as possible within the limits of the information given to you. All workings must be submitted.   **(23 marks)**

---

76   (Question 2 of examination)

2   (a)   The United Kingdom Accounting Standards Board (ASB) has for some years been issuing draft parts of what it eventually intends as a substantive 'Statement of Principles'.

Required

What is the purpose of the Statement of Principles?   **(6 marks)**

(b)   Brief extracts from issued drafts from the Statement of Principles are given in Appendix 1 at the end of the paper and you should study them carefully.

You are given four brief situations, as follows.

(1)   Firm A has paid £10,000 to buy a patent right, giving it the right to sole use, for 5 years, of a manufacturing method which saves costs.

(2)   Firm B is the freehold legal owner of a waste disposal site. It has charged customers for the right to dispose of their waste for many years. The tip is now full, and heavily polluted with

chemicals. If cleaned up, which would cost £5 million, the site could be sold for housing purposes for £3 million.

    (3)   Firm C has paid £1 million towards the cost of a new hospital in the nearby town, on condition that the hospital agree to give priority treatment to its employees if they are injured at work.

    (4)   Firm D has signed a contract to pay its managing director £100,000 per year for the next three years. He has agreed to work full-time for the firm over that period.

Required

For each of the situations 1 to 4 above you are required to state, with reasons and explanation, whether the situation creates an asset or a liability within the definitions given in Appendix 1. [Situations 1 and 3, 2 marks each; situations 2 and 4, 4 marks each.]   **(12 marks)**

(c)   It is clear from Appendix 1 that items meeting the definitions of asset and liability are not automatically to be recognised in financial statements.

Required

Give an example of

(i)   an asset item,
(ii)   a liability item

which meets the given definition but would not normally be recognised in financial statements. Explain your illustrations briefly.   **(4 marks)**
    (Total 22 marks)

---

77   (Question 3 of examination)

3   You are given the following information about Firm X a private company and a wholesaler.

	Firm X 1994	Firm X 1995	Industry Average 1995
Current ratio	1.7	1.5	1.3
Acid test ratio	0.9	0.9	0.9
ROCE (before taxation)	18%	18%	18%
ROOE (before taxation)	20%	22%	15%
Gearing (debt over equity)	50%	60%	30%
Debtors age	25 days	35 days	30 days
Creditors age	40 days	60 days	40 days
Stock age	70 days	65 days	70 days
Gross profit %	27%	25%	23%
Net profit %	11%	12%	10%

[ROCE = Return on capital employed]
[ROOE = Return on owner's equity]

Required

Write a report to the shareholders of Firm X which highlights important points revealed or suggested by these figures relating to apparent management policies in the year 1995 and to possible future implications. You may assume that there has been no inflation over the relevant periods.   **(15 marks)**

EXTRACTS FROM DRAFTS OF ASB STATEMENT OF PRINCIPLES

Assets are defined as follows:

Assets are rights or other access to future economic benefits controlled by an entity as a result of past transactions or events.

Liabilities are defined as follows:

Liabilities are an entity's obligations to transfer economic benefits as a result of past transactions or events.

Recognition is the process of incorporating an item into the primary financial statements. It involves depiction of the item in words and by a monetary amount and the inclusion of that amount in the statement totals.

An item should be recognised in financial statements if:

(a)   the item meets the definition of an element of financial statements; and

(b)   there is sufficient evidence that the change in assets or liabilities inherent in the item has occurred (including, where appropriate, evidence that a future inflow or outflow of benefit will occur); and

(c)   the item can be measured at a monetary amount with sufficient reliability.

End of Question Paper

EXAMINER'S COMMENTS

General comments

The results for this paper were again disappointing. 19% of candidates obtained an overall mark of 30% or less ie, 20 or more marks below the pass mark.

The MCQ section is largely designed to test basic technical skills. Results in this section are significantly higher than in the more integrative and applied questions discussed below, but have themselves again fallen slightly compared with the previous diet.

Question 1: was a typical incomplete records question for a sports club. Thorough understanding of basic double-entry and the ability to think simple transactions through to a logical conclusion were the essence in obtaining a good mark.

Many candidates did reasonably well in this question, although the subscriptions caused problems. However a large number of candidates had little or no idea of what the question was asking for. A startling number just listed all receipts and payments under the headings of income and expenditure, thus treating the transfer to deposit account as a charge for the year! Approximately 8% of candidates got either 0 or 1 out of 23 for this question.

Question 2: (a) asked the purpose of the ASB's Statement of Principles.

The Examination Review Board commented that this would have been a straightforward question for students who had properly read the *Students' Newsletter,* and more difficult for those who had not. It was clear that many candidates had not.

2(b) required application of given definitions of assets and liabilities to four simple situations.

The suggested solution should be studied carefully. Many 'wrong' answers were in fact intelligently argued and markers gave some credit for this.

2(c), distinguishing between definition and recognition of an asset, allowed the good candidate some quick and easy marks, but many failed to see the point.

Question 3: was generally poorly answered. This question gave a table of financial ratios and asked for an analysis and report.

Candidates must realise that rewriting the ratios and numbers in narrative form one at a time ('P is larger than last year but Q has fallen since last year but less than the industry average') is *not* an analysis. Inter-relationships and implications need to be explored.

ANSWERS TO JUNE 1996 EXAMINATION

75 (Answer 1 of examination)

1   All figures are given in £'s

Summary subscriptions account

	£		£
Opening balance	10	Opening balance	40
Opening balance	230	Bank	11,000
Closing balance	200	Closing balance	90
Income for period	10,690		
	11,130		11,130

Bar and cafe results

Sales		20,000
Opening stock	7,000	
Purchases (9,000 + 800 − 1,000)	8,800	
	15,800	
Closing stock	5,000	
		10,800
Profit (gross)		9,200

Sale of sportswear

Sales		5,000
Opening stock	3,000	
Purchases (4,500 + 450 − 300) × ⅔	3,100	
	6,100	
Closing stock	4,000	
		2,100
Profit (gross)		2,900
Loss on sportswear transferred		1,500
Profit		1,400

Hire of sportswear

Rentals		3,000
Opening balance	750	
Additions of cost $(4{,}500 + 450 - 300) \times \frac{1}{3}$	1,550	
	————	
	2,300	
	————	
Closing stock at valuation	1,000	
		1,300
		————
Surplus		1,700
		————

General income and expenditure account

Subscriptions $(10{,}720 - 30)$		10,690
Bar and cafe profit		9,200
Sale of sportswear		1,400
Hire of sportswear		1,700
Interest on deposit account		800
		————
		23,790
		————
Rent of clubhouse	6,000	
Heating oil $(1{,}000 + 4{,}000 + 200 - 700)$	4,500	
Grounds person	10,000	
Depreciation	500	
	————	
		21,000
		————
Net surplus		2,790
		————

AB Sport and Social Club balance sheet as at 31.12.95

	£	£
Fixed assets		
Equipment for grounds person		
Cost		5,000
Depreciation		4,000
		————
		1,000
		————
Current assets		
Heating oil	700	
Bar and cafe stocks	5,000	
New sportswear	2,000	
Hire sportswear	1,500	
Subscriptions due	90	
Bank		
Current account	1,300	
Deposit account	16,000	
	————	
	26,590	

Current liabilities

Bar and cafe	800
Sportswear	450
Heating oil	200
Subscriptions prepaid	200
	1,650

	24,940
	25,940

Accumulated fund b/f	23,150
Surplus for year	2,790
	25,940

---

76   (Answer 2 of examination)

2   (a)   The Statement itself, as issued in draft, describes its role as follows (candidates are not expected to know this in detail).

(1)   This Statement of Principles sets out the concepts that under-lie the preparation and presentation of financial statements for external users. The purpose of the Statement of Principles is to:

(a)   assist the Board in the development of future accounting standards and in its review of existing accounting standards:

(b)   assist the Board by providing a basis for reducing the number of alternative accounting treatments permitted by law and accounting standards;

(c)   assist preparers of financial statements in applying accounting standards and in dealing with topics that do not form the subject of an accounting standard;

(d)   assist auditors in forming an opinion whether financial statements conform with accounting standards;

(e)   assist users of financial statements in interpreting the information contained in financial statements prepared in conformity with accounting standards; and

(f)   provide those who are interested in the work of the Board with information about its approach to the formulation of accounting standards.

In other words we can say that the Statement sets out to provide a framework, a set of internally consistent definitions, assumptions and conventions which will underpin and inform accounting practice in general and accounting standards in particular. Through general applicability, these notions should then make life easier for all the parties listed in (a) to (f) above, and should ensure that standards are properly consistent with each other as they will all emanate from the same agreed starting position.

(b)   (1)   Firm A has clearly acquired an asset. There is a past event, control, and future economic benefits (through cost savings) are expected. Tangibility is not required.

(2)   The situation with firm B is rather more complicated. What is clear is that the tip is not an asset. There is control and there has been a past event, but there is no expected 'access to economic benefit'. What is less clear is whether or not there is a liability. If, as may well in

practice be the case, there is a legal requirement on firm B to clean up the site so as not to leave it in a dangerous condition, then the situation would give rise to a liability (of £2 million) as there would be a net obligation to transfer economic benefits of this amount.

(3)   This would certainly not be regarded as an asset. It seems difficult to argue that there is a 'right or other access to future economic benefits', and there is without doubt a lack of 'control' by firm C over the actions of the hospital.

(4)   Intuitively, this looks in common sense terms like a liability. However this is not the case. A liability would result as a result of the 'past event' of the managing director actually working. Since the three years of work is all in the future this is not the situation, and so no liability exists. Similarly, at this point, there is no asset in existence either.

(c)   (i)   Development expenditure which fails to meet the criteria for possible capitalisation set out in SSAP 13, would be an example of an asset not being recognised. It certainly meets the criteria for asset definition, at least in the minds of the directors approving the expenditure, but involves too much uncertainty for the recognition criteria.

(ii)   A contingent liability which is remote, within the meanings of SSAP 18, is a good example of a liability which is not recognised, again because there is inadequate likelihood of future outflow.

Note: other examples are possible and will be marked on their merits.

---

77   (Answer 3 of examination)

3   AC Ountant & Co
        4 Main Street
        Toytown

Report to Shareholders of Firm X

It is perhaps dangerous to be too dogmatic from the limited information available to us. Nevertheless a number of logical inferences can be made. The current ratio of Firm X has fallen compared with the previous year, although it is still above the industry average. The acid test ratio, however, has held constant. The likely explanation for this is that stock levels have fallen in relative terms, a possibility fully consistent with the fall in the stock turnover period.

The ROCE is constant. The ROOE is higher than the ROCE and has increased in 1995 compared with 1994. This is consistent with the increase in gearing ratio from 50% to 60% (on the assumption that the relevant interest rates are below 18%). All of these figures are higher than the industry averages, and the high gearing ratio seems particularly advantageous to the return attributable to you as shareholders. However from a lender perspective the gearing ratio, now twice the industry average, may be of considerable concern. It is very much in your interests as shareholders to ensure that the company retains a high level of creditworthiness.

Debtors payment period has increased, and creditors payment period has sharply increased together, as already mentioned, with a reduction in stock holding period. Note also that there has been a reduction in the gross profit margin. All this is consistent with a sharp increase in trading volume, related to a cut in prices, allowing debtors longer to pay (possibly increasing the risk of losses through bad debts), leading to pressure on liquidity which has resulted in the sharp increase in the time taken to pay creditors.

On the other hand, the constant acid test ratio together with a creditors increase relatively greater than the debtors increase implies an increase in cash balances.

There are several warning signs here which need to be watched very carefully. There seems to have been a dash for growth, leading to liquidity uncertainties in the short term and to a gearing position significantly more exposed than the norm in the industry. However, profits and earnings for shareholders have improved. It has worked so far!

If you have any particular further queries please let us know.

Alex Ountant

DECEMBER 1996 QUESTIONS

Note: **With effect from June 1997, there will no MCQs in the examination.**

The Multiple Choice Questions set under the old examination format until December 1996 were not released by the examiner. Some sample items were issued in 1994 and are reproduced with the June 1994 examination questions on page 161.

Section B - ALL THREE questions are compulsory and MUST be attempted.

78   (Question 1 of examination)

The book-keeper of a small limited company, Whoops Ltd, has produced a trial balance for you as at 30 November 1996. All figures are in £000s.

	Dr	*Cr*
Premises	140	
Equipment - cost 30 November 1996	130	
- depreciation 30 November 1996		47
Creditors control		36
Debtors control	53	
Purchases	206	
Sales		402
Sundry expenses including depreciation	94	
Ordinary shares of 20 pence each		50
10% preference shares of 20 pence each		20
15% debentures		40
Profit and loss balance 1 December 1995		38
Bank	3	
Cash	3	
New issue account		30
Suspense account	7	
Stocks at 1 December 1995	27	
	663	663

You are given the following information.

(i)   Debenture interest for the 6 months to 31 May has been paid and charged to sundry expenses. No dividends have been paid in the year. A dividend of 10 pence per share on the ordinary share capital as at 30 November 1996 is to be proposed.

(ii)   The balance on the new issue account consists of the proceeds of an issue of 30,000 20 pence shares in December 1995, at a price of £1 each. The book-keeper was not sure how to treat this item, but has properly dealt with the money received.

(iii)   The book-keeper has extracted lists of individual creditors ledger and debtors ledger balances, with the following totals.

Debit balances:	debtors ledger	£50,000
	creditors ledger	£2,000
Credit balances:	debtors ledger	£3,000
	creditors ledger	£40,000

You discover the following errors.

(1)   A sales credit note of £2,000 has been entered consistently as if it was a sales invoice.

(2)   The debtors control account balance has been wrongly totalled and is understated by £3,000.

(3)   The list of debit balances on the sales ledger has also been wrongly totalled and is understated by £1,000.

(4)   The balance due to XANTHIPPE Inc. of £2,000 included in the creditors ledger, has been omitted from the list of ledger balances.

(5)   Contra items of £4,000 during the year between creditors and debtors ledgers have been omitted from both control accounts, though correctly included in the individual ledger accounts.

If, after dealing with the above, there are any remaining differences between control accounts balances and lists of individual balances then the control accounts should be adjusted to equal the totals of the individual ledger balances by transfer to or from the suspense account.

(iv)   The premises are to be revalued to £150,000 as at 30 November 1996.

(v)   Closing stocks at 30 November 1996 are £34,000.

(vi)   The bank statement shows a balance of £3,000 overdraft as at 30 November 1996. Examination reveals that a cheque for sundry expenses, entered in the cash book as £4,000, was in fact for £5,000 and had been accepted by the bank as such. Unpresented cheques at 30 November 1996 all received by the bank between 1 and 10 December 1996, were £2,000 in total. Bank charges shown in the bank statement as charged on 30 November 1996, complete the reconciliation between cash book and cash statement.

(vii)   Any remaining balance on the suspense account should be transferred to sundry expenses.

Required:

Prepare trading, and profit and loss accounts, and balance sheet, in good order, for internal purposes in as clear and helpful a presentation as possible. All workings, which may be in any form, are to be submitted and must be clearly and logically presented. Ignore taxation.

(25 marks)

79	**(Question 2 of examination)**

(a)   Explain the accruals (or matching) convention, the prudence (or conservatism) convention, the consistency convention, and the going concern convention as used in financial accounting.

(8 marks)

(b)   SSAP 2, Disclosure of Accounting Policies, refers to possible 'inconsistency' between the accruals (matching) and the prudence conventions.

What is this inconsistency, and how does SSAP 2 require accountants to deal with it?

(2 marks)

(c)   The 'Definition of Terms' section of SSAP 13, Accounting for Research and Development, is reproduced in Appendix A.

What is the required accounting treatment according to SSAP 13 in relation to each of the three broad categories referred to in Appendix A?

(6 marks)

(d) Snod plc spends £1,000,000 on machinery and equipment for a new laboratory intended to be used for pure research.
How should this £1,000,000 be treated in its financial statements?

(2 marks)

(e) Are the requirements of SSAP 13, Accounting for Research and Development, consistent with the three conventions of accruals, prudence and consistency, and with the requirements of SSAP 2, Disclosure of Accounting Policies, as discussed in a) and b) above? Explain your answer carefully.

(6 marks)
(Total: 24 marks)

---

80   (Question 3 of examination)

(a) Outline the information needs of the following groups of users of financial statements:

- shareholders;
- management;
- employees.

(6 marks)

(b) Explain the extent to which a company's published financial statements are useful to each of the above user groups.

(5 marks)
(Total: 11 marks)

Appendix A

The following definition is used for the purpose of this statement:

Research and development expenditure means expenditure falling into one or more of the following broad categories (except to the extent that it relates to locating or exploiting oil, gas or mineral deposits or is reimbursable by third parties either directly or under the terms of a firm contract to develop and manufacture at an agreed price calculated to reimburse both elements of expenditure):

(a) pure (or basic) research: experimental or theoretical work undertaken primarily to acquire new scientific or technical knowledge for its own sake rather than directed towards any specific aim or application;

(b) applied research: original or critical investigation undertaken in order to gain new scientific or technical knowledge and directed towards a specific practical aim or objective;

(c) development: use of scientific or technical knowledge in order to produce new or substantially improved materials, devices, products or services, to install new processes or systems prior to the commencement of commercial production or commercial applications, or to improving substantially those already produced or installed.

ANSWERS TO DECEMBER 1996 EXAMINATION

78   (Answer 1 of examination)

Notes and Workings   *Marks*

(i)   Transfer £3,000 from sundry expenses to debenture interest expenses. Accrue a further £3,000 debenture interest expenses.

(ii)   Close the new issue account by transfer of £6,000 to ordinary shares and £24,000 to share premium.

(iii)

	Debtors Control			*Debtors Ledger Balances*		
balance	53	4	sales (1)	dr	50	
suspense (2)	3	4	contra (5)	cr	(3)	5
		4	suspense	cr (1)	(4)	
		44	balance	dr (3)	1	
	—	—			—	
	56	56	Corrected		44	
	—	—			—	

	Creditors Ledger			*Creditors Ledger Balances*		
contra (5)	4	36	balance	cr	40	
balance	40	8	suspense	dr	(2)	
	—	—		dr (4)	2	
	44	44			—	
	—	—	Corrected		40	
					—	

(iv)   Open revaluation reserve

(vi)

	Bank Account					
balance	3	1	sundry expenses	Bank (old)	(3)	3
balance	5	7 *	bank charges	Unpresented	(2)	
	—	—				
	8	8	Corrected		(5)	
	—	—			—	

* balancing figure.

(vii)

	Suspense Account				
balance	7	3	debtors control		2
debtors control	4	16 *	sundry expenses		
creditors control	8				
	—	—			
	19	19			
	—	—			

* balancing figure.

Trading and Profit and Loss Account - Whoops Ltd   Marks
Year ended 30 November 1996
All figures £'000s

Sales			398
Opening stock		27	
Purchases		206	
		——	
		233	
Closing stock		34	199
		——	
Gross profit			199
Office expenses (94 + 1 - 3 + 7 + 16)			115
			——
Operating profit			84 6
Debenture interest			6
			——
Net profit			78
Preference dividends		2	
Ordinary dividends		28	30
		——	
Retained profit for year			48
Profit and loss balance b/f			38
			——
Retained profit c/f			86
			——

Balance Sheet of Whoops Ltd   Marks
Year ended 30 November 1996
All figures £'000s

Premises			150
Equipment - cost		130	
- depreciation		47	83
		——	
			233
Current assets			
Stock		34	
Debtors		44	
Cash		3	
		——	
		81	
Current Liabilities			
Creditors	40		
Debenture interest	3		
Dividends - preference	2		
- ordinary	28		
Bank overdraft	5		
	——		
	78	3 6	
	——	——	
Net assets			236
			——

	Marks
Ordinary shares of 20 pence each	56
Preference shares of 20 pence each	20
Share premium	24
Revaluation reserve	10
Retained profits	86
Owner's equity	196
15% Debenture	40
Capital employed	236
	Layout 3

---

79   (Answer 2 of examination)

Marks

(a)   The matching or accruals convention is that profit determination is a process of matching or relating against revenue the expenses incurred in earning that revenue. The prudence convention refers to the accounting practice of recognising all possible losses, but not anticipating possible gains. This will tend to lead to an understatement of profits and to an understatement of asset values with no corresponding understatement of liability. Consistency in financial accounting is the practice of applying the same accounting rules, methods or procedures in each similar case. This is designed to avoid manipulation of reported results, and to facilitate comparison within and between firms over different accounting periods. The going concern convention is the assumption that an enterprise will continue in operation for the foreseeable future, and will not need to significantly curtail its operations. It is a logical pre-requisite of the matching convention, allowing expenses to be deferred.

4×2

(b)   SSAP 2 states that 'where the accruals concept is inconsistent with the prudence concept, the latter prevails'. The inconsistency in essence is that the matching convention requires the carrying forward of current expenditure, as assets, in order that it can be matched against the corresponding future revenue. Such 'assets' are uncertain and represent losses of varying degrees of possibility; they are therefore not recognised, on the grounds of prudence.

2

(c)   Paragraphs 24 to 27 of SSAP 13, Accounting for Research and Development, are as follows (candidates who give these points clearly in their own words will be fully rewarded).

Expenditure on pure and applied research should be written off in the year of expenditure through the profit and loss account.

Development expenditure should be written off in the year of expenditure except in the following circumstances when it may be deferred to future periods.

(a)   there is a clearly defined project, and

(b)   the related expenditure is separately identifiable, and

(c)   the outcome of such a project has been assessed with reasonable certainty as to:

    (i)   its technical feasibility, and

    (ii)   its ultimate commercial viability considered in the light of factors such as likely market conditions (including competing products), public opinion, consumer and environmental legislation, and

6

(d)   the aggregate of the deferred development costs, any further development costs, and related production, selling and administration costs is reasonably expected to be exceeded by related future sales or other revenues, and

(e)   adequate resources exist, or are reasonably expected to be available, to enable the project to be completed and to provide consequential increases in working capital.

In the foregoing circumstances development expenditure may be deferred to the extent that its recovery can reasonably be regarded as assured.

If an accounting policy of deferral of development is adopted, it should be applied to all development projects that meet the criteria in paragraph 25.

(d)   SSAP 13 paragraph 23 states that the cost of fixed assets acquired or constructed in order to provide facilities for research and development activities over a number of accounting periods should be capitalised and written off over their useful lives through the profit and loss account. Thus the £1,000,000 should be treated in principle as normal fixed assets, and not as part of normal pure research expenditure. Its expected useful life should of course be related to its anticipated function.

2

(e)   The concept of capitalising development expenditure is certainly consistent with the accruals convention; the requirement to write off all pure and applied research expenditure immediately is certainly consistent with the prudence convention; it can also be logically argued that the restrictions on capitalising development expenditure, limiting this to carefully defined circumstances, are also consistent with the prudence convention. However, the 'cut-off' point between the two is surely arbitrary. It could certainly be argued that to capitalise any development expenditure, prior to successful sales of the product, fails to allow 'prudence to prevail'. It can also be logically suggested, to take the other direction, that rational management must expect future return from current investment in research, and therefore that all research expenditure should in principle be capitalisable, at least in certain circumstances.

4

What is very clear is that there are problems with the application of the consistency convention. The SSAP is quite explicit that, under the defined circumstances, development expenditure *may* be capitalised. Although some consistency within the firm is achieved by paragraph 27 already quoted, it is obvious that, since different firms in similar circumstances are allowed to act in different ways, SSAP 13 allows a lack of consistency, and therefore a lack of comparability between firms, in this respect, which is surely contrary to both usefulness and convention. It is perhaps noteworthy that the revised International Standard, IAS 9, replaces the word 'may' with the word 'should'.

2

There is considerable scope for different views on the precise configuration of several of these points. All such views, provided they are properly supported, will be marked on their merits.

Flexible marking will be required for 2(e)

80   (Answer 3 of examination)

(a)   Shareholders are the providers of risk capital and they and their advisers are concerned with the risk inherent in, and return provided by, their investments. They need information to help to determine whether they should buy, hold or sell shares. Shareholders are also interested in information that enables them to assess the ability of the enterprise to pay dividends.   2

Management are the people who have to take decisions, both day-to-day and strategic, about how the scarce resources within their control are to be used. They need information that will enable them to predict the likely outcomes of alternative courses of action. As part of this process, they will need feedback on the results of their previous decisions in order to extend successful aspects of the decisions, and to adapt and improve the unsuccessful aspects.   2

Employees and their representative groups are interested in information about the stability and profitability of their employers. They are also interested in information that helps to assess the ability of the enterprise to provide remuneration, retirement benefits and employment opportunities.   2

(b)   There is of course scope for different arguments here. One obvious point to make is that published financial statements are not intended to be useful to management, who have easy access to information which is much more relevant and timely for their needs. Both shareholders and employees are probably generally interested in similar issues, i.e. of stability, liquidity and long and short-term profitability, though it should be noted that the major content and presentation of published financial statements focuses on shareholders very much more than on employees.   1   2

The extent to which typical published financial statements succeed in providing effective information on 'stability, liquidity and long and short-term profitability' is highly debatable. Certainly trends can be established, and various ratios calculated, considered and compared. But the generally arbitrary and semi-backward-looking implications of traditional conventions and practices raise doubts about the direct relevance of much financial accounting data to such users.   2

Flexible marking will be required for 3(b).

Student Questionnaire

Because we believe in listening to our customers, this questionnaire has been designed to discover exactly what you think about us and our materials. We want to know how we can continue improving our customer support and how to make our top class books even better - how do you use our books, what do you like about them and what else would you like to see us do to make them better?

1 Where did you hear about the ACCA Official Series?

☐ Colleague or friend   ☐ Employer recommendation   ☐ Lecturer recommendation
☐ AT Foulks Lynch mailshot   ☐ Conference   ☐ ACCA literature
☐ Students' Newsletter   ☐ Internet   ☐ Other ....

2 Do you think the ACCA Official Series is:

☐ Excellent   ☐ Good   ☐ Average   ☐ Poor   ☐ No opinion

3 Please evaluate AT Foulks Lynch service using the following criteria:

	Excellent	Good	Average	Poor	No opinion
Professional	☐	☐	☐	☐	☐
Polite	☐	☐	☐	☐	☐
Informed	☐	☐	☐	☐	☐
Helpful	☐	☐	☐	☐	☐

4 How did you obtain this book?

☐ From a bookshop   ☐ From your college   ☐ From us by mail order
☐ From us by telephone   ☐ Internet   ☐ Other ....

5 How long did it take to receive your materials?   .... days.

☐ Very fast   ☐ Fast   ☐ Satisfactory   ☐ Slow   ☐ No opinion

6 How do you rate the value of the sections of the Accounting Framework Revision Series?

		Excellent	Good	Average	Poor	No opinion
1	Syllabus and examination format	☐	☐	☐	☐	☐
2	Analysis of past papers	☐	☐	☐	☐	☐
3	General revision guidance	☐	☐	☐	☐	☐
4	Examination techniques	☐	☐	☐	☐	☐
5	Key revision topics	☐	☐	☐	☐	☐
6	Updates	☐	☐	☐	☐	☐
7	Practice questions and answers	☐	☐	☐	☐	☐
9	The New Syllabus Examinations with the examiners' own answers	☐	☐	☐	☐	☐

Continued/...

7 Have you purchased any other ACCA Official Series' titles?
If so, please specify title(s) and your rating of each below:

Title	Excellent	Good	Average	Poor	No opinion
....	☐	☐	☐	☐	☐
....	☐	☐	☐	☐	☐
....	☐	☐	☐	☐	☐
....	☐	☐	☐	☐	☐

8 Have you used publications other than the ACCA Official Series?
If so, please specify title(s) and your rating of each below:

Title and Publisher	Excellent	Good	Average	Poor	No opinion
....	☐	☐	☐	☐	☐
....	☐	☐	☐	☐	☐
....	☐	☐	☐	☐	☐
....	☐	☐	☐	☐	☐

9 Will you buy the ACCA Official Series material again?

☐ Yes   ☐ No   ☐ Not sure

Why? ....

10 Please write here any additional comments you might have on any of the above areas or tell us what you would like us to do to make the books even better:

....

....

....

....

11 Your details: these are for the internal use of the ACCA and AT Foulks Lynch Ltd only and will not be supplied to any outside organisations.

Name
....

Address
....

....

Telephone
....

Do you have your own e-mail address?	☐ Yes	☐ No	
Do you have access to the World Wide Web?	☐ Yes	☐ No	
Do you have access to a CD Rom Drive?	☐ Yes	☐ No	

Please send to:

Quality Feedback Department
FREEPOST 2254
AT Foulks Lynch Ltd, 4 The Griffin Centre, Staines Road, Feltham, Middlesex, TW14 0BR.

Thank you for your time.

ACCA
AT FOULKS LYNCH

HOTLINES	AT FOULKS LYNCH LTD
Telephone: 0181 844 0667 Enquiries: 0181 831 9990 Fax: 0181 831 9991	Number 4, The Griffin Centre Staines Road, Feltham Middlesex TW14 0HS

Examination Date:	Publications			Distance Learning	Open Learning	
June 97 ☐ December 97* ☐ *Please note that the FA97 Revision Series for taxation papers will be published in June.	Textbooks	Revision Series	Lynchpins	Includes all materials, helpline & marking	Materials	Helpline & Marking
Module A - Foundation Stage						
1 Accounting Framework	£17 ☐	£9.95 ☐	£5 ☐	£79 ☐	£99 ☐	£20 ☐
2 Legal Framework	£17 ☐	£9.95 ☐	£5 ☐	£79 ☐	£99 ☐	£20 ☐
Module B						
3 Management Information	£17 ☐	£9.95 ☐	£5 ☐	£79 ☐	£99 ☐	£20 ☐
4 Organisational Framework	£17 ☐	£9.95 ☐	£5 ☐	£79 ☐	£99 ☐	£20 ☐
Module C - Certificate Stage						
5 Information Analysis	£17 ☐	£9.95 ☐	£5 ☐	£79 ☐	£99 ☐	£20 ☐
6 Audit Framework	£17 ☐	£9.95 ☐	£5 ☐	£79 ☐	£99 ☐	£20 ☐
Module D						
7 Tax Framework (FA96)	£17 ☐	£9.00 ☐	£5 ☐	£79 ☐	£99 ☐	£20 ☐
8 Managerial Finance	£17 ☐	£9.95 ☐	£5 ☐	£79 ☐	£99 ☐	£20 ☐
Module E - Professional Stage						
9 ICDM	£18 ☐	£9.95 ☐	£5 ☐	£79 ☐	£99 ☐	£20 ☐
10 Accounting & Audit Practice	£20 ☐	£9.95 ☐	£5 ☐	£79 ☐	£99 ☐	£20 ☐
11 Tax Planning (FA96)	£18 ☐	£9.00 ☐	£5 ☐	£79 ☐	£99 ☐	£20 ☐
Module F						
12 Management & Strategy	£18 ☐	£9.95 ☐	£5 ☐	£79 ☐	£99 ☐	£20 ☐
13 Financial Rep Environment	£18 ☐	£9.95 ☐	£5 ☐	£79 ☐	£99 ☐	£20 ☐
14 Financial Strategy	£18 ☐	£9.95 ☐	£5 ☐	£79 ☐	£99 ☐	£20 ☐
POSTAGE UK Mainland	£2.00/book	£1.00/book	£1.00/book	£5.00/subject	£5.00/subject	
NI, ROI & EU Countries	£5.00/book	£3.00/book	£3.00/book	£15.00/subject	£15.00/subject	Postage free
Rest of world standard air service	£10.00/book	£8.00/book	£8.00/book	£25.00/subject	£25.00/subject	
Rest of world courier service	£22.00/book	£20.00/book	£14.00/book	£47.00/subject	£47.00/subject	

SINGLE ITEM SUPPLEMENT: If you only order 1 item, INCREASE postage costs by £2.50 for UK, NI & EU Countries or by £10.00 for Rest of World Services

TOTAL	Sub Total £					
	Postage £					
	Total £					

All details correct at time of printing.

Order Total £

DELIVERY DETAILS
Student's name (print)
Address

Postcode
Telephone   Deliver to home ☐
Company name
Address

Postcode
Telephone   Fax
Monthly report to go to employer ☐   Deliver to work ☐

PAYMENT OPTIONS
1. I enclose Cheque/PO/Bankers Draft for £_____
   Please make cheques payable to AT Foulks Lynch Ltd.

2. Charge Access/Visa Acc No: Expiry Date |__|__|__|

   |__|__|__|__|__|__|__|__|__|__|__|__|__|__|__|

Signature   Date

DECLARATION
I agree to pay as indicated on this form and understand that AT Foulks Lynch Terms and Conditions apply (available on request). I understand that AT Foulks Lynch Ltd are not liable for non-delivery if the rest of world standard air service is used.

Signature   Date

Please Allow:	UK mainland	- 5-10 workdays
	NI, ROI & EU Countries	- 1-3 weeks
	Rest of world standard air service	- up to 6 weeks
	Rest of world courier service	- 10 workdays

Notes: All delivery times subject to stock availability. Signature required on receipt (except rest of world standard air service). Please give both addresses for Distance Learning students where possible.

Source: ACRSF7